Illustrations on the Moral Sense

Illustrations on the Moral Sense

Francis Hutcheson

Edited by Bernard Peach

The Belknap Press of
Harvard University Press
Cambridge, Massachusetts
1971

Distributed in Great Britain by Oxford University Press, London
Library of Congress Catalog Card Number 71–135545
SBN 674–44326–8
Printed in the United States of America

For Amby

Preface

Francis Hutcheson's *Illustrations on the Moral Sense* is significant not only historically but also for its relevance to current and continuing problems of moral philosophy. Unfortunately, except for the brief excerpts in the appendix to the first volume of L. A. Selby-Bigge's edition of the *British Moralists*, published in 1897, and the somewhat longer selections in D. D. Raphael's edition published in 1969, it has not appeared in print since the eighteenth century. My hope is that this new edition will call attention to Hutcheson again, support the claim that he deserves a more important place in the history of ethics than he has yet been granted, and enable those who are interested in moral philosophy to profit from his contributions to normative ethics and metaethics. His views on the nature of our knowledge of moral matters and his theory of justification are the focus of my attention in the introduction, although many other topics are equally deserving of critical examination.

It is a pleasure to acknowledge the help I have had. Support and encouragement have come from the John Simon Guggenheim Foundation, the American Philosophical Society, and the Duke University Council on Research. I wish to thank my colleagues at Duke University for invaluable discussions of issues treated in the introduction, and Charles A. Baylis and R. L. Clark for reading the manuscript. My special thanks go to R. W. Binkley, who criticized two earlier drafts so thoroughly that I am tempted to suggest that its inadequacies are his. R. L. Clark's article, "On What Is Naturally Necessary," (*The Journal of Philosophy*, 1965), P. W. Taylor's *Normative Discourse* (Englewood Cliffs: Prentice-Hall, 1961), R. M. Chisholm's *Perceiving* (Ithaca: Cornell University Press, 1957), and W. K. Frankena's article, "Hutcheson's Moral Sense Theory" (*Journal *of the History of Ideas,* 1955) and his book, *Ethics* (Englewood Cliffs: Prentice-Hall, 1963) have also been of great help.

I am grateful to Jon N. Moline for help with the Greek and with the footnotes, to Linda Davis, who typed long hours during periods when there were many other demands on her time and attention, to Constance Palmer for her work during the final phases of preparation of the manuscript, to Louise Johnson for typing the final revision of the introductory essay, to Emerson Ford of the Duke Library, for his help in tracing the various editions, and to Florence Blakeley, also of the Duke Library, for expert help in problems of reference.

I dedicate this book to my wife, Amby, who has always made it possible for me to live a life, in accordance with Hobbes's phrase, "so as not to grow weary of it," even while preparing new editions of eighteenth-century books.

B. P.

Contents

Editor's Introduction

Francis Hutcheson played a central role in the rich development of British moral philosophy in the eighteenth century, and his writings are relevant to current issues in ethics. In the eighteenth century his criticism of the egoism of Hobbes and Mandeville prompted countertheories supporting egoism on both theological and psychological grounds and thus led to developments in theological voluntarism, the association of ideas, and utilitarianism. As a result, his influence runs through a line which includes John Gay, David Hartley, Jeremy Bentham, and the Mills. On the other hand, Hutcheson made explicit the divergent strains previously implicit in reactions to Hobbes both by showing the rationalists that they needed to clarify and develop their theories and by developing his own theory of the moral sense. Under the impetus of his criticism of such early rationalists as Samuel Clarke, William Wollaston, and Gilbert Burnet, rationalistic theories were developed by John Balguy and Richard Price and modified by Thomas Reid. And his own theory of the moral sense, originally suggested by Shaftesbury, was in turn developed by David Hume and had a strong influence upon Adam Smith.

Historically, Hutcheson's first two volumes were the most influential of his writings. The first, entitled *An Inquiry into the Original of Our Ideas of Beauty and Virtue,* was published in 1725. It contained separate essays on the two subjects. The second was published in 1728 and also contained two essays, *An Essay on the Nature and Conduct of the Passions and Affections and Illustrations on the Moral Sense*. In the *Inquiry into Virtue* Hutcheson was concerned to refute egoism and to argue that there is impartial benevolence which is immediately approved. The psychology of the *Inquiry* is improved in the *Essay on the Passions*, and the doctrine of the moral sense is clarified and developed in the *Illustrations*. The *Illustrations* is, in fact, primarily an essay in metaethics, which makes it of greater interest to present ethicists than to writers of the nineteenth century who were more concerned with the development of normative ethical systems.

Hutcheson illustrates the moral sense in two ways. In his controversy with the rationalists, with whom he had not dealt in the earlier essays, he argues that they must appeal to the moral sense in order to account for the significance of moral judgments. In the positive development of his own theory, he shows how an appeal to the moral sense enables him to handle some of the main problems of ethics.

In normative ethics, he takes up the problems of the degree to which an act is meritorious if its motive is effective and whether or not an act may be virtuous without regard for the Deity. His main problems, however, are with the epistemology of morals: What are the respective roles played by reason, sense, or emotion in moral judgments? What gives moral concepts their significance? Is there a fundamental principle of ethics? If so, what is the basis of its ultimacy, and how is this to be recognized?

Hutcheson deals with these questions by analyzing, interpreting, and arguing against the rationalists' answers, and by developing his own based on the moral sense. In the process he explores issues which are of concern to present-day nonnaturalists as well as naturalists, and to noncognitivists as well as cognitivists. Hutcheson himself develops a noncognitive view of the significance of moral judgments and a theory of justification combining both cognitive and noncognitive features. The result is a theory of subtlety and power that deserves the attention of contemporary ethicists and justifies the elevation of Hutcheson to a level of greater importance in the history of ethics than he now occupies.

Hutcheson's Life and Writings

Hutcheson was born August 8, 1694, in Drumalig in northern Ireland. After attending two dissenting academies in Ireland, he entered the University of Glasgow in 1711. He completed both arts and theological courses, probably in 1717; then he returned to Ulster and was licensed as a probationary preacher by the Presbyterians in 1719. His brief period of preaching, although successful on the whole, was not without its moments of failure. While substituting for his father, for example, he outraged the congregation by preaching that a benevolent God would admit the souls of heathens into heaven if they followed their consciences. His auditors preferred, so they told his father, to hear the good old doctrines of election, reprobation, original sin, and faith. His preaching career ended when he accepted the invitation of a group of Presbyterians in Dublin to establish a private academy there. This was probably in 1720 or 1721.

At the Dublin Academy Hutcheson's interests turned gradually from theology to philosophy, influenced by natural inclination and by new friends, who included Lord Molesworth, friend and admirer of Shaftesbury, and Edward Synge, friend of Berkeley and enthusiast for the "new philosophy" of Locke.[1] In 1725 he married a Miss Mary Wilson—a marriage that proved eminently satisfactory in all respects except the death in infancy of six of the seven children born.

In addition to the four essays already mentioned, Hutcheson contributed in 1725 and 1726 six "letters" to the *Dublin Journal*—three criticizing Hobbes and three criticizing Mandeville. They were, in effect, articles in the general areas of ethics and aesthetics. In 1725 he contributed two letters to the *London Journal* in an exchange with Gilbert Burnet, who, as an ex-

1. From 1721 to 1724, both Berkeley and Hutcheson lived in Dublin and were mutual friends of Synge. It is very likely, therefore, that they knew each other, although I know of no direct evidence that they ever met.

ponent of the rationalist cause, had challenged Hutcheson's doctrine of the moral sense. Because the *Illustrations* grew directly out of this exchange, the entire correspondence is transcribed in the appendix.

In 1730 Hutcheson accepted appointment as professor of moral philosophy in the University of Glasgow. His inaugural lecture, *De Naturali Hominum Socialitate*, was published that same year. He wrote *A System of Moral Philosophy* between 1735 and 1737, though it was not published until 1755, nine years after his death. In 1735 he published a pamphlet, "Considerations on Patronage, Addressed to the Gentlemen of Scotland." In 1742 *Metaphysicae Synopsis Ontologiam et Pneumatologiam complectens* and *Philosophiae Moralis Institutio Compendiaria Ethices et Jurisprudentiae Naturalis Elementa continens* appeared, which are "compends" in the manner of the day, growing out of materials used in his lectures. The compendium on morals was translated as *A Short Introduction to Moral Philosophy* and published in 1747. Between the *System* and the *Introduction*, Hutcheson translated the *Meditations of Marcus Aurelius* and added extensive notes.[2]

Claims by students, friends, and family, administrative duties, and his campaign against conservative elements in the university brought his writing to an end several years before his early death in 1746.

Hutcheson was widely read not only in Britain but also on the Continent, particularly in Germany. The *Inquiry* reached a fourth edition in 1738 and was translated into French in 1749, into German in 1762. The *Essay* reached a fourth edition in 1756 and was translated into German in 1760. By 1780 *Metaphysicae Synopsis* had gone through seven editions, including one in Strasbourg. The *Introduction* had a fifth edition in 1772. The *System* was translated into German in 1756, the year after its publication in Glasgow. The general demand for Hutcheson's books is indicated by

2. His colleague, James Moor, professor of Greek, translated the first two chapters. It was published in 1742.

the Foulis catalogue for 1772: it listed eight publications, five of which were editions of his works.

In Britain his influence upon Hume was pervasive enough to lead A. N. Prior, writing in 1949, to assert that "there is little or nothing in Hume's moral philosophy that cannot be traced to Hutcheson, but in Hume it is all more clear and pointed."[3] Hutcheson's theories were modified by Adam Smith, his student at Glasgow, in Smith's doctrines of sympathy and the impartial spectator. Hutcheson's views on economics, originally presented in lectures that later became the *System* and the *Introduction*, also had great influence upon Hume, as well as upon Smith.[4]

He contributed to the development of utilitarianism by regarding the pleasurable and painful consequences of actions as morally significant, by working out a moral calculus, and by providing the utilitarian formula that "that action is best which procures the greatest happiness for the greatest numbers."[5] His calculus computed morality in terms of the motives and ability of the agent, the felicific consequences of the act, and the number of people affected. It was criticized by Archibald Campbell, professor of ecclesiastical history in St. Andrews, for failing to recognize that approval of benevolence by the moral sense is disguised self-love and for not properly incorporating the functions of "degree, duration, and consequents" in calculating the morality of the act.[6] The unknown author of *An Inquiry into the Origins of the Human Appetites and Affections Showing How Each Arises from Association . . .*[7] claimed that any such calculus must recognize the quantitative equality of units of pleasure of equal in-

3. *Logic and the Basis of Ethics* (Oxford: Clarendon Press), p. 31.

4. Cf. W. L. Taylor, *Francis Hutcheson and David Hume as Predecessors of Adam Smith* (Durham, N.C.: Duke University Press, 1965).

5. *Inquiry Concerning Moral Good and Evil* (Glasgow, 1772), section III, par. 8.

6. *An Inquiry into the Original of Moral Virtue . . .* (Westminster, 1728); noted in W. R. Scott, *Francis Hutcheson* (Cambridge: Cambridge University Press, 1900), p. 261.

7. Lincoln, 1747; noted in Scott, *Francis Hutcheson,* p. 264.

tensity and duration and must emphasize the role of association in accounting for the development of the moral sense and its approval of benevolence from native self-love.

These proposals are similar to those of John Gay in his *Dissertation Concerning the Fundamental Principle of Virtue or Morality*.[8] Gay's essay expressed the reaction to Hutcheson of a special class of English theologians who combined Hobbes's psychological egoism with theological voluntarism in support of orthodox Christianity. Generally, they argued as follows: What is good is what God wills to be good. In fact God wills the happiness of mankind to be good. To get men to act for the general happiness, He creates and sustains a system in which present or future rewards or punishments are objects of men's selfish desires. Gay argued, in particular, that the so-called moral sense is acquired. Men think favorably of benevolent actions and are moved to perform them, according to Gay, because in childhood they were pleasurably rewarded for doing so, and this association becomes firmly fixed during the normal course of maturation. Gay's egoism and his doctrine of the association of ideas received powerful development from David Hartley (1705–1757) and through him entered the stream of utilitarianism and the writings of Bentham and the Mills.

Thomas Reid's first publication[9] was a reaction against Hutcheson's calculus and an attempt to specify what is necessary if a concept is to admit of quantification. A critic and modifier of the moral sense theory, Reid nevertheless agreed with Hutcheson's refutation of egoism, his emphasis on the constitution of man as the foundation of our first principles in theoretical and practical knowledge, the analogy between morality and aesthetics, and the propriety of appealing to ordinary language to settle philosophical issues. Reid's

8. Dublin, 1731; reprinted in *The English Philosophers from Bacon to Mill*, ed. E. A. Burtt (New York: Modern Library, 1939).

9. "An Essay on Quantity," *Philosophical Transactions of the Royal Society* 45 (1748): 505.

doctrine of common sense and its role in morals is an attempt to combine elements from the school of reason and the school of sentiment.

Whether Hutcheson or Reid is rightly to be called the father of Scottish philosophy, the line of influence runs from them to the Scottish school: and into the nineteenth century in both Scotland and the United States, although Hutcheson's name fades away in the process. Hutcheson's immediate influence in America is evident in Jonathan Edwards. Until recently he has been thought of as a fiery Puritan preacher who merely made an apology for Calvinism, but he is now coming to be recognized as a theologian and philosopher of importance. His book on the freedom of the will is gaining recognition as a piece of analysis that would credit any contemporary philosopher. It is in his short treatise entitled *The Nature of True Virtue*,[10] however, that the influence of Hutcheson is most apparent. He refers explicitly to Hutcheson in three places, giving him credit for the doctrine that beauty is a kind of agreement constituted by the blending of uniformity and variety, and the doctrine that particular differences in moral judgments do not argue against a moral sense common to mankind. He agrees with Hutcheson and Hume that there is a natural affection for the welfare of others, although he denies that this, in itself, can be the foundation of true virtue. He affirms, as I understand Hutcheson and Hume to, that the language of morals is primarily an expression of moral sentiments. He also accepts a version of the concept of fittingness or justice which is a modified version of Hutcheson's doctrine that the degree of virtue is a matter of proper proportion between the love given by and the love returned to intelligent beings. According to Edwards, this kind of natural love is limited to family, friends, community, or the like, thus lacking the inclusiveness required of true virtue. This inclusiveness is found in a higher, spiritual or divine moral sense that, if granted

10. 1765; reprint ed., Ann Arbor: University of Michigan Press, 1960. The book was written in 1755.

to man by the grace of God, enables him to love, and to enjoy loving, intelligent Being in general.

Edwards, then, while accepting Hutcheson's emphasis upon sentiment and feeling, his analogy between aesthetics and morals, his appeal to a sense of beauty and a moral sense, and his expressive theory of moral judgments, differs from him by making an appeal to theology a necessary part of his conception of true virtue. He attributes a much more restricted role to positive benevolence even in the natural and lower kind of virtue. In other writings, in fact, he even asserts that there is no natural motivation except self-love.

Edwards seems to have been aware of the difficulties in this emphasis upon feeling rather than reason as the basis of moral judgments. In the final chapter of *The Nature of True Virtue,* he answers an implicit criticism of his own view which is similar to some criticisms of Hutcheson made by Burnet and other rationalists: if moral judgments are verbal expressions of the feelings of the moral sense, then they are arbitrary. Edwards replies that moral judgments are made in accordance with a determination of mind which is given by God's grace. Thus, they are more in agreement with the necessary nature of things than any other alternative. In fact, despite Edwards' Calvinism, he virtually denies that God could have given a contrary determination of mind that still would have agreed with the nature of things. This response is in some respects like Hutcheson's response to the criticism made by Burnet that if the frame of our nature had been different, we might have judged malevolence rather than benevolence virtuous. Hutcheson's treatment of the issue, however, is not so predominantly theological.

Just as Edwards had been influenced by Samuel Clarke and Joseph Butler, as well as by Hutcheson, so his influence on American ethics extended well into the nineteenth century. It worked against the view, widely held in America, that men know moral virtue and obligation by particular insights of reason and in favor of views which emphasized sentiment and experience. The long-range effect of this emphasis was to support utilitarian theories and to contribute to the strength of teleological theories generally.

The Scottish school had lines of influence that ran to the Continent as well. Its effect upon late-eighteenth-century German epistemology and metaphysics has become well known through the case of Kant's awakening by Hume. In moral philosophy its general influence was so pervasive, according to one author, that it penetrated into sermons, catechisms, and children's books.[11] Hutcheson's view, following Butler, that a balance of the various affections within the individual is possible and in turn contributes to the well-being of the entire species, gave added strength, for a time, to the philosophy of Christian Wolff, with its emphasis upon perfection.[12]

Although there are different interpretations of its exact nature, there is little question that the influence of Hutcheson upon Kant was strong, particularly in Kant's precritical ethics. One of Kant's earliest references to Hutcheson appeared in the announcement of his lectures for the winter semester of 1765–66: "The attempts of Shaftesbury, Hutcheson, and Hume, which, although unfinished and deficient, have none the less progressed farthest in the search for the first principle of all morality, will receive that precision and supplementation which they now lack."[13] This early evalu-

11. Hermann Julius Theodor Hettner, *Literaturgeschichte des achtzehnten Jahrhunderts,* in drei Theilen; Erster Theil: Geschichte der englischen Literatur 1660–1770 (Braunschweig, 1865). Noted in T. Fowler, *Shaftesbury and Hutcheson* (London, 1882), p. 237.

12. Cf. Gustav Zart, *Einfluss der englischen Philosophen seit Bacon auf die deutsche Philosophie des 18. Jahrhunderts* (Berlin, 1881). Noted in Fowler, *Shaftesbury and Hutcheson,* p. 237, and Scott, *Francis Hutcheson,* p. 267.

13. *Kants Gesammelte Schriften* (Berlin: Prussian Academy, 1905–1936), 21 vols., II, 311–312. Quoted in P. A. Schilpp, *Kant's Pre-Critical Ethics* (Evanston: Northwestern University Press, 1960), p. 8.

ation of Hutcheson is entirely consistent with Kant's later classifications of Hutcheson's "moral feeling" as a heteronomous principle in the *Fundamental Principles of the Metaphysics of Morals,* and as an "internal, subjective, practical, material principle of determination taken as the foundation of morality" in the *Critique of Practical Reason.* (Par. VIII, Theorem IV, Remark 2)

Kant also suggests a promising interpretation of Hutcheson on the moral sense. In his precritical *Inquiry into the Distinctness of the Principles of Natural Theology and Morals,* in the Fourth Reflection, entitled "Of the Distinctness and Certainty of which the Primary Grounds of Natural Theology and Morals are Capable," Kant argues that there are formal and material moral principles and also primary and secondary moral principles. At the time of writing this essay, 1764, he considered the primary formal principle to be 'Do the most perfect thing that can be done by you.' As examples of primary material principles of practical knowledge he gives 'I ought to promote the greatest total perfection,' 'I ought to act according to the will of God,' and 'Love him who loves you.' These material principles, Kant said, must be "connected with" the primary formal moral principle if any definite obligation is to follow. He does not explain the nature of the connection beyond saying that the material principles "stand under" the formal principles or are "directly subsumed" by them. "If an action is directly thought of as good without surreptitiously containing another particular good which can be found in it by analysis, and because of which it is called perfect, it follows that the necessity of this action is an indemonstrable material principle of obligation. For instance, 'Love him who loves you' is a practical proposition which certainly and directly stands under the supreme formal and affirmative rule of obligation. For since it cannot be shown by further analysis why a particular perfection inheres in mutual love, this rule is not proved practically, i.e., by tracing it back to the necessity of another perfect action. Rather, it is directly subsumed under the universal rule of good actions."[14]

Kant is saying that proof of the practical necessity of an action can be carried just so far. Then nothing can be done except to show that it immediately and directly stands under or is subsumed under the primary formal principle of morals. The connection Kant has in mind could perhaps be understood as being an instance of some general class of actions, and his argument could perhaps be understood as the claim that demonstrability comes to an end in morals when an action has been shown to be an instance covered by an ultimate principle.

At this point Kant was not satisfied with his own views on the grounds of ultimate principles. But he gives credit to Hutcheson for assistance up to this point when he says, "Just as in theoretical philosophy, so also in the practical, we should not so readily consider something indemonstrable when it is not. Nevertheless, these principles [Kant presumably refers to what he calls indemonstrable material principles] cannot be dispensed with, for as postulates they contain the foundations of the rest of the other practical propositions. In this respect, under the name of the 'moral feeling,' Hutcheson and others have provided a start toward some excellent observations."[15] In a subsequent passage he formulates a problem not unlike one which concerns Hutcheson in the *Illustrations:* "From this it can be seen that, although it must be possible to achieve the highest degree of philosophical evidence in the primary bases of morality, the supreme principles of obligation must first be defined with more certainty. In this respect the task is greater in practical than in speculative philosophy, since it is still to be settled whether it is simply the cognitive faculty or whether it is feeling (the primary inner ground of the appetitive

14. *Critique of Practical Reason and Other Writings in Moral Philosophy,* trans. and ed. L. W. Beck (Chicago: Chicago University Press, 1949), p. 284.

15. Kant, *Critique of Practical Reason,* p. 285.

faculty) which decides the basic principles of practical philosophy."[16]

The ambiguity of Kant's phrase, "in this respect," makes his meaning unclear. He might mean that Hutcheson had provided a start toward some excellent observations about the foundations of practical propositions, the way in which certain propositions are the foundations of others, the indemonstrability of the primary material principles of morals, or the status of such principles as postulates. Nor is it entirely clear how Kant interprets Hutcheson on the role of the moral sense in all this. If he understands Hutcheson to hold that the ultimacy of an ultimate principle of morals is indicated by the approval of the moral sense, by "moral feeling" in his terminology, then I believe that he is on the right track and provides the basis for a correct interpretation of Hutcheson. I shall attempt to develop such an interpretation in the next section.

Hutcheson's influence in France was not extensive. Victor Cousin (1792–1867) taught the Scottish philosophy at the Sorbonne and wrote a history which displayed understanding and appreciation of Hutcheson.[17] Theodore Simon Jouffroy (1796–1842), lecturing in the 1830s, pointed out to his students that moral philosophy was more cultivated in the seventeenth and eighteenth centuries in Britain than in any country in Europe. His interpretations, measured, insightful, and gentlemanly, exhibit an appreciation of Hutcheson but do not indicate any marked influence, most of his attention being given to Bentham.[18]

Meanwhile, by the middle of the nineteenth century, notice of Hutcheson in England had shrunk to a point that Whewell, lecturing on the history of moral philosophy in England, devoted only a small part of a short chapter to him.[19] Even there his attention is directed to

16. Ibid.

17. *Cours d'Histoire de la Philosophie Morale du XVIIIième Siècle* (Paris, 1839–1840).

18. Theodore Simon Jouffroy, *Introduction to Ethics*, translated from the French by William H. Channing, 2 vols. (Boston, 1865).

19. William Whewell, *Lectures on the History of Moral Philosophy in England* (London, 1852).

the way in which Hutcheson's appeal to the moral sense was "degrading" to the cause of virtue. Sir James Mackintosh, in the seventh edition of the *Encyclopaedia Britannica,* gave him somewhat better coverage. James McCosh, from the vantage point of the presidency of the College of New Jersey in Princeton, gave a much fuller summary of his system, with extensive attention to his epistemology, metaphysics, and logic. His conclusion, however, is similar to Whewell's: "By bringing down morality from the height at which the great ethical writers of ancient and modern times had placed it, he prepared the way for the system of Adam Smith and even for that of Hume . . . Error has been committed, God's law has been lowered, and the avenger has come."[20]

Hutcheson was, in fact, better understood and more appreciated by his contemporaries and immediate successors than by subsequent philosophers. It may well be that this very influence has obscured his name. Where calculation and pleasurable and painful consequences are emphasized, Bentham and the later utilitarians have come down through the history of moral philosophy; where an emphasis on motives, impartiality, and "the general view" is important, Hume, Adam Smith, and Kant; psychology of emotions, again Hume and Smith, with Hartley and associationist psychology coming in later; attention to the authority of ordinary language in morals, Reid; the separation of theology and morality, again Hume; the psychological bases of moral judgments, Shaftesbury and again Hume. Even the reason-sentiment controversy is associated with Hume's name rather than Hutcheson's.

It is the doctrine of the moral sense that has remained quite firmly attached to his name, although here, too, he is often lost between Shaftesbury and Hume. If someone were asked who was responsible for the view that moral distinctions are not based on reason but on a moral sense, he would probably say that it was Hume. Even if Hutcheson received proper credit, however,

20. *The Scottish Philosophy* (New York, 1875), pp. 85–86.

there would be a likelihood of misunderstanding or a distortion of its significance. Because the moral sense theory has been closely associated with the refutation of the egoism of Hobbes and Mandeville and with subjectivism and naïve realism in moral knowledge, its role in the controversy with rationalism has not been fully appreciated. Yet it is in this controversy that Hutcheson probably has the greatest interest for the present-day reader.

Some faint echoes of rationalist criticisms have been heard in the brief notice taken of Hutcheson by historians such as Whewell and McCosh in the nineteenth century. They fail by far, however, to do justice to the breadth and depth of the issues which Hutcheson raises, such as the autonomy of ethics, the relation between normative ethics and metaethics, the meaning of ethical terms, and the grounds of moral judgments. Hutcheson's approach to these issues is common sensical, psychological, and epistemological. He never moves far from the language in which moral discourse is ordinarily conducted, stays close to the emotional experiences associated with circumstances that elicit moral judgments, and is concerned with the epistemological ground of moral distinctions and the relation between these grounds and the justification of moral judgments.

Several recent writers have discussed Hutcheson with an appreciation of his relevance to these topics. D. Daiches Raphael has argued that Hutcheson's attempt to set up an empiricist theory of the epistemology of morals is a failure;[21] E. Sprague has argued that Hutcheson's appeal to the moral sense is an indirect way of underscoring a view which he considers correct, namely, that the foundation of any system of morality is provided by the pleasure afforded those who live by it.[22] I have argued that Hutcheson's treatment of obligation conforms to some of the distinctions shown by

21. *The Moral Sense* (Oxford: Clarendon Press, 1947).
22. "Francis Hutcheson and the Moral Sense," *Journal of Philosophy* 51 (1954): 794.

W. K. Frankena to be necessary in holding that 'ought' implies 'can.'[23] W. K. Frankena has argued that Hutcheson holds a certain kind of noncognitive theory of moral judgments, is perhaps the first noncognitivist in the history of English-speaking ethical theory who is at all clear and thorough, and has more to say to contemporary cognitivists and noncognitivists than they have yet recognized.[24] W. T. Blackstone has supported Frankena's interpretation with an examination of Hutcheson's later books and has drawn some interesting comparisons with contemporary theories.[25]

The *Illustrations* makes its most significant current contribution to the general problem of justification, not only because Hutcheson's distinction between exciting and justifying reasons has extensive implications, but also because it displays in a striking way both the power and the difficulties of a metaethical framework that attempts to remain thoroughly empirical. Accordingly, after summarizing Hutcheson's position, I shall offer an interpretation of his theory of justification in terms of his controversy with the rationalists and his appeal to the moral sense analogy. I shall argue that the moral sense must be interpreted in a way that accords to it a variety of functions in the justification of moral judgments and a quite sharply restricted role in the justification of the adoption of basic moral principles. And since most of the metaethical parts of *Illustrations* were written in direct response to letters from Gilbert Burnet, I shall make extensive use of that correspondence.

23. "Methods of Analysis in Ethics: Francis Hutcheson and W. K. Frankena on Obligation and Ability," *Methodos,* vol. 6, no. 24 (1954): 287.

24. "Hutcheson's Moral Sense Theory," *Journal of the History of Ideas,* vol. 16, no. 3 (June 1955): 356.

25. "Hutcheson's Moral Sense Theory and its Significance for Emotivism in Contemporary Ethics," *Methodos,* vol. 11, no. 43–44 (1959): 245; *Francis Hutcheson and Contemporary Ethical Theory* (Athens: University of Georgia Press, 1965).

Summary of Hutcheson's Position

Hutcheson's general epistemology is a modified version of Locke's empiricism. He holds that the content of knowledge is provided by experience, either in ideas of sensation, reflection, or both, or by "accompanying" ideas. Every species of simple idea requires a sense. Expressed in a later terminology, he holds that the explanation of the significance of concepts, terms, propositions, or judgments requires a reference to some human experience, sensory, emotional, affective, or conative.

In his epistemology of morals, Hutcheson holds that the idea of virtue, or moral goodness, accompanies certain ideas of sense and reason. When we learn that an action is benevolent in motive or tendency, we find ourselves experiencing a unique kind of pleasure. This is a new simple idea and must, therefore, in accordance with his version of Locke's empiricism, have as one of the necessary conditions of its occurrence the existence of an appropriate sense. Since no other sense can account for this particular kind of pleasure, it must be a moral sense. This is supported by the need for a special language, the language of morals, to express properly the unique kind of pleasure experienced by the moral sense. Thus, moral terms, concepts, propositions, and judgments have their significance provided by the reactions of the moral sense. Without it, there would be only moral indifference. As Hutcheson expressed it in his letter of October 9, "moral good and evil would have been to us unknown." In language made familiar by Hume, moral distinctions are not derived from reason but from a moral sense.

In these respects, then, Hutcheson has virtually removed reason from playing any role in the origin or significance of moral concepts. In general, he limits the role of reason to knowledge of empirical truths, usually defining reason as the power to find out such truths, sometimes as the perception of such truths, and sometimes even limiting it to "the sagacity we have about means." Thus, reason, for Hutcheson, neither moves us to pursue one end rather than another nor shows us that we ought to pursue any given end. Despite this restriction, reason in the form of factual knowledge plays an important role in his general theory of justification. It is the moral sense, however, that is fundamental. Hutcheson holds that the moral sense is similar and functions in similar ways in all men unless something interferes. It provides the basis for anyone to take the moral point of view and apply moral terminology significantly to actions or persons. It thus provides the basis for the transition from descriptive terminology about the motives and tendencies of actions and persons to normative terminology that evaluates them from the moral point of view. It is, in short, the link for Hutcheson between "is" and "ought." Approval by the moral sense is the basis for the moral justification of actions.

Hutcheson distinguishes between exciting reasons and justifying reasons in an attempt to unravel the confusions in the rationalists' appeal to reason in claiming that virtue consists in conformity to reason or truth. Exciting reasons appeal to self-interest; they presuppose the existence of motives stemming from selfish affections and have nothing directly to do with moral justification. Justifying reasons, on the other hand, establish the virtue, moral goodness, or moral obligatoriness of actions. Hutcheson maintains that in the process of regressive moral justification, in giving more and more general or basic justifying reasons, we must finally come to the fundamental principle of morals—namely, that benevolence is virtuous. And, his empiricism apparently leading him to ignore Burnet's claim that this principle is self-evident to reason, he holds that it does not formulate an insight of reason but expresses the ultimate approval of the moral sense. Moral distinctions are, therefore, according to Hutcheson, autonomous. They cannot be reduced to or derived from self-interest, contrary to Hobbes and Mandeville; they cannot be reduced to the will of God, contrary to

Locke, Berkeley, and other Christian moralists, or to self-evident truth, contrary to Burnet, Clarke, Wollaston, and other rationalists.

This irreducibility of the reactions of the moral sense to the assertion of true statements points in turn to the noncognitive foundation of Hutcheson's theory. Approving by the moral sense is not cognizing, describing, or ascribing. Thus, the verbal forms in which the approving is expressed do not formulate, state, or assert cognitions, descriptions, or ascriptions. They express the special pleasure or pain that is felt by the moral sense. The moral sense ultimately approves benevolence of motive or tendency. This is expressed in the fundamental moral principle that benevolence is virtuous. This principle is neither self-evident to reason nor an empirical generalization. It expresses in appropriate moral terminology the moral ultimacy of the approval of the moral sense. Hutcheson's theory is, therefore, noncognitive as to the role of the moral sense and the meaning of the fundamental moral principle.

Yet reason, cognition, and truth have an important role in his theory. This is evident in his views on the correction of the moral sense. The moral sense, according to Hutcheson, tends always to react in the same way so long as its disposition to approve benevolence is not on any given occasion interfered with by ignorance, mistaken belief, prejudice, or the like. When such interference occurs, it is properly the function of reason to find this out and remove the ignorance, correct the belief, or take note of the prejudice. The subsequent reaction of the moral sense under these altered conditions may be said to be a correction of the moral sense, even a correction of the moral sense by reason. It is still the reaction of the moral sense that is morally significant, according to Hutcheson, not the information provided by reason. It does not follow, as Burnet argues, that reason is the moral faculty, that it discovers moral qualities, recognizes moral distinctions, or overrules the moral sense. A changed reaction by the moral sense in the light of new or more accurate information may be said to be a corrected reaction if it occurs after the acquisition of fuller knowledge about motives and consequences and with greater impartiality, if it is more consistent with other reactions in similar circumstances, more readily generalizable, or less affected by other factors that interfere with its appropriate functioning. In short, reason is concerned with the information and circumstances that are relevant to justification, but the justification is provided by the reaction of the moral sense as expressed in the language of morals. Hutcheson makes this evident in a passage which emphasizes this aspect of the moral sense analogy:

> must we not own that we judge of all our senses by our reason and often correct their reports of the magnitude, figure, color, taste of objects and pronounce them right or wrong, as they agree or disagree with reason? This is true. But does it then follow that extension, figure, color, taste, are not sensible ideas, but only denote reasonableness or agreement with reason? Or that these qualities are receivable antecedently to any sense, by our power of finding out truth? Just so a compassionate temper may rashly imagine the correction of a child, or the execution of a criminal, to be cruel and inhuman; but by reasoning may discover the superior good arising from them in the whole. And then the same moral sense may determine the observer to approve them. But we must not hence conclude that it is any reasoning antecedent to a moral sense which determines us to approve the study of public good any more than we can in the former case conclude that we perceive extension, figure, color, taste antecedently to a sense. All these sensations are often corrected by reasoning as well as our approbations of actions as good or evil, and yet nobody ever placed the original idea of extension, figure, color or taste in conformity to reason.[26]

Thus, although both the basic principle of morality and particular moral judgments are basically noncognitive and emotive in nature, they are not irrational or

26. Pages 134–135.

arbitrary, according to Hutcheson. Not only can particular actions be justified by the reactions of the moral sense, but the reaction of the moral sense is itself subject to conditions of correctness and justification. When its reactions are expressed in the language of morals, they are expressions of emotion, to be sure, but not merely expressions of emotion. They are presented in a public language in a public arena with the expectation that others will accept them or agree with them. They are not self-evident; they do not describe actions or attribute properties to them and are consequently neither true nor false in that sense. They are not empirical statements making assertions of fact, so they cannot be proved either deductively or inductively. Yet, both particular moral judgments and fundamental principles are, according to Hutcheson, justifiable in an orderly and systematic way in accordance with considerations which would lead anyone who took the same point of view and took the same things into consideration to come to the same conclusion.

For Hutcheson, then, contrary to the rationalists, ethical agreements or disagreements are agreements or disagreements in specifically moral attitudes, not in belief or knowledge. Yet his views on the role of reason in the correction of the moral sense provide a place for objectivity and validity in his general theory of regressive moral justification. In this respect he is like the rationalists despite his noncognitivism.

Hutcheson's theory of justification extends beyond his theory of regressive moral justification, although a part of this lacks detailed development. When Burnet challenges Hutcheson's basic principle, we do not find Hutcheson taking refuge in an appeal to self-evidence or to arbitrary decision. He argues that the moral sense theory as based upon the principle of benevolence is superior to its rivals on the basis of criteria which are appropriate for such general evaluations—criteria such as clarity, intelligibility, "answering the appearances," and the like. This is the part of his general theory of justification which I shall call "vindication" and within which it is possible to identify a negative, polemical phase, his criticism of rival theories, and a positive, constructive phase, the formulation of his own theory, which includes his normative ethics as well as his metaethics.

In this positive phase of vindication, Hutcheson is developing a "proof" of his fundamental principle in the broad sense of offering reasons for accepting it (and the moral system based on it) that are more cogent than those for accepting others. A further aspect of this proof is indicated, although not developed in detail, by his reply to Burnet's criticism that on the moral sense theory, if our affections changed, then virtue would change. He says, in effect, that you cannot give a moral justification of the acceptance of a moral theory. We know, Hutcheson says, that a life in which the moral sense functions as it does is a happier life than one in which it approved, say, malevolence. Burnet, within the rationalist framework, takes this as an admission that reason, knowledge, truth, and the unchanging natures of things constitute the foundations of morals, and he makes such a point in his letter of December 25. Hutcheson repeats his statement in *Illustrations*, however, so apparently he did not think that such a justification of his fundamental principle undermined his general theory. In short, he does not offer a moral justification for the acceptance of his theory, but a justification in terms of what we can observe about life in general, where he claims to find his theory exemplified.

Hutcheson's Theory of Justification: An Interpretation

Burnet's letters drove a wedge into the selfish-benevolence controversy, which had been Hutcheson's main concern up to that time. They contributed to the development of a new dimension of ethical discussion by espousing the cause of reason without espousing egoism

—a position that Hutcheson had not recognized in his first letter of response. In addition, they forced him to take into account another school of thought in the evaluation of ethical theories. His controversy with Hobbes and Mandeville had been concerned mainly with the psychology of motivation; now he was challenged by the "school of reason" from a standpoint that made epistemological questions central.

Unfortunately for that school, their spokesmen at this time were not unusually able, although two of them, Samuel Clarke and William Wollaston, were in their day highly regarded and widely read authors. Hutcheson finds that they and Burnet are vague, unclear, and ambiguous, and that he must interpret their doctrines, whether critical or constructive, before he can reply.

Hutcheson's Interpretation and Criticism of Rationalism

I: Virtue as conformity to truth. Burnet had said that virtue consists in "conformity to truth." A possible interpretation of this is that an action is virtuous if a true statement can be made about it. Hutcheson is apologetic about even suggesting this, because it offers no way to distinguish one act from another, let alone acts that are morally significant from those that are not. Yet from his letters, it is apparent that Burnet does intend it seriously, for he attempts to support the view by claiming that it is not conformity to any single true proposition which makes an act virtuous, but conformity to "the whole chain and compages of truth." His example goes a long way, however, toward confirming Hutcheson's belief that the rationalists wanted to develop an ethical theory on the basis of the categories of truth and falsity, and failed to recognize the problem of introducing moral concepts. Burnet says that an action may fail to be morally good because a truth about it (for example, 'that such and such an action gives me pleasure') may "contradict and interfere" with other truths (for example, 'that, though it pleases me, it hurts another'). He misses Hutcheson's point that he has offered no explanation of why contradiction or interference is morally significant.

Hutcheson finds that Wollaston's attempt to work out a theory in which actions are considered assertions or denials of true propositions, and therefore either virtuous or vicious, runs afoul of the same difficulty. He cannot provide a means of distinguishing acts or assertions which are morally significant from those which are not. Wollaston's basic premise was that "no act (whether word or deed) of any being to whom moral good and evil are imputable (i.e., intelligent and free) that interferes with any true proposition, or denies anything to be what it is, can be right."[27] He augmented this with a postulate that a proposition may be affirmed or denied by deeds as well as words and a definition of a true proposition as one which expresses things as they are. He then argued that it is wrong, for example, for a man to steal a horse from another man, because in doing so he denies that the horse belongs to the other man. His act is wrong, according to Wollaston, because it is "acting a lie," or uttering a falsehood by an action. As Hutcheson points out after an analysis of some of the key concepts left unclear in the theory, however, Wollaston has failed, in this case and in others, to explain why a lie is wrong. If he introduces moral terminology into his propositions and moral significance into certain actions that are interpreted as the assertions, denials, or contradictions of these propositions, then he must account for the moral significance of the original propositions. This is something that Hutcheson maintains Wollaston cannot do in terms of the concepts of truth, falsity, and contradiction. Hutcheson may be interpreted as finding that at worst, Wollaston has confused logical inconsistency with factual falsity, factual falsity with moral turpitude and, in some cases, has compounded those confusions by confusing moral

27. *Religion of Nature Delineated* (London, 1724), p. 16.

turpitude with logical inconsistency; at best, he has failed to account for the moral significance of the propositions whose affirmations and denials, agreements and disagreements he offers as morally significant. A sympathetic interpretation of Wollaston makes it possible to absolve him of the first charge by interpreting his theory as an attempt to develop an analogy between morality and logic in an effort to exhort people to virtuous conduct.[28] But there is no way to absolve him of the second.

II: Virtue as fitness. If Burnet's "conformity to truth" and Wollaston's "signification of truth" fail to establish any basis for the moral significance of propositions, Hutcheson considers that Clarke's "fitness" is on the right track, but incomplete. Clarke spoke frequently of "absolute and antecedent fitness," exemplifying it in one passage by saying "'tis undeniably more fit, absolutely and in the nature of the thing itself, that all men should endeavor to promote the universal good and welfare of all, than that all men should be continually contriving the ruin and destruction of all."[29] Hutcheson asks whether this fitness is simple or complex. If it is complex, then it should be definable in a way that makes it clear and intelligible, something he finds the rationalists have not done. If it is indefinable, then it is simple. If it is simple, then it must be the perception of some sense, this being the "necessary explication" which Hutcheson supplies to supplement Clarke.

Here, as elsewhere, Hutcheson's empiricism and the influence of Locke are evident. In general, throughout his ethics he rejected the rationalism that appealed to innate ideas or to knowledge that was independent of empirical observation. Reason, according to Hutcheson, may discover empirical truth. It may discover means to ends, but it cannot set ends; neither can it motivate or

28. See my article on Wollaston in the *Encyclopedia of Morals*, ed. Vergilius Ferm (New York: Philosophical Library, 1956), p. 642.

29. *The British Moralists*, ed. L. A. Selby-Bigge (Oxford: Clarendon Press, 1897), II, 5

oblige us to pursue them. And most importantly for the present context, reason cannot be the "original" or any new kind of simple idea whatsoever. It cannot originate a new simple idea by creating or inventing one, even by "receiving" one. Such ideas are, in the Lockean tradition, received only by some external or internal sense in accordance with the general doctrine that it is through sensory experience that we gain all the materials of knowledge.

The empiricism that is the basis of this criticism of Clarke leads Hutcheson to overlook the possibility that reason can become aware of simple ideas and the suggestion, made by both Clarke and Burnet, that 'It is fitting' can sometimes express the same thing as 'It is right' or 'It is obligatory.' His criticism also shows, however, how powerful an argument he has against the rationalists if the Lockean premises are granted: if fitness denotes a new simple idea, it *must* originate in sense. In this hypothetical anticipation of Clarke's answer and in his own statement that "the words election and approbation seem to denote simple ideas," we may well have the first suggestion in British philosophy that some moral ideas are simple.[30] It constituted a weapon against the rationalists which did not go unused or undeveloped by Hume and subsequent empiricists. Not surprisingly, then, John Balguy, Richard Price, Thomas Reid, and others who questioned the conclusions in ethics reached by Hutcheson and Hume attempted to develop an alternative epistemology in which the understanding perceives moral distinctions, but without returning to the doctrine of innate ideas.

Cudworth had, in fact, attempted to develop such an epistemology before Hutcheson. But his books were not published until after Hutcheson wrote, and many of his most important contributions remain in manuscript even today. Burnet suggested in his letter of April 10 that we sometimes "perceive truth or right by a kind of natural penetration and sagacity of the mind" and re-

30. Frankena, "Hutcheson's Moral Sense Theory," p. 364.

peated the suggestion in his definition of knowledge in the letter of July 31. He also distinguished demonstrative from self-evident knowledge in his letter of August 7 and claimed in his letters of November 27 and December 25 that we have self-evident knowledge of a moral principle. But a theory of knowledge according to which simple moral ideas can be directly and originally available to reason was not developed until 1758 by Richard Price in his *Review of the Principal Questions in Morals.*

Hutcheson's criticism that the rationalists had not defined or explained their key terms applied more to Clarke than to Burnet, who offered various definitions and explanations under Hutcheson's prodding. Burnet differs from Clarke in maintaining that 'fit' is a term which is always relative to an end. The phrase, "absolute antecedent fitness in the nature of things . . . antecedent to any end," is, he says, "absolute nonsense." The term 'antecedent,' he explains, means only "antecedent to the actual constitution of things"—for example, if "the perfectly wise and good author of nature should produce any rational agents, it was always antecedently fit that they should use the best means to happiness, since their happiness must be the chief end for which the wise and good author would bring them into being."[31] Anything is morally fit, then, according to Burnet, only in relation to its end, which must be a reasonable end or an end willed by God.

Hutcheson replied that Burnet is giving a circular explanation or else must escape from the circle by an appeal to the moral sense. Burnet replied in his letters of November 27 and December 25 that he meant that it is fitting to do what God wills not because it is what God wills, but because what God wills is wise and reasonable. Burnet considers it self-evident that God wills it best that all be happy. Hutcheson's empiricism was apparently so strong that he felt it unnecessary to discuss the claim that moral principles could be self-evident. He

31. Letter of July 31.

does not consider it in *Illustrations*. Leaving this omission aside, I think we can agree with Hutcheson that the rationalists had left the concept of fittingness and other concepts in an unclear and unsatisfactory state whether or not we accept the empiricism on which he based his criticisms.

It could be suggested that Hutcheson did a better job of portraying at least part of what the rationalists were after than they did. In section 6 of the *Illustrations*, he offers a way to compute the relation of good temper and love which may be regarded as an exposition of the nature of fitness and its degrees. His basic principle is that it is fitting to apportion one's love to the value of its object. In particular, "the most virtuous temper is that in which the love equals its causes, which may therefore be expressed by unity."

The rationalists were fond of appealing to an analogy between mathematics and moral philosophy. Wollaston in particular, but also Clarke and Burnet, frequently asserted that we can be as certain of principles, arguments, and conclusions in the latter as in the former. Thus, they would be inclined to accept the suggestion that degrees of fittingness can be calculated in a mathematical manner. Clarke might well agree that if a man deserved four units of love from his son-in-law and received only three, then the son-in-law displayed only three-fourths of the goodness of temper that was fitting to the situation. He might even agree that the son-in-law was only three-quarters as virtuous as he should have been, or that it would have been perfectly fitting for him to have given four units of love, or that this would have been perfectly virtuous. In short, Clarke and Hutcheson might agree that the notions of fitness and virtue have close interrelations of meaning, and that if one of them is clear, or defined, the other can be defined or made clear. They would differ about the grounds for this, Hutcheson maintaining that any such explication must include reference to the moral sense, and Clarke maintaining that whatever we know about virtue and fitness we know by reason, not by sense.

Sometimes Clarke expresses this by saying that some particular fitness is "without dispute" or that it would be "impertinent and insolent" to dispute it. He also speaks of such fitnesses as "evident," "manifest," or "plain and self-evident."

III: Virtue as conformity to reason. Burnet, in his letter of July 31, has given a more detailed version than Clarke's of the relationships between fitness and reason. Here, as well as in other places, he lays great stress on the general rationalistic doctrine that conformity to reason is fundamental to virtue. Hutcheson finds this doctrine unclear. He does not find clear distinctions, for example, among reason as a power or faculty, "being found out by reason," and "a reason (ground) can be given," nor between 'ground' and 'cause.' And, again, the rationalists' use of 'conformity' is not clear.

As part of his attempt to interpret the rationalists on these points, he introduces the important distinction between exciting and justifying reasons: "But what is this conformity to reason? When we ask the reason of an action we sometimes mean, 'What truth shows a quality in the action exciting an agent to do it?' Thus, 'Why does a luxurious man pursue wealth?' The reason is given by this truth, 'Wealth is useful to purchase pleasures.' Sometimes for a reason of actions we show the truth expressing a quality engaging our approbation. Thus the reason of hazarding life in a just war is that 'It tends to preserve our honest countrymen or evidences public spirit.' The reason for temperance and against luxury is given thus, 'Luxury evidences a selfish, base temper.' The former sort of reasons we will call exciting and the latter justifying. Now we shall find that all exciting reasons presuppose instincts and affections, and the justifying presuppose a moral sense."[32]

He argues that in neither sense can the rationalists establish that reason (our power of finding out true propositions) provides the final reason (ground) either

32. Page 121.

for excitement or for justification. Where the question 'Why did he (you, they, I) do it?' is successively asked, Hutcheson maintains that the final answer will take some form of reference to instinct or the affections—for example, 'He was moved by kindly desires' or 'It is his nature to act from self-interest.' Where the question 'Why was it virtuous (morally good) for him (you, them, me) to do it?' is successively asked, the final answer will involve some direct or indirect reference to the moral sense—for example, 'Because of approval of the moral sense' or 'Because the motive was benevolent.' Again, Hutcheson's case against the rationalists appeals implicitly to the general empirical doctrine that new or simple ideas cannot be received by reason. Whatever is known by reason—that is, any awareness we have by means of our power to find out true propositions—will be complex or derivative, according to Hutcheson. Awareness of a motive to election will be an awareness of something like a kindly desire or a desire for one's own pleasure. These are simple, original, or nonderivative ideas. Therefore, according to Hutcheson, the motivation provided by exciting reasons cannot be a function of reason. In a similar way, awareness of approbation is a simple idea. Therefore, the justification provided by justifying reasons cannot be a function of reason either.

With this distinction and its implications, Hutcheson has raised the general problem of the roles of reason and sentiment in moral judgments. An adequate consideration of his treatment of the topic will take us beyond the passages specifically concerned with the phrase "conformity to reason." His claim that justifying reasons presuppose the moral sense leads to a consideration of his replies to the rationalists' criticisms of his doctrine of the moral sense. In one part of these replies, he appeals to an analogy between the moral sense and the sense of sight that has extensive implications for the general topic of reason and sentiment, for his theory of justification, and for the status of basic moral principles.

Many of Burnet's criticisms of the moral sense are vague and metaphorical. For example, it provides "too uncertain a bottom to venture out upon in the stormy and tempestuous sea of passions and interests and affections," and it may be "deceitful and wrong" or a "wrong sense." Hutcheson must therefore interpret the criticisms before he attempts to answer them.

In his letter of October 9, Hutcheson formulates what he considers to be two of Burnet's objections. He presents the first as a problem of self-reference: How can the moral sense judge whether the moral sense is morally right or wrong? Burnet explicitly disavows this interpretation in his letter of December 25. Hutcheson apparently considered his answer worth emphasizing, however, since in section 1 of *Illustrations* he reasserts that the moral sense cannot judge its own moral rightness or wrongness. Apparently he and Burnet agree that if the acceptability of the ultimate basis of moral judgments is challenged, that challenge is not about moral qualities and does not call for a moral justification. Burnet forgets this, however, in some of his arguments for reason being the foundation of morals. Hutcheson observes it in his consistent refusal to admit that regressive justification in morals goes beyond the moral sense and the principle of benevolence.

Hutcheson's positive reply to the objection, understood as a request for an explanation of how we do judge the moral sense, is that we can tell that a life in which benevolence receives ultimate approval is better than one in which malice does. In the first kind of life, approval of actions would bring pleasurable consequences, in the latter, painful ones. Thus, his reply implicitly admits the possibility of the moral sense being constituted otherwise than it now is. Two points here are important for later stages of his theory of justification: first, it is sensible to appeal to the concept of a total life which one might be able to contemplate and, at least hypothetically, choose or reject; second, preference or choice for such a life represents the operation of exciting reasons, which are generalized and rationally grounded.

Hutcheson's version of Burnet's second objection is that if all moral ideas depend upon the constitution of our senses, then all constitutions would have been equally good in the eyes of God—an absurd consequence. This raises some specific theological issues which are not immediately relevant to his theory of justification, but two points do emerge. Although he considers morals and theology logically independent of one another, if he were put in a position where he had to deal with their relations, he would argue from morals to theology, not the other way.

In contrast to his brief and superficial treatment of the issue in his letter of October 9, section 4 of the *Illustrations* indicates that he considers Burnet's objection that the moral sense may be "wrong" to be ambiguous, complex, and puzzling. In the process of considering alternative interpretations on his way to the one that raises the most serious difficulties, he makes a number of points which have significance for his theory of justification: We can be as certain as we are of the continuation of gravitation that our senses will remain the same and that therefore we will continue to approve what we now approve if the actions approved are undertaken with sincere effort to promote public good and if we take into account the impossibility of predicting with certainty all their natural consequences. We cannot be certain that everyone will approve what we approve, although it is probable that they will (for example, it is probable that when we are free from prejudice, our judgments are sound rather than not, and therefore that approvals based on the belief, say, that an action is publicly useful, will agree). And finally, a theory that accepts a moral sense does not supersede any reasoning of moralists, either ancient or modern, but instead makes it possible to give an explication of the "reasonableness" that is supposed to be independent of affections and sense.

These replies to alternative interpretations of Burnet's objection bring Hutcheson finally to the one which Burnet may have intended. In any case, it is the one which presents the greatest difficulties and to which Hutcheson devotes the greatest attention: Isn't it possible that the condition of the moral sense may vary from time to time, so that it does not always represent its objects as they are? For example, might it not approve what is vicious, or might it not approve at one time what it disapproves at another? In short, isn't the moral sense fallible?

The Moral Sense Analogy

Hutcheson meets this version of Burnet's objection in a passage which is central to the entire argument of *Illustrations*. Basically an appeal to an analogy between the moral sense and the ordinary senses, such as vision, it shows that he is aware of differences as well as similarities. It has significant implications for his distinction between exciting and justifying reasons and is, in fact, crucial to a correct understanding of the role played by the moral sense in Hutcheson's general theory of justification.

> . . . we must remember that of the sensible ideas, some are allowed to be only perceptions in our minds and not images of any like external quality, as colors, sounds, tastes, smells, pleasure, pain. Other ideas are images of something external, as duration, number, extension, motion, rest. These latter, for distinction, we may call concomitant ideas of sensations and the former purely sensible. As to the purely sensible ideas, we know they are altered by any disorder in our organs and made different from what arise in us from the same objects at other times. We do not denominate objects from our perceptions during the disorder but according to our ordinary perceptions or those of others in good health. Yet nobody imagines that therefore colors, sounds, tastes are not sensible ideas. In like manner many circumstances diversify the concomitant ideas. But we denominate objects from the appearances they make to us in an uniform medium when our organs are in no disorder and the object not

very distant from them. But none therefore imagines that it is reason and not sense which discovers these concomitant ideas or primary qualities.

Just so in our ideas of actions. These three things are to be distinguished. 1. The idea of the external motion, known first by sense, and its tendency to the happiness or misery of some sensitive nature, often inferred by argument or reason, which on these subjects suggests as invariable eternal or necessary truths as any whatsoever. 2. Apprehension or opinion of the affections in the agent, inferred by our reason. So far the idea of an action represents something external to the observer, really existing whether he had perceived it or not, and having a real tendency to certain ends. 3. The perception of approbation or disapprobation arising in the observer according as the affections of the agent are apprehended kind in their just degree or deficient or malicious. This approbation cannot be supposed an image of anything external more than the pleasures of harmony, of taste, of smell. But let none imagine that calling the ideas of virtue and vice perceptions of a sense upon apprehending the actions and affections of another does diminish their reality more than the like assertions concerning all pleasure and pain, happiness or misery. Our reason often corrects the report of our senses about the natural tendency of the external action and corrects rash conclusions about the affections of the agent. But whether our moral sense be subject to such a disorder as to have different perceptions from the same apprehended affections in an agent at different times, as the eye may have of the colors of an unaltered object it is not easy to determine. Perhaps it will be hard to find any instances of such a change. What reason could correct if it fell into such a disorder I know not, except suggesting to its remembrance its former approbations and representing the general sense of mankind. But this does not prove ideas of virtue and vice to be previous to a sense more than a like correction of the idea of color in a person under the jaundice proves that colors are perceived by reason previously to a sense.[33]

In speaking of the qualities of objects, Hutcheson stood within a long tradition which had been most recently developed by Locke, who held that primary quali-

33. Pages 163–164.

ties such as figure and motion are inseparable from physical objects and that secondary qualities are the powers of objects to bring about such ideas as color, taste, and aroma by acting upon our sense organs. Locke concluded that our ideas of primary qualities "resemble" the characteristics of independently existing objects, but that our ideas of secondary qualities do not. Our knowledge of objects and their qualities is gained, according to Locke, through experience by means of simple or complex ideas. Simple ideas, such as those of solidity, figure, and color, are "original"—that is, temporally and logically prior to complex ideas, such as those of a tomato or a triangle. To have any simple idea requires a sense, according to Locke, because reason cannot give rise to new simple ideas. Hutcheson uses Locke's theory in the development of his analogy but modifies it and departs from it. I shall consider the analogy under four headings: (1) primary and secondary qualities, (2) the use of appraisive terminology, (3) the correction of sense, and (4) defeasibility.

Primary and secondary qualities. It is not clear what Hutcheson means by "concomitance." Interpreted in one way, it specifies a respect in which the ideas of approbation and disapprobation are like the ideas of the primary qualities of physical objects in Locke's theory. Thus, 'X is colored, so [concomitantly] X is extended' would have as its moral analogue, 'X is approved, so [concomitantly] X is virtuous.' Because of the suggestion that the concomitant idea is derived from the purely sensible idea, however, this would be a departure from the Lockean tradition, according to which secondary qualities are derivative from primary qualities and the ideas of secondary qualities correspondingly derivative from the ideas of primary qualities. In any case, Hutcheson clearly considers the ideas of approbation and disapprobation similar to the ideas of secondary qualities, which, according to the Lockean tradition, are not images of anything external to the perceiver but modifications of the perceiver himself. In the case of objects, our original ideas are simple and purely sensible, according to Hutcheson, and our concomitant ideas are dependent upon them in some unspecified way, even though they are also sensible since they are altered by disorders in the sensory organs. In the case of actions, however, our original ideas are complex, because they include observation of motion, knowledge of its effects, and knowledge of motives.

With respect to the terminology applicable to objects and to actions, Hutcheson's analogy introduces further modifications of Locke's views. Hutcheson holds that we may correctly apply the terminology of both secondary and primary qualities (of both purely sensible ideas and concomitant ideas) to objects according to the appearances they make to us under "normal conditions." If we assume, as he seems to suggest, that there are also normal conditions for the moral sense, then the analogy amounts to his maintaining that it is as proper to apply the term 'virtuous' to an action on the occasion of approving it for its benevolent motive and beneficent consequences as it is to apply the terms 'red' and 'spherical' to an object, say a tomato, on the occasion of its appearing to us red and spherical under normal conditions.

There are differences between Locke and Hutcheson, however, with regard to the nature of visual and moral ideas. The idea of red, for Locke, is a simple idea of sensation received through the sense of sight; the idea of sphericity is a simple idea of sensation received through the sense of sight or the sense of touch. Moral approval, although a simple idea, is clearly not an idea of sensation for Hutcheson. Nor does it quite fit either of Locke's two other categories of simple ideas—ideas of reflection, or ideas of both sensation and reflection. Locke did not talk about a distinct moral pleasure. He classified the idea of pleasure in general as a simple idea of both sensation and reflection, not as a simple idea of reflection alone, giving as his reason that it "joins [itself] to almost all our ideas both of sensation and reflection."[34] The idea of moral approval is, then, what Hutcheson would call, in his modification of Locke, an "accompanying" idea. Despite the difficulty of classifying the idea of moral approval according to Locke's scheme, it can be said quite definitely that moral approval is an idea of an internal sense for Hutcheson, and that it accompanies certain other ideas of sensation and reflection which show that an action had benevolent motives or beneficent consequences.

Since no distinct bodily organ is involved in internal accompanying ideas, no organ besides the ones required for sensation is involved in any such idea. Consequently, the healthy state of the sensory organ has no analogue in the case of our moral ideas of actions, although with some interpretation, an analogy can still be drawn.

Hutcheson characterizes a sense as "a determination of the mind to receive any idea from the presence of an object which occurs to us independent on our will,"[35] It is the involuntary occurrence of the idea rather than the operation of a physical organ that he is emphasizing when he speaks of a "perception of approbation." If we consider the experience (perception) of approval and disapproval in the case of actions to be the counterpart of the appearance in the case of objects, the analogy would run as follows: On the occasion when, under normal conditions, an object appears to be red independently of any volition on our part, we correctly denominate the object 'red.' Just so, on the occasion when, under normal conditions, the motive and consequences of an act elicit approval independently of any volition on our part, we correctly denominate the act 'virtuous.'

For Hutcheson, the moral counterpart of the sensory organ would seem to be the whole person; and the coun-

34. *An Essay Concerning Human Understanding* (Oxford, 1894), II, vii, 2.

35. *Inquiry into the Original of Our Ideas of Moral Good and Evil*, 4th ed. (London, 1738), p. 113. Also Selby-Bigge, *British Moralists*, I, 74.

terparts of the normal conditions of health, location, and medium of transmission of sensory stimuli would be knowledge of the motives and consequences of the actions, impartiality, consistency, and "representing the general sense of mankind," a phrase which he does not explain and which is ambiguous enough to encourage a number of different interpretations. It could be a recommendation to imagine what it would be like if someone else was in my position and to consider whether he would have the same reactions, which should serve as a reminder that moral approvals and disapprovals ought not to vary unless there are morally significant differences in the cases. This would underscore the condition of consistency. It could be a suggestion to consider what it would be like if everyone reacted in the way I am reacting and whether the resulting circumstances would be desired or desirable. It could mean that it is reasonable to assume that there would be a general agreement among people about the circumstances in which moral terminology would be appropriately used. It could be a reminder that the point of moral principles and judgments, and of actions in accordance with them, is to enable people to get along together. It could be taken to indicate that approvals and disapprovals that carry moral significance cannot be dependent upon the special circumstances of individuals. This would underscore the condition of impartiality. It could be a recommendation that the person approving or disapproving should look at the case from several different points of view, not only his own. He may be reminding us that approvals and disapprovals with moral significance are not just for the moment or the particular case, but for a lifetime and for cases not yet encountered. Such cases, we may continue to interpret, involve other people. Therefore, in considering what kind of total life we really want to live and the place in it that will be occupied by our moral system, we need to take into account the general sense of mankind.

For convenience I shall use the term 'generality' so far as possible instead of Hutcheson's phrase "representing the general sense of mankind," and I shall suggest which of these possible interpretations seems most appropriate in context. We may say, then, that Hutcheson apparently gives us four conditions for the normal functioning of the moral sense: knowledge, impartiality, consistency, and generality.

If there is an analogy between vision and the moral sense in terms of causal relations, it would presumably be that a quality of an action causes us to have the idea of approval by acting upon the moral sense. Hutcheson sometimes seems to be asking a question which would be answered by finding such a causal relation; for example, he asks "What quality determines our approbation of one action rather than of the contrary action?" At one point in his attempts to interpret the rationalists, he seems to assert that the quality of benevolence in an action causes the idea of approval in the moral sense: "If the meaning of the question, 'Is not the end of public good more reasonable than private?' be this, 'Does not every spectator approve the pursuit of public good more than private?' the answer is obvious that he does. But not for any reason or truth but from a moral sense in the constitution of the soul."

Such an interpretation carries further the analogy with the causal view of the nature of sense perception. It is based on a doctrine about sense perception that Hutcheson evidently believed. It is consistent with his views about the involuntary nature and the sensory basis of our purely sensible ideas and our ideas of approval and disapproval. Just as it would be on Locke's view proper, although somewhat artificial, to say that the quality of sphericity in the tomato causes me to have the idea of the sphericity of the tomato, so it would be proper to say that the quality of benevolence in the motive of an act causes me to approve the act. If we try to continue the analogy in Locke's terms, however, a disanalogy appears. For Locke, the idea of sphericity is caused "by impulse" of particules which have the power to "agitate our animal spirits." Hutcheson would not consider that the idea of moral approval is caused in this way.

His doctrine would be more satisfactorily expressed by saying 'When I learn that the motive of the act was benevolent, then I find myself approving the act.' Stated in this way, the analogy does not carry over. A corresponding statement comes out as some kind of nonsense: 'When I understand that a tomato is spherical, I find myself having the idea of sphericity.' We might try another version: 'When I understand that an object is a tomato, I find myself having an idea of sphericity.' But this seems to be at least false, if not nonsensical. The analogy is sufficient, however, to support certain similar conditional statements. 'If I did not have a moral sense, I would not have the idea of approving an action for its benevolent motive.' 'If I did not have a sense of sight (or touch), I would not have the idea of sphericity.'

The analogy arises from the presence of certain necessary or sufficient conditions in both cases which support the use of causal language up to a point. The disanalogy includes at least a difference in the nature and relations of these conditions. For example, in the case of objects, a certain minute structure in the object is a necessary condition for the occurrence of an idea of sphericity. In the case of actions, some thought, belief, or opinion about the action is a necessary condition for the occurrence of the idea of moral approval. The former might be taken to be a case of efficient causation, but hardly the latter.

Another interpretation also needs to be guarded against in view of Hutcheson's causal language. If we say that Hutcheson considered the causal relation to be the same in our ideas of actions and in our ideas of objects, then we would also have to say that for him the judgment, 'A is virtuous,' formulates a belief about a causal power of an act, not a moral appraisal of it. Yet he clearly intends it to be a moral appraisal. Furthermore, if 'A is virtuous' means for Hutcheson, 'There is a quality in A which causes me or every spectator to approve it,' then if someone challenged the judgment, Hutcheson should meet the challenge by arguing that he himself, or every spectator, does in fact approve.

But Hutcheson never suggests that we should justify a judgment by gathering statistics about the reactions of one or many, actual or possible, spectators. I conclude, therefore, that the analogy in terms of causal relations is limited enough to deny that 'A is virtuous' means the same as 'A causes me to feel approval,' and that Hutcheson did not intend the analogy to support the subjective theory to which such an interpretation would lead.

Appraisive terminology. I turn, therefore, to a consideration of the analogy in terms of appraisive terminology. Hutcheson introduces such terminology as a matter of course in discussing our ideas of action, but he makes no explicit use of it in discussing our ideas of objects. Therefore, at certain points I shall proceed in terms of what might be said if he had introduced appraisive terminology in the latter case. Just as there is descriptive terminology for dealing with actions, so there is appraisive terminology for dealing with objects, and it will be instructive for our general understanding of Hutcheson to pursue his analogy in these terms. Since the terminology for dealing with objects is usually descriptive and that for dealing with actions often appraisive, it is not unreasonable to expect several disanalogies to appear.

In the case of our ideas of objects, whatever other problems there may be, if we have the appropriate term for what we perceive, there is no need to introduce a new term. We see a red tomato and say, leaving aside questions of artificiality, that it is a red tomato. In the case of our ideas of actions, even if we do have the appropriate term for what we perceive, we still need to account for the introduction of ethical terms. We see a man handing some money to a member of the Salvation Army and say that the act is virtuous, thus introducing a new term.

Someone might claim that a new term *is* introduced in the case of our perception of objects. For example, if an object appears in normal conditions to be red, spherical, juicy, green stemmed, somewhat tart, many-seeded, and so on, then we may appropriately apply the term 'tomato.' The disanalogy still remains, however, since 'tomato' is a summary term used to describe or identify the object in place of the longer list, and the term introduced is a predicate noun. 'Virtuous' is a predicate adjective used to appraise the action, not a summary term used to identify or describe it.

We can find an analogy, however, by introducing explicitly appraisive terminology into the language of our ideas of objects. As the counterpart of the shift from 'benevolent' to 'virtuous,' we would have a shift from 'appearing' to, say, 'worthy of belief,' 'credible,' or 'evident.' Appearing red under normal conditions would then be a 'credibility-making characteristic' as benevolence is a 'virtue-making characteristic.' As the analogue of 'A is benevolent, so A is virtuous,' we would have 'O appears red under normal conditions, so it is credible that O is red.' There is still a disanalogy, however, in at least two respects. Appearing red is only a credibility-making characteristic for the proposition that the object is red, not that it is a tomato. And there is a difference in the point at which the normative elements become explicit: In the case of the denomination of objects, the application of the visual term—even the correct application of it—does not in itself explicitly introduce anything normative. It is necessary to add that the object's being red is credible. In the case of actions, to say 'A is virtuous,' whether correct or not, is to say something normative—that it is right to do A, that A ought to be done, that it is appropriate to regard A as a standard for morally good conduct. It is not necessary to add anything further.

It might be replied that the disanalogy is only apparent, that to say 'O is red' is to say 'O is red is worthy of being believed,' just as much as to say 'A is virtuous' is to say 'A is worthy of being done.' This would hardly be borne out by any appeal to what a person would usually intend when he said the one or the other; but that objection aside, there is a difference in the way the appraisive terms apply. Introducing the appraisive epistemic term requires the use of a higher level of language than the ethical term. The epistemic term applies to a proposition which applies to an object, whereas the moral term applies directly to the action. It is the action that is worthy of being done; it is the proposition about the object that is worthy of being believed.

There is further disanalogy in terms of the experiences of the two senses and the nature of the terms applied. The application of the normative term 'virtuous' is the expression of what the moral sense experiences—namely, its feeling of approval—and the application of the descriptive term 'benevolent' is not. The application of the descriptive term 'red' is the expression of what the visual sense experiences, and the application of the normative term 'credible' is not.

I conclude from these analogies and disanalogies that one of the main functions of the concept of the moral sense for Hutcheson is to provide a ground for the transition from the application of descriptive terms to the application of normative terms. It is because we feel approbation for benevolent motives and beneficent consequences that it is appropriate, according to Hutcheson, to apply the term 'virtuous.' This feeling of approbation ("distinct perception of pleasure"), being a simple idea, must, according to his theory of knowledge, be received by some sense. Because a moral judgment that the action is virtuous is the appropriate way to express this feeling ("perception"), it follows that the sense is a "moral sense."

This argument, again, brings out the positive implications of his earlier arguments against the rationalists. Moral ideas, being new or simple, cannot originate in reason but must originate in sense. Being a distinct species of idea, their origin can only be accounted for by a distinct sense. That they are distinct Hutcheson supports by distinguishing the moral sense from the senses of beauty, honor, and public duty and by claiming that the experiences of moral approval and disapproval are special in themselves. On my present interpretation, their distinct character is shown by the need for a distinct language in order to express such approval appropriately—that is, the language of virtue and vice or of morality generally.

In his analogy there is no counterpart of the normative role in the visual sense or in any of the ordinary senses. In *A Short Introduction to Moral Philosophy* he introduces a "sense of veracity" and even says that it is an "immediate sense," but he describes it as an awareness of an injunction to speak the truth. The sense of veracity that would be the analogue of the moral sense would need to provide the ground not for the transition from something's appearing red to its being red, but for the transition from something's appearing red to its being credible that it is red. The "concomitance" between purely sensible ideas and ideas of primary qualities might be interpreted as his bridge in the first case, although he might insist that the concomitant idea for purely sensible redness is, say, extension. But for the second case he would need to hold that when the sense of veracity is pleased or in some way affected by the appearance a thing makes to us, we can take this as an indication that the belief is credible that the thing is as it appears. And when this indication is suitably qualified, we can take such an appearance as a credibility-making characteristic.

The closest Hutcheson comes to expressing such a view is to say that there is pleasure in the recognition of truth. He does not suggest, however, that this pleasure is an indication of truth or credibility. If he were to extend his analogy along these lines, it is quite apparent that the sense of veracity would call for an interpretation similar to one I have previously suggested for the moral sense. Just as the moral sense may refer to the relevant characteristics of a person who is functioning in ways that are morally appropriate, so the sense of veracity might refer to the relevant characteristics of a person who is functioning in ways that are epistemically appropriate.

If he were to pursue such a development, we might expect a further analogy to emerge. He says, for example, that if we look at actions which are in fact considered virtuous, we see that they all flow from benevolent motives. He thus suggests that we seem to know what actions are virtuous before we know, explicitly at least, what makes them so. This is one way of interpreting his emphasis on the immediate and involuntary nature of our approvals and disapprovals. The analogous point in perception is that we seem to know what propositions or beliefs about objects are credible before we know, explicitly at least, what makes them so.

In the terminology of a later period, both senses would have preanalytic and postanalytic functions. For example, the preanalytic role of the moral sense is indicated by passages in which Hutcheson says that a person without a moral sense would be (morally) "indifferent," and that without a moral sense there would be no perception of morality. His statement that to a person without a moral sense, moral distinctions would be entirely unknown permits both preanalytic and postanalytic interpretations. And his doctrine that the moral sense enables the explication of our ideas of morality attributes a postanalytic role to the moral sense. One might say that Hutcheson has a view of the moral sense in which it is said of some person that "he has no moral sense" when this means that he looks at everything in terms of whether it will bring him pleasure or pain, whether it will benefit his business, how it will affect the gross national product, or the like, but never looks at anything from the standpoint of whether it is morally right or wrong.

I conclude that Hutcheson's concept of the moral sense may in certain cases extend widely enough that it becomes, in effect, the whole person insofar as he regards actions, consequences, and motives from the moral point of view. I shall speak in more detail of the moral point of view shortly. Here I have meant at least this much: A person who has a moral sense is morally sensitive. He finds himself reacting to certain actions with approval or disapproval. This may be quite immediate and involuntary, even uncritical. When he expresses these approvals and disapprovals, he does so in the language of 'virtue' and 'vice,' 'morally good' and 'morally evil,' 'right' and 'wrong,' and the like, which as a matter of social development and practice are the appropriate terms to use. If he is faced with the need to explain what he means or to justify what he has said, he can do so by appealing, sooner or later, directly or indirectly, to experiences of approval and disapproval and their circumstances.

Correction of the moral sense. When Hutcheson considers the analogy from the standpoint of error and correction, he is doubtful that the moral sense is similar to the visual sense in the errors it might make or in the ways in which it might be corrected. If we look into the details and implications of this apparent disanalogy, we find that Hutcheson is not a subjectivist, an objectivist, or an empirical intuitionist, and that the doctrine that the moral sense approves benevolence, which I shall refer to as the doctrine of approval, is neither logically necessary nor empirically contingent.

Hutcheson's hesitation indicates that he is puzzled about the kind of problem he is facing. On the one hand, he might be puzzled about the nature of the error—whether it might be a mistake of fact, of logic, or of some other kind. On the other hand, he might be puzzled about the nature of the correction—whether it might be done by replacing a false moral proposition with a true one, by curing some disorder in the moral sense, by bringing the moral sense into accordance with a standard of correctness, or by some other method.

It seems unlikely that he would consider an error of the moral sense to be a simple logical mistake. He recognizes two kinds of possible errors: inconsistent approvals and approvals of malevolence. He does not suggest, however, that there is a formal fallacy in either case, or that reason—in the form of the knowledge and application of the rules of formal logic—could correct them if they occurred.

Someone might claim, nevertheless, that making inconsistent approvals involves a kind of logical mistake. Jonathan Edwards argued, for example, that thieves who, being brought to justice, call their informers vicious, are inconsistent because "when they put themselves in the place of those who injured them, they approve the same things they condemn."[36] This argument makes implicit use of a principle of universalizability that some writers might claim is a logical principle. Formulated in one usual way, however, it is not a principle of logic. Hutcheson might point out that the formulation 'What is right for one person must be right for any similar person in similar circumstances' has moral content. So it could be at most a principle of "the logic of moral discourse," not of the logic of discourse in general. He would ask 'What means this word, "right?"' and argue that his question can be satisfactorily answered only by some appeal to the moral sense. Thus, neither a mistake nor a correction could be identified in purely formal terms. If the principle of universalizability is formulated in a way that makes it free of a moral context, then it comes closer to qualifying as a principle of logic, but its moral relevance comes into question. Consider it in the form 'A person who makes a universalizable judgment about anything logically commits himself to making a similar judgment about anything exactly like it or similar to it in the relevant respects.' Hutcheson could point out that this is not sufficient in itself to establish the correctness of the approval over the disapproval, or the converse. He could say to the rationalists, including Wollaston, that they apply such principles of reason only to human beings capable of free intelligent choice and normal human experiences. And, *this* is why logical principles may be morally significant—not because they are themselves the foundations of morals, but because they can be ap-

36. *The Nature of True Virtue*, pp. 106–107.

plied to situations which involve the pleasures and pains that people may experience and the good and evil they may increase or diminish by their actions.

In the case suggested by Burnet in which the mistake is approving malevolence, the same general results appear. If Hutcheson considered the doctrine of approval to be true by definition, then the approval of malevolence by the moral sense would have to be corrected by reason in the form of knowledge that this is logically impossible. Perhaps we could reject this out of hand. For, although Hutcheson is puzzled as to whether the moral sense could make a mistake, he does not say that it is logically impossible. In the final interpretation, however, such a mistake cannot be ruled out easily or quickly, because Hutcheson quite clearly wants to maintain that the doctrine has some kind of necessity. The reason for rejecting this form of error and correction comes from Hutcheson's ridicule of the rationalists on a somewhat similar point. He pointed out that one interpretation of their doctrine that virtue consists in conformity to reason reduces to the explicitly repetitive tautology that virtue is virtue, "a wonderful discovery!" If Hutcheson held that it is true by definition that the moral sense approves benevolence, then he would have to admit that it reduces to the tautology that the moral sense approves what the moral sense approves. Thus, whatever necessity Hutcheson may consider the doctrine of approval to have, it is not the kind that would make it a contradiction in terms to say that the moral sense approved malevolence. Nor would the correction of such a mistake consist in a perception by reason that a term means what it means and not another thing. I conclude that Hutcheson's position is that it is logically possible for the moral sense to make a mistake, that if it does it is not a simple logical mistake, that it would not be corrected by reason in the form of replacing statements that are logically false by statements that are logically true. In short, I believe Hutcheson does not consider the doctrine that the moral sense approves benevolence a simple logical necessity.

Would a mistake be some kind of factual mistake to be corrected by factual knowledge, and would the doctrine of approval consequently be an empirical generalization? Consider a case in which the facts were the reactions of my own moral sense. A mistake of inconsistency would be a case in which at one time I felt approval of an act and at another felt disapproval of that very same act. Could reason, in the form of a more careful introspective recollection, discover that what had seemed to be painful was really pleasurable, or the converse? Such an appeal to introspection is dubious on psychological and epistemological grounds, and Hutcheson never suggests this as the way to go about correcting a mistake if it should occur.

Could a more careful gathering of information about the reactions of others in the community, nation, or world correct inconsistent approvals or the approval of malevolence? Hutcheson would agree that such a gathering of statistics is a proper function of reason, but he would point out that in themselves, statistics cannot determine which feelings are correct or incorrect. If some additional principle were introduced—for example, that we are approving correctly only if we approve or disapprove what most people approve—Hutcheson would point out that you still have to answer the question 'For what reason is it right to approve what all or most people approve?' The answer he would give, as I understand him, is definitely not 'Because the feelings of the majority determine what is right.' If Hutcheson were to use this approach, he would answer 'Because you find that in the general sense of mankind actions are considered to be right, virtuous, morally good, or obligatory according to whether they are benevolent in motive or tendency.' Such approval, he would continue, is not a perception of reason in the form of introspective or statistical knowledge.

This indicates to me that Hutcheson is not a subjectivist, either personal or transpersonal. It would be inaccurate to attribute to him the view that a moral judgment, such as 'Hazarding life in a just war is virtuous,' means the same thing as 'My moral sense (or the moral sense of others, or the moral sense of the majority) approves of hazarding life in a just war.' The latter is not for him a different way of saying the former. If it were, then a mistake in the former would be corrected by making some true statement about the latter. Furthermore, to say that it did mean the same thing would imply that Hutcheson considered a moral judgment to be a report, perhaps somewhat disguised, about the affective reactions of ourselves or others. Among other reasons for rejecting such an interpretation is the one that it would nullify the normative function of the moral sense, which, I have argued, is one of its main roles for Hutcheson.

Perhaps the facts involved in error and correction are not about subjective states or reactions, however, but about simple, objective qualities or characteristics of the action or the agent. According to a common interpretation of Hutcheson, the moral sense is directly aware of virtue or moral goodness in a person or action. Without going into the details of the nature of error and correction on this interpretation, there are at least four considerations against it. First, the problem of error and correction could not even arise, because the moral sense is held to be a kind of intuitive faculty, empirical in nature, to be sure, but presumably incapable of making mistakes. Second, this interpretation makes the moral sense conform to Hutcheson's definition of reason rather than to his definition of sense. Third, in the analogy, as well as in other passages, Hutcheson makes quite clear that he does not consider moral qualities to be objective at all. And finally, as Frankena has shown,[37] the terms 'sense,' 'perceive,' and 'apprehend,' which now lend themselves to this interpretation, did not necessarily indicate any kind of direct cognition of objective qualities either in Hutcheson's usage or in eighteenth-century usage generally.

These considerations indicate to me that about simple moral qualities, Hutcheson is not an objectivist, a de-

37. Ibid., pp. 368–369.

scriptivist, or a naive realist. That is, moral terms do not refer to or describe simple, objective characteristics that are intrinsic to other persons or actions. For that reason, as well as because of his distinction between sense and reason, moral properties cannot be directly intuited by the moral sense. In fact, I might add, the whole concept of error by a sense and correction by reason threatens to obliterate his basic distinction between sense and reason.

Perhaps the facts involved in error and correction are neither subjective, nor objective and simple, but objective and complex. Many of the foregoing reasons against subjectivism and objectivism of simple moral qualities apply with appropriate variations to this interpretation as well. In addition, no factual knowledge is in itself sufficient, according to Hutcheson, to account for its own moral significance. Just as Hutcheson says to Burnet that when anyone claims that an action is in conformity to God's will, a question still remains as to why this should justify it morally, so he says (although not quite so patently) that when anyone claims that an action contributes to the welfare of humanity, the same question remains. His answer is that in the latter case no less than in the former, something beyond the knowledge of the complex characteristic is necessary to account for the moral relevance of the factual information. It is the approval of the moral sense that makes an action's contribution to the welfare of humanity a good reason for judging it to be virtuous; it is the approval of the moral sense that makes the fact relevant to the moral justification of the act. Suppose, then, that an action conforms to the will of God. This could be a good reason for considering it virtuous, according to Hutcheson, only if such conformity contributes to the general welfare, this, in turn, being approved by the moral sense. The moral sense, therefore, determines what facts are relevant to moral justification.

Hutcheson would agree that the complex objective characteristic of conforming to the will of God or contributing to the general welfare could be perceived by reason. He would also agree that the truth or falsity of a proposition ascribing such a property to an action could be ascertained by reason. Thus, we might believe that an action had a given characteristic when it did not, and we would then be believing a proposition that was false. It would be a function of reason to find this out and to correct the mistake by substituting a true proposition for the false one. But none of this, according to Hutcheson, is a correction of the moral sense by reason. It is the correction of a mistaken belief by a correct one, by accurate knowledge. It could be exemplified by replacing a false statement, such as 'A conforms to the will of God' or 'A contributes to the general welfare,' with a true one, such as 'A flouts the will of God' or 'A contributes to the general ill.' According to Hutcheson, nothing in these corrections, taken in themselves, has moral significance. That enters only when moral attitudes and feelings about these facts are introduced by the reactions of the moral sense.

Since the reactions of the moral sense do not consist in belief or knowledge, however, a mistake and correction of the moral sense cannot consist in having a statement formulating a false belief corrected by being replaced by a statement formulating a true one. For example, a mistake of inconsistency might be a case in which my moral sense both approves and disapproves of an action that was done from a motive to contribute to the general welfare. A mistaken approval might be a case in which my moral sense approves of an action that was done from a motive to contribute to the general ill. Both these mistakes would be corrected by bringing my moral sense to approve consistently of actions that are motivated by a concern to contribute to the general welfare. The correction of the moral sense, then, according to Hutcheson, cannot *consist in* some perception of reason—that is, in finding out some true proposition. If my analysis of Hutcheson on the matter of error and correction is right, it consists neither in finding out a true proposition about my subjective reactions or those of others, nor in finding out any truths of logic.

The reason for this, in summary, is very simple: none of them can be, in themselves, propositions with any morally significant content.

This does not mean, of course, that there is no way in which the moral sense can be corrected. There are many ways in which many things can be corrected: you can correct a criminal or a compass, a child or a chess strategy, a belief or a barometer, a person or a page proof, a fault or a figure, a sum or a supposition, a report or a recipe. Within this variety is one main sense of 'correction' with various possible modifications: something which is not in accordance with a standard of correctness is changed so that it is.

Mistaken perceptions of reason will be formulated in false statements and will be corrected by being replaced by true statements. Beliefs, sums, suppositions, and reports work similarly. The standard from which they diverge, when mistaken, is the standard of "the truth." As I understand Hutcheson, mistaken reactions of the moral sense will not be formulated in false propositions, although characteristically they will be expressed in some kind of verbal form; they will be inconsistent approvals or approvals of the wrong thing. The standard from which they diverge is the standard of "approval of benevolence." They will be corrected by being brought into conformity with that standard. Such a correction does not consist, however, in a perception of reason. It is more like the correction that might be made of a compass or a barometer. Just as a mislocated magnet might interfere with the functioning of a compass or a change in altitude might interfere with the functioning of a barometer, self-interest, lack of relevant information, or too restricted a viewpoint might interfere with the functioning of the moral sense. If we know about the misplaced magnet or the change in altitude and know how to adjust the magnets of the compass or the tension against the capsule of the barometer, then we can correct them. In this sense, it could be said that we have corrected them "by reason"—that is, our knowledge enables us to change them so that they conform to the

standards of "indicating magnetic north" or "measuring atmospheric pressure as if at sea level." We might say that reason has been able to bring about the correction or has caused the correction to be brought about. Only in this sense would Hutcheson admit that reason can correct the moral sense. We know by reason, for example, that a thing cannot both be and not be something in the same respect and at the same time. In the light of this knowledge, this "perception of reason," the moral sense may change in its reactions so that it reacts always in the same way to the same action, although this, in itself, as indicated earlier, does not assure correctness. We may know by reason that according to the general sense of mankind, actions are considered to be morally right if they are approved for their benevolence of motive or tendency toward beneficent consequences. Our knowledge may influence the moral sense in such a way that the approval of malevolence is changed to an approval of benevolence. That is, in general, reason might correct the moral sense by bringing about changes in its reactions. For example, being a fearful man like Thomas Hobbes, I may morally disapprove of an act of hazarding life in a just war. Reason may inform me that this act contributes to the welfare of my innocent countrymen and thus to the general welfare, and that it was undertaken from that motive. I may then find that I morally approve of the act. The correction is not itself a perception of reason, but a change from disapproval to approval; it brings the reaction of the moral sense into accordance with the standard of approving benevolence. Knowing that the act did contribute to the general welfare and that its motive was to that end *are* perceptions of reason, but they do not *constitute* the correction, according to Hutcheson. They cause the change to occur that does constitute the correction.

If we consider the verbalized form of the change, this may be clearer. I express the reaction of my moral sense at one time by saying 'I disapprove of his act of hazarding life in a just war.' I express this reaction at

another time by saying 'I approve of his act of hazarding his life in a just war.' Granting that the act is done from a benevolent motive, the second expression would be, according to Hutcheson, a correction of the first; but it is not a perception of reason. This is evident if you consider the agreement and disagreement of the judgments with the two relevant standards. Both verbal forms are equally in accordance with the standard of truth. Thus, the second is not a correction of the moral sense by reason in the sense of replacing a false statement with a true statement; the correction is not a perception of reason, even though the change which constitutes the correction is brought about by a perception of reason. With respect to the standard of approving benevolence, however, they do differ. The reaction of the moral sense is brought into accordance with the standard of approving benevolence after having diverged from it. It can be said that this is brought about by factual knowledge of the nature of the motive—that is, by a perception of reason. But, Hutcheson points out at the end of the passage in which he draws the analogy, "This does not prove ideas of virtue and vice to be previous to a sense more than a like correction of the ideas of color in a person under the jaundice proves that colors are perceived by reason previously to a sense."

According to Hutcheson, then, the analogy does not have the cognitive consequences claimed by Burnet. Hutcheson holds, in effect, that we apply the language which is appropriate to the sensory, perceptual, and epistemic point of view to objects according to the appearances they make to us under normal conditions, and that we may modify or adapt what we say about objects according to what we know or may subsequently learn about these conditions. Thus, Hutcheson would say that a person who, on the basis of sense perception, judged that an object was yellow would probably change his judgment if he learned he was "under the jaundice," using one of the standard examples of the day. "Just so in our ideas of actions": we apply the language which is appropriate to the moral point of view to actions accord-

ing to our approvals under normal conditions, and we may modify or adapt what we say about actions according to what we know or may subsequently learn about these conditions. Thus, Hutcheson would also say that a person who, on the basis of observing the inflicting of pain upon a child, judged the actions to be morally wrong would probably change his judgment if he realized that, due to his emotion of the moment, he had failed to consider the mother's concern for the child's long-term welfare. But just as subsequent modifications in our judgments about objects do not entail that we have a priori concepts or a priori knowledge of objects, neither do subsequent modifications in our judgments about actions entail that we have a priori concepts or a priori knowledge of actions. As I read Hutcheson, approval and disapproval occur in one set of circumstances of knowledge, information, impartiality, consistency, and generality, or another. When these circumstances change, then we approve or disapprove again; we do not learn from reason some moral truth which we did not know before. Although the approval may be different if the circumstances are different, this does not mean that the moral sense itself finds out and asserts true propositions. Nor does it mean that reason has corrected the moral sense by reaching some true conclusion about moral matters which replaces, removes, or shows to be false some conclusion which the moral sense had previously reached. The appropriate function of reason is confined to the marshalling of relevant information to the determination of how well or ill justified the reaction of the moral sense may be.

If the information concerns motives and consequences of actions, then it is relevant, because these are the matters to which the moral sense reacts either favorably or unfavorably. These are the considerations in the light of which moral approval or disapproval occurs. But the approval and disapproval belong in one epistemological category, the knowledge and information about motives and consequences in another. Moral approval and disapproval, expressed in the language of 'virtue' and 'vice,' cannot be a true proposition found out by reason according to Hutcheson's version of the nature of sense and reason.

The sense in which moral judgments can be said to be correct or incorrect, better or worse, appropriate or inappropriate will be a matter of justification, then, not a matter of the correction of sense by reason or one of reason discovering moral qualities or asserting true moral propositions. For Hutcheson, a correct, or corrected, moral judgment—one which is better or more appropriate than another—is still the expression of the approval or disapproval of the moral sense.

Because this approval may be expressed under a variety of conditions, its "correctness" will have to be judged in terms of those conditions. In general, if it can be supported by justifying reasons, then it is correct, and if not, not. A correct moral judgment for Hutcheson, therefore, is the expression in appropriate language of an attitude, emotion, feeling, or "perception" of approval which can be initially justified by an appeal to certain facts and principles and ultimately justified in terms of certain facts about actions, motives, and consequences and certain principles about benevolence, the moral sense, and virtue. We need now to look more closely at those principles.

Defeasibility. Hutcheson does not consider the doctrine that the moral sense approves benevolence a plain logical necessity. He admits that the moral sense might approve something other than benevolence. Nor does he consider the doctrine to be a simple empirical generalization. The moral sense being inconsistent in its approvals or approving something other than benevolence does not, for Hutcheson, falsify the doctrine, make it less probable, or demand any modification of it. The doctrine does not state that the moral sense will probably approve benevolence, or that it will approve some percentage of benevolent acts. Yet there are elements of both necessity and contingency in the doctrine as Hutcheson conceives it. The nature and relationship of these elements can be clarified by distinguishing the disposition of the moral sense to approve benevolence from the occasions on which it does so. I suggest that the necessity inheres in the generic relationship between the moral sense and its disposition to approve, and the contingency in the occasions on which approval may or may not occur. For Hutcheson, it is necessarily the case that the moral sense is disposed to approve benevolence, that it has a tendency to approve benevolence if and when it should appear, that it is benevolence-approbative. Yet he recognizes that there are different occasions on which this disposition may manifest itself, that it may be subject to the influence of many factors, some of which may be favorable, some not, and that some factors may actually prevent approval. Expressed in current language, the doctrine that the moral sense approves benevolence is necessary, but *defeasibly* so.[38]

Most simply, a defeasibly necessary principle is a statement of what will happen unless something prevents it.[39] On this interpretation, then, when Hutcheson says that the moral sense approves benevolence, he means that the moral sense will approve benevolence unless something prevents it. The relationship between the moral sense and its disposition to approve benevolence is necessary. It would not be the moral sense if it were not disposed to approve benevolence. Even though Hutcheson admits that God could have made man differently, he insists that He *did* make man

38. See R. L. Clark, "On What Is Naturally Necessary," *Journal of Philosophy* 61 (1965): 613; Donald Paul Snyder, "Causation, Predication, and Modal Logic" (Ph.D. diss., Duke University, 1964); G. E. M. Anscombe and P. T. Geach, *Three Philosophers* (Oxford: Blackwell, 1961), p. 102; P. T. Geach, "Dr. Kenny on Practical Inference," *Analysis* 26, no. 3 (1966): 76; George Pitcher, "Hart on Action and Responsibility," *Philosophical Review* 69 (1960): 226–235; W. Haas, "Defeasibility," *Mind* 66 (1957): 543–544, and "Value Judgments," ibid. 62 (1953): 512–517; H. L. A. Hart, "The Ascription of Responsibility and Rights," *Proceedings of the Aristotelian Society* 49 (1948–49), reprinted in *Logic and Language,* ed. A. Flew (Oxford: Blackwell, 1955), pp. 145–166.

39. Clark, "On What Is Naturally Necessary," p. 615.

with a moral sense disposed to approve benevolence. More accurately, Hutcheson holds that the doctrine of approval, in its dispositional form, is necessary, relative to the world and human nature as constituted by God. As I interpret him, Hutcheson holds that there is no empirical evidence available in the world as it is constituted—no special case or set of circumstances—that would require him to deny the doctrine or admit that it is false.

On the other hand, the doctrine may be understood in terms of particular occasions—for example, when Molly Macauley learns that Dan McCann is hazarding his life in a just war. Such occasions may vary in many ways, not only in terms of the circumstances of the person making the judgment, but also in terms of what he is judging. Thus, Hutcheson is pointing out that many different factors, such as ignorance, passion, or habit, may affect the moral sense on any given occasion, complicating the manifestation of the disposition to approve benevolence. Current terminology refers to these as "defeating" circumstances. Hutcheson speaks of them as factors which could "counteract" the moral sense.

The difficulty about the status of Hutcheson's doctrine of approval is thus resolved. It is not in any simple way straightforwardly necessary from the logical point of view, nor is it in any simple way straightforwardly contingent from the empirical point of view. Given the nature and proper functioning of the moral sense, it is necessarily benevolence-approbative. It is the nature of the moral sense to be disposed to approve benevolence in the way that it is the nature of a thief to be disposed to steal. Just as it may occur on a given occasion, however, that a thief will not steal a particular car because of conscience, disinterest, fatigue, illness, lack of time, or the like, so it may occur on a given occasion that a moral sense will not approve a particular act of benevolence because of vindictiveness, self-interest, or ignorance. Just as it is not required that we deny or consider false the general doctrine that thieves steal, so it is not required that we deny or consider false the general doctrine that the moral sense approves benevolence.

Hutcheson is quite definite about what should be done if such defeat were to occur. He does not suggest that we consider the principle false, that we have made some mistaken inference, or that we have come to an incorrect conclusion by reasoning. He suggests that we should look for the counteracting circumstances and then see whether our approval does not change (or at least whether the aberrant approval or disapproval cannot be accounted for).

A further consideration also makes it appropriate to interpret Hutcheson's doctrine in terms of defeasible necessity. One of the main purposes of the contemporary doctrine is to enable one to analyze the nature of laws or lawlike generalizations without encountering certain paradoxes. In brief, the theory of defeasibility avoids the paradoxes by accepting premises that affirm a necessary connection between being a certain kind of thing and having a certain property or disposition and a conclusion that denies the manifestation of that property or disposition on a given occasion. Thus, it is not contradictory (or nonsensical) to assert, for example, that sugar is soluble and that this piece of sugar is now immersed in water and not dissolving. Another example more pertinent to Hutcheson's analogy would be this: 'My visual sense enables me to observe the colors of objects; I am now looking at object O, but I am not observing its color.' To express Hutcheson's point more aptly, the final statement needs to be reformulated as 'I am not observing its true color' or 'I am not seeing its actual color.'

From the standpoint of defeasibility, interference, or counteraction, the analogy applies quite widely, not only to things like sugar and its properties and vision and its capacities, but also to the moral sense. Thus, Molly Macauley's moral sense is, relative to the world and human nature as constituted by God, necessarily benevolence-approbative. That on February 29 she will approve

Dan McCann's act of hazarding his life in a just war is, relative to the preceding statement, also necessary, but capable of being counteracted, or prevented from occurring by interfering circumstances, such as passion, habit, or self-interest. When such a defeat occurs, Hutcheson never suggests that we should consider the doctrine of approval false or falsified. Instead, he suggests that we should look for interfering circumstances and then see whether our approval does not change.

Any approval, according to Hutcheson, is made in the light of a variety of considerations. When something seems to go wrong, it is appropriate to examine the circumstances, not in order to find some true moral judgment to replace a false one, but in order to see whether some circumstance formerly neglected, obscured, misconceived, or omitted might not lead to a different approval. In the analogy he explicitly advises us to consider former approbations with a concern for consistency, and to take into account the general sense of mankind. According to my former interpretation, such consistency and generality are two among the factors which set the "normal conditions" for the operation of the moral sense. The doctrine of approval then read 'The informed, consistent, impartial, generalized moral sense approves benevolence.' According to the present interpretation, they indicate areas in which circumstances might arise to defeat the approval of benevolence by the moral sense. The doctrine now reads 'The moral sense, on a given occasion, will approval benevolence unless affected by ignorance, prejudice, inconsistency, particularity, or the like.' On the former approach, it would seem that Hutcheson considered his list of normal conditions exhaustive. On the present approach, a more plausible interpretation is that the factors specified are the beginning of a list of possible interfering conditions which could be indefinitely long.

As such a beginning, they specify some of the conditions determining whether the approval of a moral sense provides a reason that justifies the application of explicitly moral terminology to actions, consequences, motives, or persons. As a first formulation, which will, of course, need explanation and qualification, we may say that for Hutcheson, when the approval of the moral sense is not defeated by interfering circumstances, then the application of 'virtue' or some other conventionally explicit moral term to the object of approval is justified.

The reference to the application of appropriate terminology brings us to another aspect of Hutcheson's analogy between the visual sense and the moral sense, which he develops only in part. If his term 'denominate' covers 'what we say' in a variety of ways, then it follows that it is appropriate to say that an object is red when it appears red in normal conditions or that an object is extended if it appears colored in normal conditions and, in general, that there is a close and significant relation between the language of appearing and the language of physical objects. This close relationship can now be said to be that statements in the language of appearing, if they are not defeated by interfering circumstances, justify statements in the language of physical objects. A similar relationship is implicit in Hutcheson's analogy between the language of sentiment and the language of morals. For example, that Dan McCann was moved to hazard his life in a just war because of a concern to preserve the lives of his honest countrymen expresses in the language of sentiment some factual information about his actions, emotions, feelings, or attitudes. On the occasion of contemplating the act and its context, Molly Macauley may judge that the act was right, morally good, or virtuous. If she does, and uses these terms, her judgment is expressed in the language of morals. And one relationship between the two languages according to my interpretation of Hutcheson, is that the statement in the language of sentiment constitutes a good reason for the judgment in the language of morals. To think that they mean the same thing is to confuse the meaning of a judgment with the reason that is appropriate to offer in support of it. As I read Hutcheson, he holds that on the occasion when it is appropriate to express the judgment in the language of morals, it is appropriate to support it with the statement in the language of sentiment. And when the statement is true, it is appropriate to express the judgment. To return to Hutcheson's language, the statement is a justifying reason for the judgment.

The process of giving higher and higher justifying reasons for an action must come to an end, according to Hutcheson; otherwise the series would be infinite and there would be no ultimate reason for an action. That benevolence is virtuous (right, morally good) is the ultimate moral principle for Hutcheson. I shall refer to it as the principle of benevolence. It is supported ultimately by the doctrine that the moral sense approves benevolence.

Both are fundamental to Hutcheson's general moral theory, and both might be called principles. They are significantly different from one another, however, as the principle of benevolence is a moral principle in the full normative sense, whereas the principle of approval is primarily descriptive and psychological. To be sure, it provides the ultimate reason for the moral significance of benevolence, and therefore it is normative in the sense that it is the ultimate good reason for considering an action to be morally good. But it is not itself a moral principle. It is a "principle of human nature" for Hutcheson in much the same way that the disposition to develop the habit of expectation from repeated experiences is a "principle of human nature" for Hume. Where it is necessary to keep this difference in mind, I shall speak of the doctrine of approval and the principle of benevolence.

It is a misinterpretation of Hutcheson to think that for him the doctrine of approval means the same thing as the principle of benevolence. They do not mean the same thing at this dispositional, indefeasible, level any more than do their specific instances—for example, the occasion of Dan McCann's action and Molly Macauley's judgment of it. To think they do would be a mistake of the same general kind, one which has led to the mistaken interpretations of Hutcheson as a moral subjectivist, naturalist, or naive realist.

Besides the difference in meaning and status between the two principles, there is a difference in defeasibility. One could hardly claim that benevolence has, by its nature, the capacity or disposition to be virtuous in precisely the same way that the moral sense has, by its nature, the capacity or disposition to approve benevolence. Despite these differences, and some others which will appear, there are significant similarities that become apparent when their nature and relations are examined more closely.

The principle of benevolence has forms which are similar to those of the doctrine of approval. For example, it also is necessary, understood in a dispositional sense. In a later terminology this could be more accurately expressed by saying that benevolence tends to be virtuous, that benevolence is a virtue-making characteristic, or that benevolence is prima facie virtuous.[40] And, like the doctrine of approval, the principle of benevolence is contingent, understood in its occurrent sense. Hutcheson would not hold that every instance, example, or occurrence of a benevolent act is an instance, example, or occurrence of a virtuous act. Just as factors may on some given occasion interfere with the functioning of the moral sense to prevent its approval of benevolence, so interfering factors may prevent a given action that is benevolently motivated from being virtuous. Thus both principles are necessary in the dispositional sense but can be counteracted on some given occasion.

There is a difference, however, in the sense in which they have "tendency." The moral sense as such tends to approve benevolence. Benevolence as such tends to be virtuous. Approval may be manifested by applause, shouting, or the like, and Hutcheson holds that it is also manifested in an awareness by the observer of a special

40. Cf. various ethical writings by W. D. Ross, e.g., *The Right and the Good* (Oxford: Clarendon Press, 1930), and by C. D. Broad, e.g., "Some of the Main Problems of Ethics," *Philosophy* 21 (1946): 99.

feeling of pleasure. These may all be considered events of a spatio-temporal kind, although there are difficulties about identifying the special feeling. It could not be said that benevolence tends to be virtuous in the same sense: The tendency of benevolence to be virtuous is not a tendency of a disposition to manifest itself in a spatio-temporal event, whether or not that event may be easy or difficult to identify on a given occasion.

This difference becomes clearer when the two principles are contrasted in terms of interference, prevention, or counteraction. The moral sense will approve benevolence unless something counteracts it, and benevolence will be virtuous unless something counteracts it. The first carries the implication that something may be prevented from happening. The second does not carry such a temporal implication; what may be counteracted or prevented is the justification of an act or judgment. The interfering circumstances in the first case would be the influence of fear, passion, habit, ignorance, or self-interest. Those in the second case would be counteracting reasons or circumstances counting against judging a benevolent action to be virtuous, such as telling a lie, stealing, or inflicting pain in the process of carrying out the act.

The difference in the defeating circumstances arises from the difference between the observer of an action and the action itself. Hutcheson ignores the difference in many cases, and this has led to lack of clarity on his part and mistaken interpretations by his critics. Basically, his theory is a "spectator theory"—something which becomes more evident and pointed in his influence on David Hume and Adam Smith. If we adhere consistently to the point of view of the observer, we find that this disanalogy disappears.

I shall not do this by emphasizing the special feeling of pleasure to which Hutcheson refers. Although this was emphasized by Hume and subsequent empiricists, it has properly been criticized as a kind of inadequacy to which empiricism in general has been subject—namely, appealing to inner states without giving any satisfactory explanation of how they are to be identified or reidentified. There is present in Hutcheson and Hume, and in subsequent empiricism generally, an appeal to language which is more continuous and sound. Hutcheson, for example, offers an analysis of obligation in terms of the circumstances in which we say that someone is obliged. He criticizes the rationalists for vagueness in their use of "'duty,' 'obligation,' 'owing,' and the meaning of the gerund or participle, 'is to be preferred.'" And of particular relevance to my present concern is his appeal in the moral sense analogy to the circumstances in which we denominate objects in accordance with the appearances they make to us in normal conditions. He implies that an appeal to the circumstances in which we explicitly speak of actions is also part of the analogy. So, without having to beg the question whether certain peculiarly moral feelings can be identified by a special hedonic quality, visceral clutch, or stomach flutter, I shall proceed to consider these principles in terms of the circumstances in which we explicitly use moral terminology.

On this interpretation, the similarity between the doctrine of approval and the principle of benevolence is more extensive, although, of course, the two retain their difference in meaning and their respective descriptive-normative status. The sense in which the respective dispositions are manifested becomes similar. The disposition of the moral sense to approve benevolence is manifested by the observer saying that he approves. The tendency of benevolence to be virtuous is manifested by the observer saying that the act is virtuous. Similarly, just as someone might observe a benevolently motivated act and not say that he approves of it, so someone might observe the same act and not say that it is virtuous. On this interpretation, both principles are necessary, but defeasibly so, and in this case they are, in addition, defeasible in the same sense, even though the defeating factors may be different.

It would be a tidy spot in Hutcheson's theory and in my interpretation of it if I could now say that, according to him, whatever would defeat the approval of a benevolently motivated act in a given case would also defeat the claim that it was virtuous. This would be an inaccurate interpretation of Hutcheson, however, because he does not find the relationship so tidy. Consider the following cases and what he would say about them. Suppose that Molly Macauley approved Dan McCann's refusal to serve his country and said that he was doing the morally right (virtuous) thing. She might be challenged by someone who said that he was not doing the morally right thing and that she only said so because she was in love with him and approved anything he did. If she could not defend her approval by showing that it was free from prejudice and by showing that ultimately his act was done out of a concern for the general welfare, and if she admitted that she did not have good reasons for applying 'morally right' ('virtuous') and withdrew it, but still approved, then her prejudice would have defeated her application of moral terminology, although not her approval. This is surely possible in fact and also in accordance with my interpretation of Hutcheson's theory.

Suppose Miss Macauley does not withdraw the application of the moral predicate. This might be a case in which she did not change her approval and did not change the moral language in which she expressed it. Or it might be a case in which she changed her approval and yet refused to change her language. Both situations seem possible, even though not common. Hutcheson could deal with the first case by saying that her prejudice is strong enough to predominate over her moral sense. As long as she remains in this condition, any use of moral terminology on her part will be distorted and inaccurate, expressing personal preference rather than moral approval. He could deal with the second case by saying that if Miss Macauley admits that she no longer approves Dan's refusal now that she has fully considered her own special relationship with him, and yet she still says that his refusal is right, then she may be regarding his action in too limited a way. She might be failing to consider its consequences, his motive, or her approvals and disapprovals in similar circumstances and the language which she used on those occasions. Perhaps if she were to take these and other factors into account, she would come to see that her reaction should, finally, be properly expressed in such terms as 'not right,' 'reprehensible,' or 'failure to meet his obligations.'

It is possible, however, that she should refuse to change her language even after taking this more general view, saying, as one might say of a conscientious objector, 'When I consider fully all the circumstances involved, I still find that I do not approve what he is doing, yet I must admit that I think he is doing the right thing,' Hutcheson's theory would enable him to interpret a case of this kind as one in which the speaker's position would be put more clearly by saying, 'From the economic, military, political, social, or national points of view, I do not approve what he is doing, but from the moral point of view, I must say that I do approve.' This, I think, is not only open to Hutcheson but does not go very far beyond what he actually says. In addition, it seems plausible in itself.

Also, we should not forget that we are concerned with defeasible relations. There are many circumstances which could interfere with approval or disapproval from the moral point of view. There are many circumstances which could interfere with the application of the term 'virtue' to an action or person. There is nothing in Hutcheson's theory which requires that exactly the same circumstances which defeat the approval of an act should also defeat the application of 'virtue' to it, or the converse—not even, as previous examples indicate, that if something does defeat the one, then something must also defeat the other. Where defeat does occur, however, Hutcheson's theory indicates that we should look for the interfering conditions and then see whether our approvals and disapprovals and our applying or withholding of moral predicates, don't change.

One of the most serious difficulties with his theory,

insofar as helping in this search is concerned, is that it seems to call for the identification of a feeling, emotion, or attitude, as such, independently of the way in which it might be expressed in language. Investigations of the apparent discrepancy between the disapproval and the application of moral terminology might reveal, for example, that the emotion, feeling, or attitude which the speaker expressed by saying 'I don't approve of his action' would be better expressed as 'I could not bring myself to do what he is doing' or 'My training has conditioned me against doing what he is doing.' If so, then there is no discrepancy between the feeling and the application of moral terminology, because the feeling is not one of moral disapproval.

Even if further investigation should reveal, however, that the feelings are moral feelings and not some other kind, matters would not be changed insofar as the general defeasibility of Hutcheson's two principles is concerned. For example, the defeat of the application of 'virtue' to a given benevolent act does not necessarily defeat approval of it by the moral sense: It is possible that someone would refuse to apply the term 'virtue' to a benevolent act because of hate for the agent ('I would never call anything *that* guy did virtuous') and either to approve or to disapprove of the action from the moral point of view. Nor does the defeat of the approval of benevolence by the moral sense necessarily defeat the application of 'virtue' to that act: It is possible that someone would not approve a benevolent act because of envy, anger, or jealousy toward the beneficiary and yet would say that it was virtuous.

Perhaps the extent of this defeasibility is not so surprising when we take into account that it is affected not only by the complications provided by the variety of possible emotional reactions, but also by the complications in applying terminology. The language of morals, perhaps even more than the language of sentiment, is an extremely complex social product whose rules and proprieties are extremely subtle and elusive. The number of factors that could intervene between a feeling of approval—even one which could with some degree of accuracy be identified as a feeling of moral approval—and the application of the term 'virtue' is surely indefinitely large. Thus, while Hutcheson would hold that 'virtue' properly applies to any action which we find ourselves approving from the moral point of view, a person might be kept from applying the term on a given occasion by pain, anger, envy, ignorance, prejudice, or the like.

It appears, therefore, not only that the two principles have both defeasible and indefeasible forms, but that the relationship between them also takes both forms. Just as it is indefeasible that the moral sense is benevolence-approbative and that benevolence is a virtue-making characteristic, so it is indefeasible that approval of benevolence by the moral sense tends to justify the claim that benevolent acts are virtuous. Equally, however, just as something may interfere with the approval by the moral sense of some given benevolent act on some occasion, and just as some given act that is motivated by benevolence may not, for some other reason, be virtuous, so the approval of some benevolent act by the moral sense may on some occasion fail to justify the claim that it is virtuous. We might summarize these principles and their relationships, as I interpret Hutcheson, in the following way: Given that some act is motivated by benevolence, then if a person considers it from the moral point of view, he will, barring interference, approve it, and this approval will, again barring interference, justify the claim that the act is virtuous, which claim, again barring interference, he will make.

Before turning to the next topic, I want to bring out more explicitly some implications of this interpretation. The first can be stated simply, even though the details are complex. The approach to Hutcheson in terms of defeasibility shows how the doctrine of approval and the principle of benevolence are neither simple logical necessities nor simple empirical generalizations and yet share some of the characteristics of both. It is an approach that avoids the morass of asking whether they are synthetic and a priori.

The second concerns the noncognitive status of the moral sense. Although the moral sense may err and may be corrected by reason, it does not follow, despite Burnet, that reason is the moral faculty, or that a moral judgment is a cognition of reason. Reason knows that the moral sense approves or disapproves. It knows that the moral sense has changed its approval to disapproval if it has. Reason knows what facts were the relevant ones in bringing about the change. Reason, therefore, even knows what corrected the moral sense. But none of these propositions that are known by reason *constitutes* the correction. The correction is a change from approval to disapproval. It is expressed by changing 'That act is morally right' to 'That act is not morally right.' To paraphrase Hutcheson, it is not the change from considering a proposition true to finding it false that constitutes the correction, it is the change in the moral sense, in the constitution of the soul, that reacts one way in one set of circumstances and another in another.

This interpretation of the moral sense indicates that Hutcheson avoids what earlier seemed to be an incoherence between his views about sense in general and the moral sense in particular. In his general distinction between sense and reason, he contrasted a passive receptivity to ideas, including ideas of pleasure and pain, with a power of finding out true (empirical) propositions; in short, he contrasted a noncognitive passivity and a cognitive activity. Yet, the subjectivist, objectivist, and naively realistic interpretations of the moral sense—its errors and corrections—threatened to make it into a cognitive faculty. My interpretation of error and correction indicates that the moral sense is not a cognitive faculty but a noncognitive, passive receptivity to a special kind of pleasure or pain. It thus maintains the distinction between sense and reason as defined by Hutcheson and keeps the moral sense among the senses in general.

Another implication of Hutcheson's view of the moral sense concerns the analogy between the language of objects and the language of actions. In my earlier discussion of the analogy between the visual and moral senses from the standpoint of the application of appraisive terminology, I was concerned to show that the analogy between the language of objects and the language of morals called for something like a sense of credibility as a counterpart of the moral sense. Here I want to call attention to the similarity of the relationship on the one hand between 'O appears red to P under normal conditions' and 'O is red,' and on the other hand, between 'P approves A under normal conditions' and 'A is virtuous.' In neither case does the first mean the same as the second. Nor does the first logically imply the second or constitute inductive evidence for it. Yet on an occasion when it is appropriate to assert the latter of either two, it is appropriate to support it, if necessary, with the former. And when the former of either two is true, it is appropriate to assert the latter. In each case it is appropriate to offer the former as a justifying reason for the latter, although there is this disanalogy: while approving a benevolent act on a given occasion may be considered the manifestation of a disposition to approve benevolence, appearing red on a given occasion could not, in the same sense, be considered a manifestation of a disposition to be red.

Just as 'P approves A,' if not defeated, is a justifying reason for 'A is virtuous,' so 'O appears red,' if it is not defeated as a justifying reason for 'O is red,' is a justifying reason for 'O's being red is credible.' Just as there are circumstances which could lead to the defeat of 'A is virtuous,' so there are circumstances which could lead to the defeat of 'O's being red is credible.' Just as one might argue against these defeating conditions in the one case by arguing that the approval of A was made without prejudice, without inconsistency, and the like, so one might argue against the defeating conditions in the other by arguing that the appearance occurred under conditions in which P's sensory organs were without disorder, the object not excessively distant, the medium of vision not unusual, or the like.

We may say, therefore, with the qualifications indicated, that for Hutcheson, there is a general analogy which might be appropriately expressed as a proportion. The language of appearing is (in certain respects) to the language of objects as the language of sentiment is (in certain respects) to the language of morals.

Finally, the interpretation in terms of defeasibility has some interesting bearings on a passage from Frankena about Hutcheson. Frankena says:

> A rationalist may object that . . . it is just an accident that it is right to do what is for the general welfare, for the moral sense might have favored something else or even the opposite. In reply Hutcheson must admit that, viewed from without, the response of the moral sense to the standard of benevolence is contingent and might have been otherwise. But he may nevertheless insist, as he seems to between the lines, that, viewed from within, this response is felt with the note of necessity which the rationalist finds in it; and that the moral sense itself (though not an outside spectator), if asked to recant, has no choice but to declaim, "Ich kann nicht anders." [41]

I suggest that the contingency is defeasibility, that there is necessity in Hutcheson's scheme (although perhaps not of a kind, or enough, to satisfy the rationalists) which is indefeasibility, and that the felt necessity is the experience of the moral sense functioning free of counteracting influences.

The Nature and Functions of the Moral Sense

Our examination of the moral sense analogy has indicated that far from considering the moral sense an ordinary sense similar to vision, Hutcheson considers it complex enough to have a variety of functions in the moral context. These range from the function of making it possible to have a simple involuntary awareness of pleasure in approving acts that are benevolent in motive or tendency to a role which is virtually indistin-

41. Frankena, "Hutcheson's Moral Sense Theory," p. 375.

guishable from the whole person in his sensitivity to moral matters. We have also found that having a moral sense is a necessary condition for giving an answer to the question 'Why was it right for him to do that?' and for making a transition from factual and descriptive terminology to normative and moral terminology. Some of its roles are preanalytic, such as enabling a person to regard an action from the moral point of view, and some are postanalytic, such as making it possible to explain the relation between knowledge of facts about actions, consequences, and motives and the application of moral terminology. Also, we have seen that, according to Hutcheson, to say that a man has a moral sense is to say that he has a disposition to approve benevolence and will do so on a given occasion unless something interferes.

These are some of the interpretations that emerge from Hutcheson's statements that the moral sense determines a person to love those who are benevolent and to approve all kind affections, that it is involuntary and immediate and perceives simple ideas, and that without it there would be no perception of morality, only moral indifference to the acts of others. Other aspects of the moral sense are indicated when he says that it is probable that the moral sense is similar in all men, and that issues about the moral sense are independent of issues about free will. Of chief interest for our concern with explanation and justification are his statements that the moral sense is necessary for the explication of our ideas of morality, that it is presupposed by justifying reasons, that it is not itself a rule but provides the basis that enables reason by reflecting on it to find out a rule, and that it does not judge itself. Against this background I want now to discuss the moral sense with explicit reference to the meaning of moral judgments, the moral point of view, regressive justification, and moral rules.

The role of the moral sense in Hutcheson's theory of the meaning of moral judgments. The basis of Hutcheson's theory of the meaning of moral judgments lies in the capacity of the moral sense to make possible the experience of a special pleasure from viewing actions which are benevolent in motive or tendency. In Lockean terms, the moral sense is capable of receiving a new simple idea, namely the unique pleasure of moral approbation. In accordance with the view held by Berkeley and made explicit by Hume—but implicit in Hutcheson—that the meaning of an idea is provided by the experience from which it is derived, this experience of approval is what gives moral concepts their moral significance. As I interpret Hutcheson, however, a moral judgment is not an assertion that such an experience of pleasure has occurred, is now occurring, or will occur, but it is the expression of the experience of pleasure in appropriate language. That is, I find him holding a nondescriptive theory of the meaning of moral judgments. The evidence that he holds this theory has in large part been given in the discussions of correction and defeasibility; in this section I shall simply make more explicit their significance for this topic.

Earlier, we saw that any mistake that the moral sense might be said to make could not be considered a simple mistake of logic or of fact, and that, consequently, a correction of the moral sense could not consist in an insight of reason in the form of logical or factual knowledge. I argued that a mistake by the moral sense could not be a mistake about my subjective feelings or those of others or about simple or complex objective characteristics of acts, the will of God, or the nature of the situation. And I argued that because the moral sense did not make mistakes by "perceiving" false propositions of these kinds, it could not be corrected by reason in the form of finding out true propositions of these kinds. If these are the cognitive forms that the moral sense theory may take,[42] then the conclusion that Hutcheson is a noncognitivist hardly seems avoidable.

Further support for this conclusion appeared in my interpretation of his doctrine of approval in terms of

42. Cf. Frankena, "Hutcheson's Moral Sense Theory," pp. 359, 365, 366.

defeasibility. On my interpretation of Hutcheson, a mistake by the moral sense is made when on a given occasion some factor defeats its approval of benevolence, bringing about the approval of malevolence perhaps, and the correction of the moral sense occurs when it then approves without being subject to that defeating factor. The point of present significance is that the correct reaction of the moral sense is still a feeling of approval, not the knowledge of some true proposition. I found, further, that the principle that benevolence is virtuous did not mean the same thing as the doctrine that the moral sense approves benevolence in general, undefeated statements in the language of sentiment being regarded by Hutcheson as good reasons for judgments in the language of morals. The significance is, again, that the meaning of moral judgments is not to be analyzed in terms of factual statements which may be true or false. Thus, 'Hazarding life in a just war is virtuous' does not mean the same thing as 'My moral sense approves of hazarding life in a just war.' But the moral judgment is the appropriate way to express my personal feeling of moral approval in standard terminology.

I pointed out that this interpretation coheres with Hutcheson's distinction between sense and reason, according to which sense is noncognitive. Add to these Hutcheson's statement that the reactions of the moral sense are immediate and nonvoluntary, and we have quite a number of reasons for concluding that, for him, the moral sense is noncognitive, moral judgments are nondescriptive, and moral judgments express the feelings of the moral sense. They do not describe the action or the agent; they do not describe or report the feelings, actual or possible, of one's self or others; nor do they assert that such feelings are now occuring, have occurred, will, would, or will probably occur. Finally, when Hutcheson says that it does not diminish the reality of virtue to say that an action is virtuous when it pleases, he is indicating that this is the appropriate way to indicate the speaker's view of the moral significance of the action. Thus, when someone says 'Hazarding life in a just war is virtuous,' he is experiencing a unique kind of pleasure in contemplating the action and is expressing this feeling by his verbal utterance. Because Hutcheson considers it highly probable that all men have a moral sense and that it is "pretty uniform," he would hold, I take it, that such a judgment implies that other observers in similar circumstances would approve the action in a similar way. And because of his conviction that it is an integral function of moral judgments specifically, and of moral philosophy generally, to affect the attitudes and actions of people, he would intend it to evoke similar approval in others. In short, he has a theory of the meaning of moral judgments that is thoroughly noncognitive.[43]

The role of the moral sense in delineating the moral point of view. Hutcheson claims that without the moral sense there would be no perception of morality, and one could only be morally indifferent to actions. This indicates to me that the moral sense provides the basis for explaining how it is possible for someone to take the moral point of view. Without a moral sense, he is claiming, one might regard people, character, actions, consequences, and motivation from the standpoint of whether they are prudent, expedient, economically sound, politically advisable, or the like, but not from the standpoint of whether they are virtuous or vicious, morally good or bad, or morally obligatory or not. Broadly stated, without the moral sense we could not have the attitudes, the concepts, or the language in terms of which to consider anything from the moral point of view. To take the moral point of view in this broad sense is to regard things from the standpoint of moral principles, standards, or rules. It is to think and judge in terms of moral categories.

43. This is not a common interpretation of Hutcheson. It seems to me, however, that the considerations I have offered in its favor are compelling or very close to it. As an additional consideration I might add that Frankena reaches a similar conclusion through a different approach. See his "Hutcheson's Moral Sense Theory."

There is also, however, a narrow sense of the phrase "the moral point of view" which identifies it with some particular moral system. One might argue in this sense that to take the moral point of view, according to Hutcheson, is to judge an act, consequence, or motive according to the kind of pleasure experienced when observing or contemplating it. It would be a mistake, I think, to attribute any such narrow sense to Hutcheson because to do so would imply, for example, that he would not admit that Clarke was taking the moral point of view when he asked whether some action was fitting to the situation. This is hardly Hutcheson's attitude when he says he does not intend to oppose Clarke but only to add a necessary explication of his use of the concept of fittingness. To me, such a statement indicates that Hutcheson considers the category of fittingness to be morally significant but Clark's use of it in formulating his own moral system to be incomplete and unclear.

One might claim that a recognition of the distinction between the broad and narrow senses of the moral point of view is implicit in his discussion of alternative moral systems in the opening remarks of *Illustrations*. Epicurus, Cicero, Hobbes, and Rochefoucauld are not failing to take the moral point of view when they attempt to formulate a moral theory in which virtuous actions are interpreted in terms of self-love. They are, in Hutcheson's opinion as I read him, making mistakes about human motivation and formulating moral theories that do not agree with certain facts about human nature and that do not, therefore, give an adequate explanation of the way their terminology indicates the moral significance of actions. His own system, which recognizes these facts and interprets virtuous actions in terms of the approval of benevolence of motive or tendency, is an alternative which he would claim has such an adequate explanation. And the rationalists offer a third alternative which attempts to explain the morality of actions in terms of conformity to reason, and again fails to provide a satisfactory explanation of the meaning of their moral terminology.

It would hardly be appropriate to maintain that according to Hutcheson these people fail to take the moral point of view in their concern to explain the morality of action; but they take the moral point of view in the broad sense. One could say, expressing it in perhaps the broadest sense possible, that they are all taking the moral point of view insofar as they deploy the language of morals in an attempt to formulate satisfactory theories about people, actions, consequences of actions, character, motives, attitudes, and the like. They differ not in their terminology or concepts but in their explanations of the moral significance of actions, the bases of the significance of the concepts and terminology, and, of particular importance for our concerns, the general principles which determine relevant facts and good reasons in the justification of actions. For Hobbes, such general principles are formulated in terms of facts concerning the preservation of one's own life, the process of satisfying one's own desires, and the avoidance of weariness; for Hutcheson, in terms of facts about benevolence of motive or tendency of actions; for the rationalists, in terms of facts about what is or can be known by reason: self-evident truth, logical necessity, and the natures and relations of things.

Although they differ about what facts are relevant to the justification of actions, these men all agree about the appropriate role of these facts. This can be stated in two ways: either they constitute the circumstances in the light of which moral predicates are properly applied to acts, or they provide the basis for considerations which would be appealed to if it became necessary to justify the application of moral predicates.

I think we may say, then, that all of these men take the moral point of view in the broad sense and differ in their moral point of view in the narrow sense—that is, in what Hutcheson calls their "schemes of morality." These two senses could easily be confused if someone considered that the only way to take the moral point of view in the broad sense is to take the point of view of his particular moral system. When Hutcheson says that

Hobbes apparently had no view of human nature other than that every man is concerned only with his own satisfaction, he suggests that Hobbes is subject to such a confusion. And Butler's remark that "benevolence and the want of it, singly considered, are in no sort the whole of virtue and vice,"[44] might be taken as a criticism of the same kind of fault in Hutcheson, although Butler does not mention him by name.

These criticisms are similar to those that might be made of anyone who espouses other limited points of view; for example, of someone who says that to look at things from the aesthetic point of view is to look at them from the standpoint of cubism, or of someone who says that to look at things from the religious point of view is to look at them from the standpoint of Calvinism, or of someone who says that to look at things from the logical point of view is to look at them in terms of the first-order calculus. It seems to me that Hutcheson is not subject to this kind of criticism. Recognizing that there are alternative and competing moral theories, he is claiming that with respect to motivation and the moral significance of his language, he has a more satisfactory explanation than Hobbes, and that with respect to the significance of moral terminology generally, he has a more satisfactory explanation than the rationalists. But he is hardly saying that his moral theory therefore defines *the* moral point of view. At most he would hold that it provides *a* moral point of view that is more adequate in specifiable respects than its chief competitors. Within this adequacy, the moral sense plays a role at two levels: first, by providing a basis for the explanation of the meaning of moral concepts and terminology that is consistent with observation of human nature; and second, by providing a basis for the development of a moral theory that deals with some of the main problems of ethics in a more satisfactory way than its competitors.

If we interpret Hutcheson's assertion that without the

44. "Dissertation on Virtue," appended to the *Analogy* (London, 1736).

moral sense there would be no perception of morality to mean that his moral theory formulates *the* moral point of view, we would have to attribute to him the claim that it is more adequate in *every* respect than *any* existing *or* possible moral theory, or even more strongly, that there is no existing or possible moral theory which is at all plausible as a competitor to his. This would be unjust. Instead we should interpret it in terms of his statement that the various moral systems put forth by the rationalists actually presuppose the moral sense. That they presuppose it, we may say for Hutcheson, is indicated by the very fact that they use the language of morals in a way that is understood by their readers. According to Hutcheson, moral language has this relatively uniform significance and intelligibility because there is a moral sensitivity in each of us which is itself fairly uniform.

In view of the confusion which may arise from a failure to distinguish the narrow and broad senses of the moral point of view, I shall continue to use the phrase "the moral point of view" in the broad sense. For the narrow sense I shall speak of a "moral scheme" in Hutcheson's terminology, or of a moral theory, moral system, or moral code.

The role of the moral sense in Hutcheson's theory of regressive moral justification. We can make the different levels of Hutcheson's theory of moral justification more explicit in the following way. An action can be justified by appealing to a principle according to which some fact about its motive or tendency is a good reason for saying that, other things being equal, it is virtuous. If that justification is challenged, a more general principle can be used, and so on. The fundamental principle is reached when this scheme of morality provides no more general principle to be appealed to in such a regress.

In terms of our earlier example, suppose Hutcheson expresses moral approval of Dan McCann's risking his life in a just war by saying that it is a virtuous act. Suppose Burnet challenges the judgment by asking why it is virtuous, how he knows it is virtuous, or what is his basis for saying it is virtuous. Hutcheson would reply that it is an act of preserving the lives of McCann's innocent countrymen. If Burnet continues to challenge, Hutcheson would respond by saying successively that this is evidence of public spirit, and that evidencing public spirit is benevolent. Risking life in a just war, preserving the lives of one's innocent countrymen, and evidencing public spirit are successively more inclusive ways of being benevolent in motive or tendency and for that reason are virtuous in a derivative way. Benevolence is virtuous in an ultimate way because it is approved by the moral sense, whose approvals and disapprovals are, according to Hutcheson, the basis for explaining how it is possible to regard anything from the moral point of view. That benevolence is virtuous is the fundamental principle of morals for Hutcheson because in his theory, it cannot be justified in the way in which it is used to justify the subordinate principles.

This hierarchical structure makes evident what Hutcheson means by saying that justifying reasons presuppose the moral sense. Its approval of benevolence is a necessary condition of their moral significance. In themselves, justifying reasons are factual statements about the benevolent motive or tendency of an act; without the approval of benevolence by the moral sense, their moral relevance would remain questionable. It is because benevolence has the ultimate approval of the moral sense that statements about various ways of being benevolent can be offered as justifying reasons for an act. In a later idiom, the moral sense provides the basis for Hutcheson's version of the autonomy of morals.

The moral sense as the basis of a rule. Hutcheson's statement that the moral sense, although not itself a rule, provides the basis on which our understanding "by reflecting upon it, may find one out," admits of different interpretations. Using the general title, "Rule of Benevolence," one interpretation is that it provides the basis for a rule of conduct that could be formulated in terms of obligation: 'Everyone ought to be benevolent.' Hutcheson would be indicating that one can find out that he ought to be benevolent by reflecting on the significance of the role of the moral sense in moral justification. This interpretation would be supported by Hutcheson's references to the "directive power" of the moral sense.

Another, more speculative interpretation would make the moral sense the basis for a rule in the logic of discourse on moral justification that governs the relation between propositions about benevolence and propositions about virtue: "From propositions of the form 'Actions of type-A are benevolent in motive or tendency,' one may derive propositions of the form 'Actions of type-A are virtuous.'" This version would be based, again, on the ultimate moral role played by the approval of benevolence by the moral sense. For example, risking life in a just war would be justified by drawing from the factual proposition that risking life in a just war is benevolent, the conclusion that risking life in a just war is virtuous, in accordance with the rule of benevolence. The rule would be not a premise in the argument but a means of showing how, from a factual premise, it is appropriate to derive a moral conclusion. This interpretation would be supported by Hutcheson's general distinction between reason and the senses and by his insistence that the moral sense does not judge itself.

If Hutcheson's statement is taken to refer to a standard rather than a rule, there is a third interpretation in which the moral sense is regarded as the basis on which the understanding may find out a standard. Rules and standards can be distinguished incompletely, but for present purposes sufficiently, in the following way. A person by his actions can conform to both standards and rules, but there can be degrees of this conformity in the case of standards and not in the case of rules. Thus, standards can be used as the basis for a rank ordering, whereas rules cannot. Rules require, permit, or forbid actions and can thus be obeyed or broken; standards do not and cannot. One may by his actions conform to the standard of benevolence not only in a variety of ways but also in a variety of degrees. As Hutcheson indicates in his discussion of merit and goodness of temper, virtue is a matter not merely of being benevolent or failing to be benevolent but of effecting an appropriate balance among one's abilities, the degree of benevolence, and the object toward which benevolence is directed. By risking his life, protecting the lives of his innocent countrymen, displaying public spirit, and being benevolent, one may be not simply virtuous, but virtuous to some specific degree. In risking his life to the full extent of his capacities, he is perfectly virtuous; equally so in protecting the lives of his innocent countrymen to the full extent of his capacities, and so on.

Benevolence is the moral standard, then, in two ways: first, by providing the standard according to which different ways of acting are different ways of being benevolent and thus constituting different justifying reasons for actions, and second, by providing the standard for judging the degree of virtuousness of a given action. The moral sense is presupposed in the case of finding out a standard in the same way it is in the case of finding out a rule. That the moral sense approves benevolence is the ultimate reason for using benevolence as a standard for judging and ranking the virtue of actions.

It is evident, then, that the moral sense is basic to Hutcheson's whole moral system: without the moral sense, judgments would not express moral approval, and we would not be able to explain how it is possible to regard actions from the moral point of view or to justify them ultimately in terms of their benevolence of motive or tendency. Despite the nondescriptive nature of moral judgments themselves and the noncognitive role of the moral sense, Hutcheson has nevertheless formulated a theory which carries justification back to fundamentals in a way that provides a place for the operation of reason and for the application of the concepts of validity and objectivity. Briefly, the process of justification can be valid or invalid and the moral sense can be correct or incorrect, and in neither case is this simply a matter of personal preference or arbitrary decision.

The process of justification can be valid or invalid not only in the general sense that it is a rational process, but also in at least two more specific senses. First, it requires the use of reason in finding out propositions about motives or tendencies that are relevant to the justification of the act in question. If these are true, then in that respect the justification is valid, and if false, invalid. Second, the process of justification may be carried out in conformity with the standards, rules, and principles set out by Hutcheson, and in that sense it can be valid. If the process fails to conform to these standards, then it is invalid. And there is a further sense in which his theory of justification provides a place for the concept of validity: although the moral sense is not itself a cognitive faculty, its reactions are responsible to, and can be modified by, changes that might occur in the knowledge gained by reason about motives or consequences.

The concept of objectivity has its place in Hutcheson's theory of justification in two, closely related senses. According to Hutcheson, the reactions of the moral sense are quite uniform throughout mankind. Its reactions are objective, then, in the sense that they are common to many if not subject to interference. More importantly, he would hold that reason and the moral sense combine to work in such a way that anyone in the same circumstances taking account of the same factors would have the same reactions and come to the same conclusions. The processes of justification are repeatable. They represent not arbitrary, limited, subjective or personal preference, but the general sense of mankind, as the terms 'virtuous' and 'vicious,' 'moral right' and 'moral wrong,' and 'moral good' and 'moral evil' in the language of morals show.

We noted earlier A. N. Prior's view that "there is little or nothing in Hume's moral philosophy that cannot be traced to Hutcheson, but in Hume it is all more clear and pointed." Nowhere is this more evident than in Hutcheson's influence on Hume on the points discussed above. This influence is particularly apparent in certain statements in Part I of the Conclusion of Hume's *Enquiry Concerning the Principles of Morals:*

> The notion of morals implies some sentiment common to all mankind, which recommends the same object to general approbation, and makes every man, or most men, agree in the same opinion or decision concerning it . . . When a man denominates another his enemy, his rival, his antagonist, his adversary, he is understood to speak the language of self-love, and to express sentiments, peculiar to himself, and arising from his particular circumstances and situation. But when he bestows on any man the epithets of vicious or odious or depraved, he then speaks another language, and expresses sentiments, in which he expects all his audience are to concur with him . . . language must . . . invent a peculiar set of terms, in order to express those universal sentiments of censure or approbation, which arise from humanity, or from views of general usefulness and its contrary. Virtue and Vice become then known; morals are recognized; certain general ideas are framed of human conduct and behaviour; such measures are expected from men in such situations. This action is determined to be conformable to our abstract rule; that other, contrary. And by such universal principles are the particular sentiments of self-love frequently controlled and limited.[45]

Although many difficulties remain, it seems to me that Hutcheson has the beginnings of a subtle synthesis of cognitive and noncognitive factors into a plausible pattern for a theory of regressive moral justification. Yet it is not the end of the line of justification for Hutcheson. If it were, then he could only reply to someone who, like Burnet, challenged his fundamental moral principle that any further request for justification is not in order or is based on misunderstanding. But he clearly

45. Oxford: Clarendon Press, 1946, pp. 272–274.

considers that Burnet's challenge is legitimate and calls for an extensive answer. The justification he gives, however, is significantly different from the regressive justification which I have been considering. It is, in fact, based on the denial that the moral sense plays a role in it at all. When Hutcheson says that the moral sense "does not judge itself," I interpret this as his way of saying that if the fundamental principles, their basis, and the whole moral system that is founded on them are challenged, then any further justification of basic principles cannot be a moral justification. I find him offering something similar to what has been called "pragmatic justification" or "vindication." How his general theory of justification leads to it will appear more clearly if we return to his criticism of rationalism and to the contrast between him and Burnet.

Vindication

A general line in Hutcheson's criticism of Burnet and the rationalists may be interpreted as follows: When Burnet attempts to run the pattern of regressive justification straight through any fundamental moral principle to "reason itself," he encounters a difficulty: either the whole process is one of moral justification from beginning to end, or none of it is. In the first case, he begs the question of whether moral distinctions originate with reason. In the second case, he cannot get moral justification at all.

Hutcheson does not make the first criticism explicit. Indeed, because of his apparent conviction that there are no self-evident truths in morals, he seems to miss altogether Burnet's claim that the fundamental principle of morals is self-evident. The second criticism is, of course, the main point of his numerous arguments that, no matter how he attempts to interpret what the rationalists have said about reason, it cannot provide a principle that is able to perform the jobs required of the fundamental principle of morals. This part of Hutcheson's criticism of the rationalists is apparently based on a belief, most evident in his discussion of Wollaston, that they are attempting to base a system of morality upon foundations of pure logic or epistemology. Such an interpretation is quite understandable in view of their claim that the principles of morals share the same unchallengeable status as the principles of mathematics. Hutcheson, on the contrary, considers that all moral principles, including those claimed to be fundamental, are open to challenge. He also considers that unless there is a shift in the process of justification at the point where the fundamental principle is challenged, further regressive justification in logical or epistemological terms will strip it of moral significance.

The difference between the two approaches to justification can be interpreted in terms of their respective attitudes toward the similarities and differences of mathematics and morals. The rationalists explicitly claimed that morality is like mathematics in terms of the certainty that could be achieved in moral knowledge. With Burnet saying that reason is the method of thinking that "discovers such truths as are not self-evident by the intervention of self-evident truths," speaking of the "regress of analysis" in search of a self-evident truth, and finally, finding one by pushing beyond the moral sense, Hutcheson may well have thought that Burnet had pushed the fundamental principle of morals so far back that it was out of the moral context altogether. Expressed in more contemporary terminology, he might have thought that Burnet viewed moral justification in terms of a deductive model in which a moral judgment is logically implied by a first level moral principle, that by a second level moral principle, and so on, even beyond the principle that it is best that the human species be happy. (I am ignoring the difference between the substantive content of their respective fundamental principles because it is not relevant to the present issue.) For Burnet says that in the "regress of analysis" (that is, in the successive appeals to more and more basic moral principles) we cannot be satisfied until we come to something self-evident to reason, that reason is the measure of the goodness or badness of our affections, that truth is the same as reason, and that in acting contrary to our apprehension of truth, we become morally evil agents. Viewed in terms of a mathematical or geometrical model, this would imply to Hutcheson that Burnet was appealing to some self-evident axiom which could not contain any moral concepts. And, of course, he would deny that Burnet's appeal "singly to Reason only" could provide any. He may have had in mind something as Wollastonian (and as bad) as this: If something is self-evident to reason, then it is true. If it is true, then it is morally right. It is self-evident that it is best that all be happy. So it is true that it is best that all be happy. So it is morally right that it is best that all be happy.

Hutcheson would probably agree that the first statement in the argument, which I shall call the principle of self-evidence, is known singly to reason only. And, as presented here, he would consider the regress of analysis as showing that Burnet considered it to be the foundation of morals. This is, of course, an unsympathetic reading of Burnet. In the light of subsequent intuitionism, it is certainly not the most appropriate one. But to someone who did not admit self-evident moral knowledge, and thus would not accept 'It is best that all be happy' as itself a moral principle, it would be a natural one.

Hutcheson, on the other hand, holds that the fundamental principle of morals provides, among other things, the substantive content which establishes the moral significance of deductive or rule-governed reasoning in morals. He does not deny that reasoning in the manner of mathematics has a place in morality. In fact, he shows us how, by using some mathematical-like rules, to calculate the degree of virtue of actions in terms of benevolence and ability (*Inquiry*, section III, par. 11) and gives us mathematical formulae for determining the goodness of temper in the first edition of *Illustrations*. He does not hold, however, that such calculations and formulae show that the moral ultimacy of the principle of benevolence is provided by its self-evidence to reason. They show what can be known with certainty if the principle is taken to be fundamental and reasoning carried out according to the rules. Burnet's mistake, according to my interpretation of Hutcheson's criticism, is to confuse conformity to the rules of valid reasoning with conformity to the standards which give some moral point to the processes of valid reasoning.

If the basis of moral significance is challenged, then, according to my interpretation of Hutcheson, it cannot be justified by a process which simply extends the process of justification that is carried out under its aegis. The adoption of the principle and the acceptance of the system of morality which is based on it must be justified if challenged; but this cannot be done by appealing to a higher principle from which they follow deductively. They must be vindicated by a much broader appeal.

Hutcheson's vindication of the adoption of the principle of benevolence includes both theoretical and practical arguments, although the line between them is not sharp. Within the theoretical arguments, it is possible to distinguish between the polemical and the constructive. We have, in effect, already considered Hutcheson's theoretical arguments: The polemic against the rationalistic theories is an indirect vindication of his own, because it reveals the inadequacy of the main alternative to it once egoism is rejected: The key concepts of the rationalistic theories are vague, unclear, or unintelligible. Attempts at interpretation result in theories which are irrelevant to moral issues, incomplete, or which require an appeal to the moral sense and the principle of benevolence. And rationalist criticisms of the moral sense are based on misconceptions of the role it plays in the moral ultimacy of the principle of benevolence and in justification.

Constructive theoretical vindication is provided by his contributions to normative ethics (for example, his theory that actions done from affection can be considered morally praiseworthy, that a regard for God is not necessary to make an action virtuous, and the like) by his contributions to metaethical theory (for example, his analysis of ethical terms, such as obligation and virtue, and of the distinction between merit and reward) by his contributions to the epistemology of morals in his development of various analogies and in his version of the defeasible necessity of the doctrine of approval and the principle of benevolence, and by his development of a theory of justification. All these may be understood to vindicate the adoption of, or commitment to, the doctrine of approval, the principle of benevolence, and the moral system based on them by setting forth their adequacy in the appropriate areas of moral philosophy. Hutcheson would not claim, however, that he has "proved" the principle of benevolence in any mathematical or deductive sense, only that he has shown that there are a great many good reasons for recognizing it as the fundamental principle of morals—proved it, perhaps, only in the larger meaning of 'proof' of which John Stuart Mill speaks near the end of the first chapter of *Utilitarianism:* "We are not to infer that its acceptance or rejection must depend on blind impulse or arbitrary choice. There is a larger meaning of the word 'proof,' in which this question is as amenable to it as any other of the disputed questions of philosophy. The subject is within the cognizance of the rational faculty; and neither does that faculty deal with it solely in the way of intuition. Considerations may be presented capable of determining the intellect either to give or withhold its assent to the doctrine; and this is equivalent to proof." [46]

The extension of his theory of justification to include practical vindication becomes apparent if we consider the case of someone who had read and understood the *Illustrations* and yet said, "Yes, but you haven't yet shown me a good reason for being benevolent." We may take this, I think, as one way of understanding Burnet's challenge. What could Hutcheson, or anyone

46. Quoted by Frankena, *Ethics* (Englewood Cliffs: Prentice-Hall, 1963), p. 90.

else, do? The answer is provided, I think, by considering the position of Hutcheson himself. It is significant that there is no need to vindicate the adoption of the principle to him: he has adopted it and found it satisfactory not only in the theoretical sense of providing a satisfactory basic principle of morals but also as the guiding principle of his conduct. Consider what we would think if we knew, or found out, that instead of being benevolent to his family, friends, and students, he was the opposite. We would, I think, have some doubts that he took the principle and its system seriously. It is appropriate, therefore, to approach this question from the standpoint of a person's whole life. At this point, Hutcheson's exciting reasons become relevant again.

In his letters and in *Illustrations*, when the question of accepting or rejecting the principle of benevolence is raised Hutcheson suggests that we consider what it would be like to live both a life in which the moral sense was operative and another in which it was not. He asks Burnet, and us, to "look into our hearts" and ask ourselves whether we would really want the one and not the other. The decision, he is indicating, involves acting in certain ways rather than others, striving for certain things rather than others, taking certain attitudes, and having certain experiences. He is appealing to the concept of a way of life in which the satisfaction of examined desires is maximized, to the concept of the kind of person, all things considered, one wants to be.

This interpretation is supported not only by the fact that Hutcheson offers alternative lives for consideration but by a number of other doctrines as well. For example, he finds that human nature is constituted so that pleasures and pains come in certain ways rather than others, and that there are emotions, experiences, and preferences characteristic of the majority of mankind. He believes that an analysis of human nature shows that we have an ability to come to clear conclusions about what we want, what kind of person we really want to be, or what kind of life we really want to live. He holds that there are various ways in which we can come to these conclusions: basically, by observing and consulting other people and ourselves. The latter is indicated by his frequent emphasis upon our ability to evaluate our desires by "consulting our own hearts" and "reflecting on our own sentiments."

Practical vindication of a principle, therefore, according to my interpretation of Hutcheson, may finally require getting the person who challenges its ultimacy as the fundamental principle of a system of morals to live the life of the moral system which is based on that principle. This calls for actual commitment to and consequent actions in accordance with the standards and rules of that system and for careful consideration of whether this life is the one which maximizes one's examined preferences.

While this concept of vindication in Hutcheson calls for an appeal to exciting reasons once again, they are not merely exciting, and their satisfaction is not merely satisfaction of desire. They are, as he indicates, examined desires which it is possible to say ought to be satisfied or which it is reasonable to satisfy, as he indicates in several passages in which he is attempting to interpret the rationalists. For example, "He acts reasonably who considers the various actions in his power and forms true opinions of their tendencies and then chooses to do that which will obtain the highest degree of that to which the instincts of his nature incline him."

To fill out the outline of vindication, we would like additional details regarding the concepts of examined desires, alternative ways of life, decision, and reasonable choice among alternative ways of life. The details are not in *Illustrations,* although his later books, *Introduction to Moral Philosophy* (1747) and *A System of Moral Philosophy* (1755), can be interpreted in a way that provides some of the needed development. If we restrict attention to *Illustrations*, the outline of the conditions of a reasonable decision about a way of life has the following form: When our decision to live a certain kind of life is taken freely, impartially, and with full knowledge, when it is acted upon with consistency and serious commitment, and when it is free of defeating factors and leads to the maximal satisfaction of examined desires, then the adoption of a moral system and its fundamental principle is vindicated by its contributions to and the part it plays in constituting such a life.

Self-Evidence of the Fundamental Principle of Morals

With this extended theory of justification it may now be possible to reply for Hutcheson to the criticism that he ignores Burnet's claim that the fundamental principle of morals is justified by being recognized to be self-evident. In one sense, no reply is possible at all; he ignored it. Although he discussed Burnet's principle that it is best that all be happy, this was part of his attempt to interpret the rationalists' doctrine that virtue consists in conformity to reason and not a direct confrontation of the claim that the principle is self-evident. Instead, he argued that the principle cannot be an exciting reason without presupposing either selfish or public affections or a justifying reason without presupposing a moral sense, neither response being relevant to the issue of self-evidence.

He could argue relevantly, however, that Burnet has failed to recognize two significant things about justification; first, that the necessity of a fundamental principle must be interpreted in terms of defeasibility, and second, that justification involves both validation and vindication. In the light of the first, it would seem inappropriate to claim that the fundamental principle is self-evident, for if we interpret the claim to be that the necessity is evident in the principle itself without reference to anything else, this is belied by the need to explain the indefeasible necessity in terms of particular cases and possible interference. In regard to the second, I have suggested that according to one interpretation of Hutcheson's criticism, Burnet fails to recognize that justification involves both validation and vindication because he thinks of it on the model of mathematical or deductive reasoning. And this, I have also suggested, leads Hutcheson to criticize him for attempting to make some self-evident and therefore nonmoral principle the fundamental principle of morals.

Burnet might reply, however, that he was not making this mistake and that instead, he is saying that justification ends with the fundamental principle of morals just because it is known to be self-evident, not because there is a further principle of self-evidence from which it follows deductively. He might say that validation ends with the fundamental principle of morals because its self-evidence indicates that it needs no further justification. Hutcheson could reply that this way of limiting justification to validation has rather disastrous consequences not only for ethics and metaethics but for morality as well. He could point to some of these consequences in a passage in which Burnet himself makes them evident: "if I could find a man of so different a make of understanding from mine that what was self-evident to me was not so to him, I should have no medium by which I could argue with him any longer on that head; but we must part and own that we cannot understand each other."[47]

If this were the case, then there would be, Hutcheson could maintain, no point in considering whether a given principle was more adequate than another, whether it accounted for the origin of moral concepts and terms and did this more satisfactorily than another, whether it provided standards for judging degrees of virtue or rules for the direction of conduct and did this better than another, or, in general, whether it was capable of performing the various functions required of a basic principle of morals and did this more satisfactorily than another. In short, the whole process of vindication, both theoretical and practical, would be pointless if the justification of the fundamental principle were simply a question of whether it was self-evident.

Whether Hutcheson would have pointed out these

47. Letter of December 25.

consequences in explaining why he ignored Burnet's claim I cannot say. I can say, however, that he could have, and that if Burnet were right, there would have been no point in writing the *Illustrations*—something which no one interested in the history of ethics or in the systematic issues of ethics could accept. For if my interpretation and development of Hutcheson's theory of justification is well founded, then in an accurate rewriting of the history of ethics, he must be awarded a place of greater importance than has so far been granted for providing the outlines of a theory of justification that displays a subtle blend of cognitive and noncognitive elements, for indicating that the categories of analytic-synthetic and a priori–a posteriori are not adequate to the task of explicating the status of fundamental moral principles, and for showing that moral controversy involves indefeasible and defeasible principles and cannot be brought to a satisfactory conclusion by an appeal to self-evidence.

A Note on the Editions and the Dating of the Correspondence with Burnet

The first edition of *An Essay on the Passions with Illustrations on the Moral Sense* appeared in 1728 and was followed by another in the same year and another in 1730. Comparison of the three editions shows that neither of the two later contains any substantive changes. For convenience, therefore, in the footnotes dealing with collation of the editions, I have referred to "ed. 1," but this is to be understood to include all three of these early editions. Hutcheson made extensive revisions in the edition of 1742, the text for posthumous editions in 1756 and 1769. I have used the Robert & Andrew Foulis edition of 1769, always comparing it with the editions of 1742 and 1756. The collation in effect, therefore, compares the editions before and after 1742. Spelling, punctuation, and capitalization have been somewhat modernized. Hutcheson's footnotes are indicated by lower case letters, editorial footnotes and insertions by brackets.

T. E. Jessop, in his *Bibliography of David Hume and of Scottish Philosophy from Francis Hutcheson to Lord Balfour,* lists posthumous editions for 1751 and 1772.[48] He indicates that he did not verify their existence by actual inspection, and I have not been able to locate them, although secondary evidence is fairly strong that they exist. He also lists a Dublin edition for 1728 which he did not verify. In this case, the evidence is quite strong that no such edition exists, as I shall indicate shortly.

The numbering of the editions is erratic, the first three not being numbered at all and the edition of 1742 being called the third on the title page. If we use the criterion proposed by Ronald B. McKerrow according to which an edition is "the whole number of copies of a book printed at any time or times from one setting-up of type," then the edition of 1742 is the fourth.[49] It is not surprising, therefore, to find Jessop in his *Bibliography* inserting "sic" after noting that the edition of 1769, printed by Robert & Andrew Foulis in Glasgow, is also identified on the title page as the third, when the edition of 1756, printed for W. Innys, J. Richardson, and others in London, is said on the title page to be the fourth.

Tracing all the editions is made difficult not only by anachronistic numbering, but also by W. R. Scott's statement that there was a Dublin edition published by John Smith and William Bruce in 1728. On the basis of an extensive search I have concluded that Scott was mistaken. He based his statement on an advertisement in the *Dublin Intelligencer* for March 23, 1728, that does not actually assert that the edition was published in Dublin.[50] I have been able to locate two editions for 1728. The first, carrying a London imprint, was "Printed

48. London, 1938, pp. 144–145.
49. *An Introduction to Bibliography* (Oxford, 1927), p. 175.
50. W. R. Scott, *Francis Hutcheson* (Cambridge, 1900), p. 53.

and *Dublin* Reprinted by S. Russell for P. Crampton."[51] The second, also carrying a London imprint, with errors of spelling, grammar, and typography of the earlier edition corrected, was "Printed by *J. Darby* and *T. Browne* for *John Smith* and *William Bruce*, Booksellers in Dublin."[52] It may have been this edition, being sold in Dublin and advertised in the *Dublin Intelligencer*, which led Scott to say that there was "an Irish edition."

These details are of more than bibliographical significance because they have a bearing on the explanation of the error in dating the Burnet correspondence.[53] The correspondence appeared in the *London Journal* from April to December of 1725, yet Hutcheson says in the preface to the *Illustrations* that it occurred in 1728, and virtually every secondary source which mentions the correspondence accepts that date. The question arises whether this is a typographical error or an error of memory. Barton Charles Cooper, the only person I know who has noticed it, thinks it was probably typographical "since it is not reasonable to suppose that Hutcheson, writing in 1728, could have forgotten that Burnet had died two years earlier."[54] But Hutcheson does not include the date of the correspondence in either of the 1728 editions I have been able to locate. Even if there is some edition of 1728 which I have not inspected, however, such as the putative Irish edition mentioned by Scott, the date is not likely to be included because there is no date given for the correspondence in the 1730 edition either. I conclude that something like sixteen years passed between the time of the correspondence and Hutcheson's insertion of its date along

51. From the title page.
52. From the title page.
53. I have discussed the details of this problem in the article "The Correspondence between Francis Hutcheson and Gilbert Burnet: The Problem of the Date," *Journal of the History of Philosophy* 8, no. 1 (January 1970): 87–91.
54. "An Examination of the Ethics of Francis Hutcheson" (Ph.D. diss., University of California at Berkeley, 1956), p. x.

with other revisions into the preface of the edition of 1742, and that uncritical secondary sources have perpetuated a mistake of his memory, not a typographical error.

The text of the Burnet correspondence is taken from the edition of 1735. It was originally prepared by Burnet, who added an introduction and a postscript to the letters, but it was not published until nine years after his death. *The Dictionary of National Biography* suggests that the collection was edited by Hutcheson.[55] There is at least a doubt about this, however, because the title page has his name misspelled and without initial or first name. Furthermore, if he had edited the collection, it would be less likely that he would have misdated the correspondence in his preface to the 1742 edition of *Illustrations*. The latter argument is weakened, however, by the fact that the 1735 edition of the letters does not include their dates. I have been unable, so far, to determine with certainty from external evidence the identity of the editor.

55. S.v. "Hutcheson, Francis."

Illustrations on the Moral Sense

AN ESSAY ON THE NATURE and CONDUCT OF THE *Passions* and *Affections.*

With ILLUSTRATIONS on the

MORAL SENSE.

By FRANCIS HUTCHESON, Professor of Moral Philosophy in the University of *Glascow*; and Author of the *Inquiry into the Original of our Ideas of* Beauty *and* Virtue.

Hoc opus, hoc studium, parvi properemus, & ampli,
Si Patriæ volumus, si nobis vivere chari. HOR.

LONDON:

Printed for JAMES and JOHN KNAPTON, and JOHN CROWNFIELD in St. *Paul's Church-Yard*; JOHN DARBY in *Bartholomew-Close*; THOMAS OSBORNE *Jun.* at *Greys Inn*; and LAUTON GILLIVER in *Fleetstreet*. M.DCC.XXX.

Preface to *An Essay on the Nature and Conduct of the Passions and Affections with Illustrations on the Moral Sense*

Although the main practical principles which are inculcated in this treatise have this prejudice in their favor, that they have been taught and propagated by the best of men in all ages, yet there is reason to fear that renewed treatises upon subjects so often well managed may be looked upon as superfluous especially since little is offered upon them which has not often been well said before. But beside that general consideration, that old arguments may sometimes be set in such a light by one as will convince those who were not moved by them, even when better expressed by another, since for every class of writers there are classes of readers adapted who cannot relish anything higher besides this, I say, the very novelty of a book may procure a little attention from those who overlook the writings which the world has long enjoyed. And if by curiosity or any other means some few can be engaged to turn their thoughts to those important subjects about which a little reflection will discover the truth and a thorough consideration of it may occasion a great increase of real happiness, no person need be ashamed of his labors as useless which do such service to any of his fellow creatures.

If any should look upon some things in this *Inquiry into the Passions* as too subtle for common apprehension and consequently not necessary for the instruction of men in morals, which are the common business of mankind, let them consider that the difficulty on these subjects arises chiefly from some previous notions, equally difficult at least, which have been already received, to the great detriment of many a natural temper, since many have been discouraged from all attempt of cultivating kind generous affections in themselves by a previous notion that there are no such affections in nature and that all pretence to them was only dissimulation, affectation, or at best some unnatural enthusiasm. And farther, that to discover truth on these subjects nothing more is necessary than a little attention to what passes in our own hearts, and consequently every man may come to certainty in these points without much art or knowledge of other matters.

Whatever confusion the Schoolmen introduced into philosophy some of their keenest adversaries seem to threaten it with a worse kind of confusion by attempting to take away some of the most immediate simple perceptions and to explain all approbation, condemnation, pleasure, and pain, by some intricate relations to the perceptions of the external senses. In like manner they have treated our desires or affections, making the most generous, kind and disinterested of them to proceed from self-love by some subtle trains of reasoning to which honest hearts are often wholly strangers.

Let this also still be remembered, that the natural dispositions of mankind may operate regularly in those who never reflected upon them nor formed just notions about them. Many are really virtuous who cannot explain what virtue is. Some act a most generous disinterested part in life who have been taught to account for all their actions by self-love as the sole spring. There have been very different and opposite opinions in optics, contrary accounts have been given of hearing, voluntary motion, digestion, and other natural actions. But the powers themselves in reality perform their several operations with sufficient constancy and uniformity in persons of good health whatever their opinions be about them. In the same manner our moral actions and affections may be in good order when our opinions are quite wrong about them. True opinions, however, about both, may enable us to improve our natural powers and to rectify accidental disorders incident unto them. And true speculations on these subjects must certainly be attended with as much pleasure as any other parts of human knowledge.

It may perhaps seem strange that in this treatise virtue is supposed disinterested yet so much pains is taken by a comparison of our several pleasures to prove the pleasures of virtue to be the greatest we are capable of and that consequently it is our truest interest to be virtuous. But let it be remembered here that though there can be no motives or arguments suggested which can directly raise any ultimate desire, such as that of our own happiness, or public affections (as we attempt to prove in Treatise IV), yet if both are natural dispositions of our minds, and nothing can stop the operation of public affections but some selfish interest, the only way to give public affections their full force and to make them prevalent in our lives must be to remove these opinions of opposite interests and to show a superior interest on their side. If these considerations be just and sufficiently attended to, a natural disposition can scarce fail to exert itself to the full.

In this *Essay on the Passions* the proofs and illustration of this point, that we have a moral sense and a sense of honor by which we discern an immediate good in virtue and honor [1] not referred to any further enjoyment, are not much insisted on since they are already laid down [1] in the *Inquiry into Moral Good and Evil* in the first and fifth sections. Would men reflect upon what they feel in themselves all proofs of such matters would be needless.

Some strange love of simplicity in the structure of human nature or attachment to some favorite hypothesis has engaged many writers to pass over a great many simple perceptions which we may find in ourselves. We have got the number five fixed for our external senses though a larger number might perhaps as easily be defended. We have multitudes of perceptions which have no relation to any external sensation, if by it we mean perceptions immediately occasioned by motions or impressions made on our bodies, such as the ideas of number, duration, proportion, virtue, vice, pleasures of honor, of congratulation, the pains of remorse, shame, sympathy, and many others. It were to be wished that those who are at such pains to prove a beloved maxim, 'that all ideas arise from sensation and reflection,' had so explained themselves that none should take their meaning to be that all our ideas are either external

[1. Ed. 1 reads: 'are not mentioned because they are so']

sensations or reflex acts upon external sensations. Or if by reflection they mean an inward power of perception, [2]as Mr. Locke declares expressly, calling it internal sensation,[2] that they had as carefully examined into the several kinds of internal perceptions as they have done into the external sensations, that we might have seen whether the former be not as natural and necessary [3]and ultimate, without reference to any other,[3] as the latter. Had they in like manner considered our affections without a previous notion that they were all from self-love they might have felt an ultimate desire of the happiness of others as easily conceivable and as certainly implanted in the human breast, though perhaps not so strong as self-love.

The author hopes this imperfect essay will be favorably received till some person of greater abilities and leisure apply himself to a more strict philosophical inquiry into the various natural principles or natural dispositions of mankind from which perhaps a more exact theory of morals may be formed than any which has yet appeared, and hopes that this attempt to show the fair side of human temper may be of some little use toward this great end.

[4]The author takes nothing in bad part from any of his adversaries except that outcry which one or two of them

[2. Ed. 1 reads: 'as I fancy they do']

[3. Not in ed. 1.]

[4. Ed. 1 reads: 'The principal objections offered by Mr. Clarke of Hull, against the second section of the second *Treatise*, occurred to the author in conversation and had apprized him of the necessity of a farther illustration of disinterested affections in answer to his scheme of deducing them from self-love, which seemed more ingenious than any which the author of the *Inquiry* ever yet saw in print. He takes better from Mr. Clarke all other parts of his treatment than the raising such an outcry against him as injurious to Christianity for principles which some of the most zealous Christians have publicly maintained. He hopes that Mr. Clarke will be satisfied upon this point, as well as about the scheme of disinterested affections, by what is offered in the *Treatise on the Passions*, Section V, and designedly placed here, rather than in any distinct reply, both to avoid the disagreeable work of answering or remarking upon books wherein it is hard to keep off too keen and offensive expressions; and also, that those who have had any of the former editions of the *Inquiry* might not be at a loss about any illustrations or additional proofs necessary to complete the scheme.']

made against these principles as opposite to Christianity, though it be so well known that they have been and are espoused by many of the most zealous Christians. There are answers interspersed in the later editions to these objections to avoid the disagreeable work of replying or remarking, in which one is not generally upon his guard sufficiently to avoid cavils and offensive expressions.[4]

The last treatise had never seen the light had not some worthy gentlemen mistaken some things about the moral sense alleged to be in mankind. Their objections gave opportunity of farther inquiry into the several schemes of accounting for our moral ideas which some apprehend to be wholly different from, and independent on, that sense which the author attempts to establish [5]in Treatise IV.[5] The following papers attempt to show that all these schemes must necessarily presuppose this moral sense and be resolved into it. Nor does the author endeavor to overturn them or represent them as unnecessary superstructures upon the foundation of a moral sense, though what he has suggested will probably show a considerable confusion in some of the terms much used on these subjects. One may easily see, from the great variety of terms and diversity of schemes invented, that all men feel something in their own hearts recommending virtue which yet it is difficult to explain. This difficulty arises from our previous notions of a small number of senses, so that we are unwilling to have recourse in our theories to any more and rather strain out some explication of moral ideas with relation to some of the natural powers of perception universally acknowledged. The like difficulty attends several other perceptions to the reception of which philosophers have not generally assigned their distinct senses, such as natural beauty, harmony, the perfection of poetry, architecture, designing, and such like affairs of genius, taste, or fancy. The explications or theories on these subjects are in like manner full of confusion and metaphor.

To define virtue by agreeableness to this moral sense,

[5. Not in ed. 1.]

or describing it to be kind affection, may appear perhaps too uncertain considering that the sense of particular persons is often depraved by custom, habits, false opinions, or company, and that some particular kind passions toward some persons are really pernicious and attended with very unkind affections toward others, or at least with a neglect of their interests. We must therefore only assert in general, 'that every one calls that temper or those actions virtuous which are approved by his own sense' and withal, 'that abstracting from particular habits or prejudices [6] that temper which desires, and those actions which are intended to procure, the greatest moment of good toward the most extensive system in which our power can reach, is approved as the highest virtue, and that the universal calm good will or benevolence, where it is the leading affection of the soul, so as to limit or restrain all other affections, appetites, or passions, is the temper which we esteem in the highest degree, according to the natural constitution of our soul; and withal, that we in a lower degree approve every particular kind affection or passion which is not inconsistent with these higher and nobler dispositions.' [6]

Our moral sense shows this [7] calm extensive affection [7] to be the highest perfection of our nature, what we may see to be the end or design of such a structure, and consequently what is required of us by the author of our nature. And therefore if any one like these descriptions better he may call virtue, with many of the ancients, *vita secundum naturam*, or 'acting according to what we may see from the constitution of our nature we are intended for by our creator.'

[6. Ed. 1 reads: 'every one is so constituted as to approve every particular kind affection toward any one which argues no want of affection toward others. And constantly to approve that temper which desires, and those actions which tend to procure, the greatest moment of good in the power of the agent toward the most extensive system to which it can reach; and consequently, that the perfection of virtue consists in "having the universal calm benevolence, the prevalent affection of the mind, so as to limit and counteract not only the selfish passions, but even the particular kind affections."']

[7. Not in ed. 1.]

If this moral sense were once set in a convincing light those vain shadows of objections against a virtuous life, in which some are wonderfully delighted, alleging that whatever we admire or honor in a moral species is the effect of art, education, custom, policy, or subtle views of interest, would soon vanish. We should then acknowledge "Quid sumus et quidam victuri gignimur."—Pers.

It is true a power of reasoning is natural to us and we must own that all arts and sciences which are well founded and tend to direct our actions, [8]if not called natural, yet are an improvement upon our nature. But if virtue be looked upon[8] as wholly artificial, there are I know not what suspicions against it, as if indeed it might tend to the interest of large bodies or societies of men or to that of their governors [9]while yet one may better find his private interest[9] or enjoy greater pleasures in the practices counted vicious, especially if he has any probability of secrecy in them. These suspicions must be entirely removed if we have a moral sense and public affections, whose gratifications are constituted by nature our most intense and durable pleasures.

Gentlemen[10] who have opposed some other sentiments of the author of the *Inquiry* seem convinced of a moral sense. Some of them have by a mistake made a compliment to the author which does not belong to him, as if the world were any indebted to him for this discovery. He has too often met with the *sensus decori et honesti* and with the *φιλάνθρωπον καὶ αναθοειδές*[11] to assume any such thing to himself.

Some letters in the London Journals in 1728,[12] sub-

[8. Ed. 1 reads: 'are, if not to be called natural, an improvement upon our nature; yet if virtue be looked upon']

[9. Ed. 1 reads: 'whereas a private person may better find his interest']

[10. Ed. 1 reads: 'I hope it is a good omen of something still better on this subject to be expected in the learned world that Mr. Butler, in his sermons at the Rolls Chapel, has done so much justice to the wise and good order of our nature; that the gentlemen,']

[11. Ed. 1 reads: '*Δύναμις αγαθοειδὴς*']

[12. The date is not in any edition before 1742. See "A Note on the Editions and the Dating of the Correspondence with Burnet" in the Preface.]

scribed Philaretus, gave the first occasion to the fourth treatise. The answers given to them in those weekly papers bore too visible marks of the hurry in which they were wrote and therefore the author declined to continue the debate that way, choosing to send a private letter to Philaretus to desire a more private correspondence on the subject of our debate. [13]He was soon after informed that his death disappointed the author's [13] great expectations from so ingenious a correspondent. The objections proposed in the first section of Treatise IV are not always those of Philaretus, though the author endeavored to leave no objections of his unanswered, but he also interspersed whatever objections occurred in conversation on these subjects, and has not used any expressions inconsistent with the high regard he has for the memory of so ingenious a gentleman and of such distinction in the world.[14]

In the references at the bottoms of pages the *Inquiry into Beauty* is called Treatise I, the *Inquiry into the Ideas of Moral Good and Evil* is Treatise II, the *Essay on the Passions,* Treatise III, and the *Illustrations on the Moral Sense,* Treatise IV.

[13. Ed. 1 reads: 'I have been since informed that his death disappointed my great expectations']

[14. Ed. 1 has two additional paragraphs: 'The last section of the fourth treatise was occasioned by a private letter from a person of the most real merit in Glasgow [identity not ascertainable either by Scott or by the present editor] representing to me some sentiments not uncommon among good men which might prejudice them against any scheme of morals not wholly founded upon piety. This point is, I hope, so treated as to remove the difficulty.

'The deference due to a person, who has appeared so much in the learned world, as M. Le Clerc would seem to require that I should make some defense against, or submission to, the remarks he makes in his *Bibliothèque Ancienne & Moderne.* [Jean le Clerc (of Amsterdam) (1657–1736), *Bibliothèque Ancienne et Moderne,* pour servir de suite aux *Bibliothèque Universelle et Choisie,* 29 vols., Amsterdam and the Hague, 1714–1730. Le Clerc's review appeared in volume 26 (1726), pp. 102–115.] But I cannot but conclude from his abstract, especially from that of the last section of the *Inquiry,* either that I don't understand his French, or he my English, or that he has never read more than the titles of some of the sections and if any one of the three be the case we are not fit for a controversy.']

Contents

Introduction

The differences of actions from which some are constituted morally good and others morally evil have always been accounted a very important subject of inquiry and, therefore, every attempt to free this subject from the usual causes of error and dispute, the confusion of ambiguous words, must be excusable.

In the following discourse happiness denotes pleasant sensation of any kind, or a continued state of such sensations, and misery denotes the contrary sensations.

Such actions as tend to procure happiness to the agent are called for shortness, privately useful, and such actions as procure misery to the agent, privately hurtful.

Actions procuring happiness to others may be called publicly useful and the contrary actions publicly hurtful. Some actions may be both publicly and privately useful and others both publicly and privately hurtful.

These different natural tendencies of actions are universally acknowledged and in proportion to our reflection upon human affairs we shall enlarge our knowledge of these differences.

When these natural differences are known, it remains to be inquired into, first, 'What quality in any action determines our election of it rather than the contrary?' Or, if the mind determines itself, 'What motives or desires excite to an action, rather than the contrary, or rather than to the omission?' Second, 'What quality determines our approbation of one action rather than of the contrary action?'

The words election and approbation seem to denote simple ideas known by consciousness which can only be explained by synonymous words or by concomitant or consequent circumstances. Election is purposing to do an action rather than its contrary, or than being inactive. Approbation of our own action denotes, or is attended with, a pleasure in the contemplation of it, and in reflection upon the affections which inclined us to it. [1]Approbation of the action of another has some little pleasure attending it in the observer and raises love toward the agent in whom the quality approved is deemed to reside, and not in the observer who has a satisfaction in the act of approving.[a] [1]

The qualities moving to election or exciting to action are different from those moving to approbation. We often do actions which we do not approve and approve actions which we omit. We often desire that an agent had omitted an action which we approve and wish he would do an action which we condemn. Approbation is employed about the actions of others where there is no room for our election.

Now in our search into the qualities exciting either our election or approbation let us consider the several notions advanced of moral good and evil in both these respects and what senses, instincts, or affections must be necessarily supposed to account for our approbation of election.

There are two opinions on this subject entirely opposite the one that of the old Epicureans as it is beautifully explained in the first book of Cicero, *de Finibus*, which is revived by Hobbes, [2]Rochefoucauld, and others

a. See Treat. II, Sect. 2, parag. ult. [*An Inquiry into the Original of Our Ideas of Beauty and Virtue in Two Treatises,* I. Concerning Beauty, Order, Harmony, Design; II. Concerning Moral Good and Evil, London, 1725. The last paragraph of section 2 reads: 'We ought here to observe that the only reason of that apparent want of natural affection among collateral relations is that these natural inclinations in many cases are overpowered by self-love, where there happens any opposition of interests; but where this does not happen we shall find all mankind under its influence, though with different degrees of strength according to the nearer or more remote relations they stand in to each other and according as the natural affection of benevolence is joined with and strengthened by esteem, gratitude, compassion, or other kind affections or, on the contrary, weakened by displicence, anger, or envy.']

[1. Ed. 1 reads: 'Approbation of the action of another is pleasant and is attended with love toward the agent.']

[2. Not in Ed. 1.]

of the last century,[2] and followed by many better writers, 'that all the desires of the human mind, nay of all thinking natures, are reducible to self-love, or desire of private happiness that from this desire all actions of any agent do flow.' Our Christian moralists of this scheme introduce other sorts of happiness to be desired, but still it is the 'prospect of private happiness, which, with some of them, is the sole motive of election. And that, in like manner, what determines any agent to approve his own action is its tendency to his private happiness in the whole, though it may bring present pain along with it; that the approbation of the action of another is from an opinion of its tendency to the happiness of the approver, either immediately or more remotely; that each agent may discover it to be the surest way to promote his private happiness to do publicly useful actions and to abstain from those which are publicly hurtful; that the neglecting to observe this and doing publicly hurtful actions does mischief to the whole of mankind by hurting any one part; that every one has some little damage by this action; such an inadvertent person might possibly be pernicious to any one, were he in his neighborhood; and the very example of such actions may extend over the whole world and produce some pernicious effects upon any observer. That therefore every one may look upon such actions as hurtful to himself and in this view does disapprove them and hates the agent. In the like manner, a publicly useful action may diffuse some small advantage to every observer whence he may approve it and love the agent.'

This scheme can never account for the principal actions of human life[b] such as the offices of friendship,

b. See Treat. III, Sect. 1. [*An Essay on the Nature and Conduct of the Passions*. Section 1 is entitled "A general account of our several senses and desires, selfish or public." With help from Butler, Hutcheson analyzes affection and desire more carefully than he had in the *Inquiry Concerning Moral Good and Evil,* distinguishing, for example, between the "public sense" and the "moral sense," between pleasure and desire, and between "ultimate" and "subordinate" desires. He reaffirms his argument of the *Inquiry* that human nature includes benevolent affections as well as egoistic ones.]

gratitude, natural affection, generosity, public spirit, compassion. Men are conscious of no such intentions or acute reflections about these actions. Ingenious speculative men in their straining to support an hypothesis may contrive a thousand subtle selfish motives which a kind generous heart never dreamed of. In like manner, this scheme can never account for the sudden approbation and violent sense of something amiable in actions done in distant ages and nations while the approver has perhaps never thought of these distant tendencies to his happiness. Nor will it better account for our want of approbation toward publicly useful actions done casually or only with intention of private happiness to the agent. And then, in these actions reputed generous, if the agent's motive was only a view to his own pleasure, how come we to approve them more than his enriching himself or his gratifying his own taste with good food? The whole species may receive a like advantage from both and the observer an equal share.

Were our approbation of actions done in distant ages and nations occasioned by this thought, that such an action done toward our selves would be useful to us, why do not we approve and love in like manner any man who finds a treasure or indulges himself in any exquisite sensation, since these advantages or pleasures might have been conferred on ourselves and tend more to our happiness than any actions in distant ages?

The sanctions of laws may make any agent choose the action required under the conception of useful to himself and lead him into an opinion of private advantage in it and of detriment in the contrary actions; but what should determine any person to approve the actions of others, because of a conformity to a law, if approbation in any person were only an opinion of private advantage?

The other opinion is this, 'that we have not only self-love, but benevolent affections also toward others, in various degrees, making us desire their happiness as an ultimate end without any view to private happiness; that we have a moral sense or determination of our mind to approve every kind affection either in ourselves or others and all publicly useful actions which we imagine flow from such affection, without our having a view to our private happiness in our approbation of these actions.'

These two opinions seem both intelligible, each consistent with itself. The former seems not to represent human nature as it is, the other seems to do it.

There have been many ways of speaking introduced which seem to signify something different from both the former opinions. Such as these, that 'Morality of actions consists in conformity to reason or difformity from it,' that 'Virtue is acting according to the absolute fitness and unfitness of things, or agreeably to the natures or relations of things,' and many others in different authors. To examine these is the design of the following sections and to explain more fully how the moral sense alleged to be in mankind must be presupposed even in these schemes.

Concerning the character of virtue, agreeable to truth or reason

Section I

Since reason is understood to denote our power of finding out true propositions, reasonableness must denote the same thing with conformity to true propositions or to truth.

Reasonableness in an action is a very common expression but yet upon inquiry it will appear very confused whether we suppose it the motive to election or the quality determining approbation.

There is one sort of conformity to truth which neither determines to the one or the other, viz., that conformity which is between every true proposition and its object. This sort of conformity can never make us choose or approve one action more than its contrary for it is found in all actions alike. Whatever attribute can be ascribed to a generous kind action the contrary attribute may as truly be ascribed to a selfish cruel action. Both propositions are equally true and the two contrary actions, the objects of the two truths, are equally conformable to their several truths with that sort of conformity which is between a truth and its object. This conformity then cannot make a difference among actions or recommend one more than another either to election or approbation, since any man may make as many truths about villainy as about heroism by ascribing to it contrary attributes.

For instance, these are truths concerning the preservation of property, 'It tends to the happiness of human society. It encourages industry. It shall be rewarded by God.' These are also truths concerning robbery. 'It disturbs society. It discourages industry. It shall be punished by God.' The former three truths have that sort of conformity to its objects which is common to all truths with their objects. The moral difference cannot therefore depend upon this conformity, which is common to both.

The number of truths in both cases may be plainly the same, so that a good action cannot be supposed to agree to more truths than an evil one, nor can an evil action be disagreeable to any truth or compages of truths made about it; for whatever propositions do not agree with their objects are not truths.

If reasonableness, the character of virtue, denote some other sort of conformity to truth it were to be wished that these gentlemen who make it the original idea of moral good antecedent to any sense or affections would explain it and show how it determines us, antecedently to a sense, either to election or approbation.

They tell us, 'We must have some standard antecedently to all sense or affections since we judge even of our senses and affections themselves and approve or disapprove them. This standard must be our reason, conformity to which must be the original idea of moral good.'

But what is this conformity of actions to reason? When we ask the reason of an action we sometimes mean, 'What truth shows a quality in the action, exciting the agent to do it?' Thus, why does a luxurious man pursue wealth? The reason is given by this truth, 'Wealth is useful to purchase pleasures.' Sometimes for a reason of actions we show the truth expressing a quality engaging our approbation. Thus the reason of hazarding life in just war is that 'It tends to preserve our honest countrymen or evidences public spirit.' The reason for temperance and against luxury is given thus, 'Luxury evidences a selfish base temper.' The former sort of reasons we will call exciting and the latter justifying.[a] Now we shall find that all exciting reasons presuppose instincts and affections and the justifying presuppose a moral sense.

As to exciting reasons, in every calm rational action some end is desired or intended. No end can be in-

a. Thus Grotius distinguishes the reasons of war into *justificae* and *suasoriae*, or these, *sub ratione utilis*. [Hugo Grotius (1583–1645), *De Jure Belli et Pacis*, Paris, 1625. The phrase, 'or these *sub ratione utilis*,' was not in the first edition.]

tended or desired previously to some one of these classes of affections, self-love, self-hatred, or desire of private misery (if this be possible), benevolence toward others, or malice. All affections are included under these. No end can be previous to them all. There can therefore be no exciting reason previous to affection.

We have indeed many confused harangues on this subject telling us, 'We have two principles of action, reason and affection or passion,[1] the former in common with angels, the latter with brutes. No action is wise, or good, or reasonable, to which we are not excited by reason, as distinct from all affections, or, if any such actions as flow from affections be good, it is only by chance, or materially, and not formally.' As if indeed reason, or the knowledge of the relations of things, could excite to action when we proposed no end, or as if ends could be intended without desire or affection.

[2]Writers on these subjects should remember the common divisions of the faculties of the soul. That there is (1) reason presenting the natures and relations of things antecedently to any act of will or desire, (2) the will, or *appetitus rationalis*, or the disposition of soul to pursue what is presented as good and to shun evil. Were there no other power in the soul than that of mere contemplation there would be no affection, volition, desire, action. Nay, without some motion of will no man would voluntarily persevere in contemplation. There must be a desire of knowledge and of the pleasure which attends it. This too is an act of willing. Both these powers are by the ancients included under the λδγος or λογικὸν μέρος. Below these they place two other powers dependent on the body, the *sensus*, and the *appetitus sensitivus*, in which they place the particular passions. The former answers to the understanding and the latter to the will. But the will is forgot of late and some ascribe to the intellect not only contemplation or knowledge but choice, desire, prosecuting, loving. Nay, some are grown so ingenious in uniting the powers of

[1. Ed. 1 adds '(i.e., strong affection)']
[2. This paragraph not in ed. 1.]

the soul that contemplating with pleasure symmetry and proportion, an act of the intellect as they plead, is the same thing with good will or the virtuous desire of public happiness.[2]

But are there not also exciting reasons, even previous to any end, moving us to propose one end rather than another? To this Aristotle long ago answered 'that there are ultimate ends desired without a view to any thing else, and subordinate ends or objects desired with a view to something else.' To subordinate ends those reasons or truths excite which show them to be conducive to the ultimate end and show one object to be more effectual than another. Thus subordinate ends may be called reasonable. But as to the ultimate ends, to suppose exciting reasons for them would infer that there is no ultimate end but that we desire one thing for another in an infinite series.

Thus ask a being who desires private happiness or has self-love, 'What reason excites him to desire wealth?' He will give this reason, 'that wealth tends to procure pleasure and ease.' Ask his reason for desiring pleasure or happiness. One cannot imagine what propositions he could assign as his exciting reason. This proposition is indeed true, 'There is an instinct or desire fixed in his nature determining him to pursue his happiness.' But it is not this reflection on his own nature, or this proposition, which excites or determines him, but the instinct itself. This is a truth, 'Rhubarb strengthens the stomach,' but it is not a proposition which strengthens the stomach but the quality in that medicine. The effect is not produced by propositions showing the cause but by the cause itself.

In like manner, what reason can a benevolent being give as exciting him to hazard his life in just war? This perhaps, 'Such conduct tends to the happiness of his country.' Ask him, 'Why he serves his country?' He will say, 'His country is a very valuable part of mankind.' Why does he study the happiness of mankind? If his affections be really disinterested he can give no exciting reason for it. The happiness of mankind in general, or of any valuable part of it, is an ultimate end to that series of desires.

We may transiently observe a mistake some fall into.[3] They suppose, because they have formed some conception of an infinite good, or greatest possible aggregate, or sum of happiness, under which all particular pleasures may be included, that there is also some one great ultimate end with a view to which every particular pleasure is desired without farther view as an ultimate end in the selfish desires. It is true, the prospect of a greater inconsistent pleasure may surmount or stop this desire; so may the fear of a prepollent evil. But this does not prove 'that all men have formed ideas of infinite good, or greatest possible aggregate, or that they have an instinct or desire [4]actually operating[4] without an idea of its object.' Just so in the benevolent affections, the happiness of any one person is an ultimate end, desired with no farther view. And yet the observing its inconsistency with the happiness of another more beloved, or with the happiness of many, though each one of them were but equally beloved, may overcome the former desire. Yet this will not prove that in each kind action men form the abstract conception of all mankind or the system of rationals. [5]Such conceptions are indeed useful,[5] that so we may gratify either our self-love or kind affections in the fullest manner, as far as our power extends, and may not content ourselves with smaller degrees either of private or public good while greater are in our power. But when we have formed these conceptions we do not serve the individual only from love to the species, no more than we desire grapes with an intention of the greatest aggregate of happiness or from an apprehension that they make a part of the general sum of our happiness. These conceptions only serve to suggest greater ends than would occur to us

[3. Ed. 1 adds: 'who in their philosophical inquiries have learned to form very abstract ideas']

[4. Not in ed. 1.]

[5. Ed. 1 reads: 'The forming such large conceptions is indeed useful']

without reflection and by the prepollency of one desire toward the greater good, to either private or public, to stop the desire toward the smaller good when it appears inconsistent with the greater.

Let us examine the truths assigned as exciting to the pursuit of public good, even by those who, though they allow disinterested affections and a moral sense, yet suppose something reasonable in it antecedently. They assign such as these, 'Public good is the end proposed by the Deity.' Then what reason excites men to concur with the Deity? It is this, 'Concurring with the Deity will make the agent happy'? This is an exciting reason indeed, but plainly supposes self-love, and let any one assign the exciting reason to the desire of happiness. Is the reason exciting to concur with the Deity this, 'The Deity is our benefactor'? Then what reason excites to concur with benefactors? Here we must recur to an instinct. Is it this truth, 'The divine ends are reasonable ends'? Then what means the word reasonable? Does it mean that 'The Deity has reasons exciting him to promote the public good'? What are these reasons? Why, perhaps 'We do not know them particularly but in general are sure that the Deity has reasons for them.' Then the question recurs, 'What reason excites us to implicit concurrence with the ends of the Deity?' The reasons which excite one nature may not excite another. The tendency of an action to the happiness of one agent may excite him but will not excite another agent to concur unless there appears a like tendency to the happiness of that other. They may say, 'They are sure the divine ends are good.' What means goodness? Is it moral or natural? If the divine ends be natural good, i.e., pleasant, or the cause of pleasure, to whom is this pleasure? If to the Deity, then why do we study the happiness or the pleasing of the Deity? What reason excites us? All the possible reasons must either presuppose some affection if they are exciting or some moral sense if they are justifying. Is the divine end naturally good to us? This is an exciting reason but supposes self-love. If we say the divine ends are morally good we are just where we began. What is moral goodness? Conformity to reason. What are the reasons exciting or justifying?

If any allege as the reason exciting us to pursue public good this truth, that 'The happiness of a system, a thousand, or a million, is a greater quantity of happiness than that of one person and, consequently, if men desire happiness they must have stronger desires toward the greater sum, than toward the less,' this reason still supposes an instinct toward happiness as previous to it. And again, to whom is the happiness of a system a greater happiness? To one individual or to the system? If to the individual, then his reason exciting his desire of a happy system supposes self-love, if to the system, then what reason can excite to desire the greater happiness of a system or any happiness to be in the possession of others? None surely which does not presuppose public affections. Without such affections this truth, 'that an hundred felicites is a greater sum than one felicity,' will no more excite to study the happiness of the hundred than this truth, 'an hundred stones are greater than one,' will excite a man, who has no desire of heaps, to cast them together.

The same may be observed concerning that proposition, assigned by some as the ultimate reason both exciting to, and justifying, the pursuit of public good, viz., 'It is best that all should be happy.' Best is most good. Good to whom? To the whole or to each individual? If to the former, when this truth excites to action it must presuppose kind affections. If it is good to each individual it must suppose self-love.

Let us once suppose affection, instincts, or desires previously implanted in our nature and we shall easily understand the exciting reasons for actions, viz., 'These truths which show them to be conducive toward some ultimate end or toward the greatest end of that kind in our power.' He acts reasonably who considers the various actions in his power and forms true opinions of their tendencies and then chooses to do that which will obtain the highest degree of that, to which the instincts of his nature incline him, with the smallest degree of those things from which the affections in his nature make him averse.

More particularly, the exciting reasons to a nature which had only selfish affections are those truths which showed what object or event would occasion to it the greatest quantity of pleasure. These would excite to the prosecution of it. The exciting truths about means would be only those which pointed out some means as more certainly effectual than any other or with less pain or trouble to the agent. Public usefulness of ends or means, or public hurtfulness, would neither excite nor dissuade farther than the public state might affect that of the agent.

If there is any nature with public affection the truths exciting to any end in this order are such as show that any event would promote the happiness of others. That end is called most reasonable which our reason discovers to contain a greater quantity of public good than any other in our power.

When any event may affect both the agent and others, if the agent have both self-love and public affections, he acts according to that affection which is strongest, when there is any opposition of interest. If there be no opposition, he follows both. If he discovers this truth, 'that his constant pursuit of public good is the most probable way of promoting his own happiness,' then his pursuit is truly reasonable and constant. Thus both affections are at once gratified and he is consistent with himself. Without knowledge of that truth he does not act reasonably for his own happiness but follows it by means not tending effectually to this end, and must frequently, from the power of self-love, neglect or counteract his other end, the public good. If there be also a moral sense in such an agent, while yet he is inadvertent to the connection of private happiness with the study of the public, he must be perpetually yet more uneasy, either through the apprehended neglect of private interest when he serves in public, or when he pursues only private interest. He will have perpetual remorse and dissatisfaction with his own temper, through his moral sense. So that the knowledge of this connection of private interest with the study of public good seems absolutely necessary to preserve a constant satisfaction of mind and to prevent an alternate prevalence of seemingly contrary desires.

Should any one ask even concerning these two ultimate ends, private good and public, is not the latter more reasonable than the former?—what means the word reasonable in this question? If we are allowed to presuppose instincts and affections then the truth just now supposed to be discoverable concerning our state is an exciting reason to serve the public interest since this conduct is the most effectual means to obtain both ends. But I doubt if any truth can be assigned which excites in us either the desire of private happiness or public. For the former none ever alleged any exciting reason; and a benevolent temper finds as little reason exciting him to the latter, which he desires without any view to private good. If the meaning of the question be this, 'Does not every spectator approve the pursuit of public good more than private?'—the answer is obvious, that he does; but not for any reason or truth but from a moral sense [6] in the constitution of the soul.[6]

This leads to consider approbation of actions, whether it be for conformity to any truth, or reasonableness, that actions are ultimately approved, independently of any moral sense? Or if all justifying reasons do not presuppose it?

If conformity to truth, or reasonable, denote nothing else but that 'an action is the object of a true proposition,' it is plain that all actions should be approved equally, since as many truths may be made about the worst, as can be made about the best. See what was said above about exciting reasons.

But let the truths commonly assigned as justifying be examined. Here it is plain, 'a truth showing an action to be fit to attain an end,' does not justify it; nor do we approve a subordinate end for any truth which only shows it to be fit to promote the ultimate end; for the

[6. Not in ed. 1.]

worst actions may be conducive to their ends, and reasonable in that sense. The justifying reasons then must be about the ends themselves, especially the ultimate ends. The question then is, 'Does a conformity to any truth make us approve an ultimate end, previously to any moral sense?' For example, we approve pursuing the public good. For what reason? Or what is the truth for conformity to which we call it a reasonable end? I fancy we can find none in these cases, more than we could give for our liking any pleasant fruit.[b]

The reasons assigned are such as these, 'It is the end proposed by the Deity.' But why do we approve concurring with the divine ends? This reason is given, 'He is our benefactor.' But then, for what reason do we approve concurrence with a benefactor? Here we must recur to a sense. Is this the reason moving to approbation, 'Study of public good tends to the advantage of the approver'? Then the quality moving us to approve an action is its being advantageous to us and not conformity to a truth. This scheme is intelligible but not true in fact. Men approve without perception of private advantage and often do not condemn or disapprove what is plainly pernicious, as in the execution of a just sentence which even the sufferer[7] may approve.

If any allege that this is the justifying reason of the pursuit of public good, 'that it is best all be happy,' then we approve actions for their tendency to that state which is best and not for conformity to reason. But here again, what means best? morally best, or naturally best? If the former, they explain the same word by itself in a circle, if they mean the latter, that 'It is the most happy state where all are happy,' then most happy for whom? the system, or the individual? If for the former, what reason makes us approve the happiness of a system? Here we must recur to a sense or kind affections. Is it most happy for the individual? Then the quality

b. This is what Aristotle so often asserts that the προαιρετόν or βουλευτόν is not the end, but the means. [This footnote not in ed. 1.]

[7. Ed. 1 has 'criminal']

moving approbation is again tendency to private happiness, not reasonableness.

There are some other reasons assigned in words differing from the former, but more confused, such as these. 'It is our duty to study public good. We are obliged to do it. We owe obedience to the Deity. The whole is to be preferred to a part.' But let these words, duty, obligation, owing and the meaning of that gerund [8] or participle,[8] is to be preferred, be explained and we shall find ourselves still at a loss for exciting reasons previously to affections or justifying reason without recourse to a moral sense.

When we say one is obliged to an action we either mean, (1) that the action is necessary to obtain happiness to the agent, or to avoid misery or, (2) that every spectator, or he himself upon reflection, must approve his action, and disapprove his omitting it, if he considers fully all its circumstances. The former meaning of the word obligation presupposes selfish affections, and the sense of private happiness; the latter meaning includes the moral sense. Mr. Barbeyrac, in his annotations upon Grotius,[c] makes obligation denote an indispensable necessity to act in a certain manner. Whoever observes his explication of this necessity (which is not natural, otherwise no man could act against his obligation) will find that it denotes only 'such a constitution of a powerful superior as will make it possible for any being to obtain happiness or avoid misery but by such a course of action.' This agrees with the former meaning, though sometimes he also includes the latter.

Many other confused definitions have been given of obligation by no obscure names in the learned world. But let any one give a distinct meaning different from the two above-mentioned. To pursue them all would be endless; only let the definitions be substituted in place of the word obligation, in other parts of each

c. Lib. i, chap. I, sect. 10.
[8. Not in ed. 1.]

writer, and let it be observed whether it makes good sense or not.[d]

Before we quit this character reasonableness let us consider the arguments brought to prove that there must be some standard of moral good antecedent to any sense. Say they, 'Perceptions of sense are deceitful; we must have some perception or idea of virtue more stable and certain. This must be conformity to reason. Truth discovered by our reason is certain and invariable. That then alone is the original idea of virtue, agreement with reason.' But in like manner our sight and sense of beauty is deceitful and does not always represent the true forms of objects. We must not call that beautiful or regular, which pleases the sight, or an internal sense, but beauty in external forms, too, consists in conformity to reason. So our taste may be vitiated. We must not say that savor is perceived by taste but must place the original idea of grateful savors in conformity to reason and of ungrateful in contrariety to reason. We may mistake the real extent of bodies, or their proportions, by making a conclusion upon the first sensible appearance. Therefore ideas of extension are not originally acquired by a sense but consist in conformity to reason.

If what is intended in this conformity to reason be this, 'that we should call no action virtuous unless we have some reason to conclude it to be virtuous, or some truth showing it to be so,' this is very true. But then in like manner we should count no action vicious unless we have some reason for counting it so, or when it is truth 'that it is vicious.' If this be intended by conformity to truth, then at the same rate we may make conformity to truth the original idea of vice as well as virtue, nay, of every attribute whatsoever. That taste alone is sweet which there is reason to count sweet; that taste alone is bitter, concerning which it is true that it is bitter; that

d. The common definition, *vinculum juris quo necessitate adstringimur alicujus rei praestandae,* is wholly metaphorical and can settle no debate precisely. [This footnote not in ed. 1.]

form alone is beautiful, concerning which it is true that it is beautiful; and that alone deformed, which is truly deformed. Thus virtue, vice, sweet, bitter, beautiful, or deformed, originally denote conformity to reason, antecedently to perceptions of any sense. The idea of virtue is particularly that concerning which it is truth, that it is virtue; or virtue is virtue; a wonderful discovery!

So when some tell us, 'that truth is naturally pleasant, and more so than any sensible perception; this must therefore engage men more than any other motive, if they attend to it,' let them observe that as much truth is known about vice as virtue. We may demonstrate the public miseries which would ensue upon perjury, murder, and robbery. These demonstrations would be attended with that pleasure which is peculiar to truth, as well as the demonstrations of the public happiness to ensue from faith, humanity and justice. There is equal truth on both sides.

We may transiently observe what has occasioned the use of the word reasonable as an epithet of only virtuous actions. Though we have instincts determining us to desire ends without supposing any previous reasoning, yet it is by use of our reason that we find out the means of obtaining our ends. When we do not use our reason we often are disappointed of our end. We therefore call those actions which are effectual to their ends reasonable in one sense of that word.

Again, in all men there is probably a moral sense, making publicly useful actions and kind affections grateful to the agent and to every observer. Most men who have thought of human actions agree that the publicly useful are in the whole also privately useful to the agent, either in this life or the next. We conclude that all men have the same affections and sense. We are convinced by our reason that it is by publicly useful actions alone that we can promote all our ends. Whoever then acts in a contrary manner we presume is mistaken, ignorant of, or inadvertent to, these truths which he might know; and say he acts unreasonably.

Hence some have been led to imagine some reasons either exciting or justifying previously to all affections or a moral sense.

Two arguments are brought in defence of this epithet, as antecedent to any sense, viz., 'that we judge even of our affections and senses themselves, whether they are morally good or evil.'

The second argument is, 'that if all moral ideas depend upon the constitution of our sense then all constitutions would have been alike reasonable and good to the Deity, which is absurd.'

As to the first argument, it is plain we judge of our own affections, or those of others, by our moral sense, by which we approve kind affections and disapprove the contrary. But none can apply moral attributes to the very faculty of perceiving moral qualities, or call his moral sense morally good or evil, any more than he calls the power of tasting sweet or bitter; or of seeing, straight or crooked, white or black.

Every one judges the affections of others by his own sense, so that it seems not impossible that in these senses men might differ as they do in taste. A sense approving benevolence would disapprove that temper which a sense approving malice would delight in. The former would judge of the latter by his own sense, so would the latter of the former. Each one would at first view think the sense of the other perverted. But, then, is there no difference? Are both senses equally good? No, certainly, any man who observed them would think the sense of the former more desirable than of the latter; but this is because the moral sense of every man is constituted in the former manner. But were there any nature with no moral sense at all observing these two persons, would he not think the state of the former preferable to that of the latter? Yes, he might, but not from any perception of moral goodness in the one sense more than in the other. Any rational nature observing two men thus constituted with opposite senses might by reasoning see, not moral goodness in one sense more than in the contrary, but a tendency to the happiness of the person himself, who had the former sense in the one constitution, and a contrary tendency in the opposite constitution. Nay, the persons themselves might observe this, since the former sense would make these actions grateful to the agent which were useful to others, who, if they had a like sense would love him and return good offices; whereas the latter sense would make all such actions as are useful to others, and apt to engage their good offices, ungrateful to the agent; and would lead him into publicly hurtful actions, which would not only procure the hatred of others, if they had a contrary sense, but engage them out of their self-love to study his destruction, though their senses agreed. Thus any observer, or the agent himself with this latter sense, might perceive that the pains to be feared, as the consequence of malicious actions, did over-balance the pleasures of this sense; so that it would be to the agent's interest to counteract it. Thus one constitution of the moral sense might appear to be more advantageous to those who had it, than the contrary; as we may call that sense of tasting healthful which made wholesome meat pleasant; and we would call a contrary taste pernicious. And yet we should no more call the moral sense morally good or evil than we call the sense of tasting savory or unsavory, sweet or bitter.

But must we not own that we judge of all our senses by our reason and often correct their reports of the magnitude, figure, color, taste of objects, and pronounce them right or wrong as they agree or disagree with reason? This is true. But does it then follow that extension, figure, color, taste, are not sensible ideas but only denote reasonableness, or agreement with reason? Or that these qualities are perceivable antecedently to any sense by our power of finding out truth? Just so a compassionate temper may rashly imagine the correction of a child or the execution of a criminal to be cruel and inhuman; but by reasoning may discover the superior good arising from them in the whole; and then the same moral sense may determine the observer to approve them. But we must not hence conclude that it is any reasoning antecedent to a moral sense which determines us to approve the study of public good, any more than we can in the former case conclude that we perceive extension, figure, color, taste, antecedently to a sense. All these sensations are often corrected by reasoning, as well as our approbations of actions as good or evil[e] and yet no body ever placed the original idea of extension, figure, color, or taste, in conformity to reason.

[9]It is manifest we have in our understanding moral ideas, or they are perceptions of the soul. We reason about them, we compare, we judge; but then we do all the same acts about extension, figure, color, taste, sound, which perceptions all men call sensations. All our ideas, or the materials of our reasoning or judging, are received by some immediate powers of perception internal or external which we may call sense; by these too we have pleasure and pain. All perception is by the soul, not by the body, though some impressions on the bodily organs are the occasions of some of them; and in others the soul is determined to other sorts of feelings or sensations where no bodily impression is the immediate occasion. A certain incorporeal form, if one may use that name, a temper observed, a character, an affection, a state of a sensitive being, known or understood, may raise liking, approbation, sympathy, as naturally from the very constitution of the soul, as any bodily impression raises external sensations. Reasoning or intellect seems to raise no new species of ideas but to discover or discern the relations of those received. Reason shows what acts are conformable to a law, a will of a superior, or what acts tend to private good or to public good. In like manner, reason discovers contrary tendencies of contrary actions. Both contraries are alike the object of the understanding and may give that sort of pleasure which arises upon discovery of truth. A demonstration that certain actions are detrimental to society is attended with the peculiar pleasure of new knowledge,

e. See Sect. 4 of this treatise.

[9. This paragraph not in ed. 1.]

as much as a like demonstration of the benefit of virtue. But when we approve a kind beneficent action let us consider whether this feeling, or action, or modification of the soul, more resembles an act of contemplation, such as this, 'When straight lines intersect each other, the vertical angles are equal,' or that liking we have to a beautiful form, an harmonious composition, a grateful sound.[9]

Thus though no man can immediately either approve or disapprove as morally good or evil his own moral sense, by which he approves only affections and actions consequent upon them, yet he may see whether it be advantageous to him in other respects to have it constituted one way rather than another. One constitution may make these actions grateful to this sense which tend to procure other pleasures also. A contrary constitution may be known to the very person himself to be disadvantageous, as making these actions immediately grateful which shall occasion all other sorts of misery. His self-love may excite him, though with[10] dissatisfaction, to counteract this sense in order to avoid a greater evil. Mr. Hobbes seems to have had no better notions of the natural state of mankind. An observer who was benevolent would desire that all had the former sort of sense; a malicious observer, if he feared no evil to himself from the actions of the persons observed, would desire the latter constitution. If this observer had a moral sense he would think that constitution which was contrary to his own strange and surprising, or unnatural. If the observer had no affections toward others, and were disjoined from their actions, he would be indifferent about their constitutions and have no desire or preference of one above another; though he might see which were advantageous to them, and which pernicious.

As to the second argument, what means 'alike reasonable or good to the Deity'? Does it mean, 'that the Deity could have had no reasons exciting him to make one

[10. Ed. 1 adds 'inward']

constitution rather than another'? It is plain if the Deity had nothing essential to his nature [11]resembling or analogous[11] to our sweetest and most kind affections we can scarce suppose he could have any reason exciting him to any thing he has done. But grant such a disposition in the Deity and then the manifest tendency of the present constitution to the happiness of his creatures was an exciting reason for choosing it before the contrary.[f] Each sort of constitution might have given

f. A late author on the *Foundation of Moral Goodness* etc., p. 9 [John Balguy (1686–1748), *The Foundation of Moral Goodness,* Part I, London, 1728], thus argues, 'If such a disposition is in the Deity, is it a perfection or is it not? Is it better than the contrary, more worthy of his nature, more agreeable to his other perfections? If not, let us not ascribe it to him. If it be, then for what reason, account, or ground is it better? That reason, account, or ground, must be the foundation of moral goodness. If there be no reason why it is better, then God is acted by a blind unaccountable impulse.' In answer, one may first ask the precise meaning of these vague words, perfection, betterness, worthiness, agreement. If these terms denote 'whatever makes the being possessed of them happier than he would be without them,' then (1) it is plain, kind dispositions are perfections to men in our present frame, are better for us than the contrary, and agree better without other powers, i.e., they tend to preserve them and procure us many enjoyments. (2) Our apprehending such dispositions in God, according to our frame, makes us esteem and love him. (3) Our knowledge of God is so imperfect that it is not easy to prove that such dispositions tend to make or preserve him happy, or to procure him other enjoyments. And yet, (4) we may have good reason, ground, or evidence, from his works and administration to believe him benevolent. (5) If he has real good will to his creatures, their perfection or happiness is to him an ultimate end, intended without further view or reason, and yet, (6) he is not acted by a blind impulse. The ultimate end is known to him, and the best means chosen, which never happen in what we call blind impulses unless one calls willing any ultimate end a blind impulse. For thus each man should desire his own happiness by a blind impulse; and God's willing to regard the fitness of things must be a blind impulse unless he have a prior reason why he wills what his understanding represents as fit rather than what is unfit; for his understanding represents both. And there must be a prior fitness or reasonableness that he should will what is fit and a yet prior fitness that he should regard the fitness of willing what is fit, and so on.

If in these questions is meant, not 'by what argument do we prove that the Deity is benevolent?' but 'what is the efficient cause of that disposition in God?' Those gentlemen must answer for us who tell us also of the reason or ground of the Divine existence, and that not as a proof that he does exist, or the *causa cognoscendi,* as the School-

[11. Ed. 1 reads 'corresponding']

men an equal immediate pleasure in present self-approbation for any sort of action; but the actions approved by the present sense procure all pleasures of the other senses and the actions which would have been approved by a contrary moral sense would have been productive of all torments of the other senses.

If it be meant, 'that upon this supposition, that all our approbation presupposes in us a moral sense, the Deity could not have approved one constitution more than another,' where is the consequence? Why may not the Deity have something of a superior kind, analogous to our moral sense, essential to him? How does any constitution of the senses of men hinder the Deity to reflect and judge of his own actions? How does it affect the divine apprehension which way soever moral ideas arise with men?

If it means 'that we cannot approve one constitution more than another, or approve the Deity for making the present constitution,' this consequence is also false. The present constitution of our moral sense determines us to approve all kind affections. This constitution the Deity must have foreseen as tending to the happiness of his creatures; it does therefore evidence kind affection or benevolence in the Deity, this therefore we must approve.

We have got some strange phrases, 'that some things are antecedently reasonable in the nature of the thing,' which some insist upon, 'that otherwise,' say they, 'if before man was created, any nature without a moral sense had existed, this nature would not have approved as morally good in the Deity his constituting our sense as it is at present.' Very true; and what next? If there had been no moral sense in that nature, there would

---

men speak, but the *causa essendi* of that Being which they acknowledge uncaused and independent. See Dr. Sam. Clarke's Boyle Lectures. [Samuel Clarke (1675–1729), *A Discourse Concerning the Being and Attributes of God, the Obligation of Natural Religion, and the Truth and Certainty of the Christian Revelation . . .* (being sixteen sermons preached in the Cathedral Church of St. Paul in the years 1704 and 1705, at the lecture founded by the Honorable Robert Boyle, Esq.), London, 1706. [This footnote not in ed. 1.]

have been no perception of morality. But 'Could not such natures have seen something reasonable in one constitution more than in another?' They might no doubt have reasoned about the various constitutions and foreseen that the present one would tend to the happiness of mankind, and would evidence benevolence in the Deity; so also they might have reasoned about the contrary constitution, that it would make men miserable, and evidence malice in the Deity. They would have reasoned about both and found out truths. Are both constitutions alike reasonable to these observers? No, say they, 'The benevolent one is reasonable and the malicious unreasonable,' and yet these observers reasoned and discovered truths about both. An action then is called by us reasonable when it is benevolent and unreasonable when malicious. This is plainly making the word reasonable denote whatever is approved by our moral sense, without relation to true propositions. We often use that word in such a confused manner; but these antecedent natures, supposed without a moral sense, would not have approved one constitution of the Deity as morally better than another.

Had it been left to the choice of these antecedent minds what manner of sense they would have desired for mankind, would they have seen no difference? Yes they would, according to their affections which are presupposed in all election. If they were benevolent, as we suppose the Deity, the tendency of the present sense to the happiness of men would have excited their choice. Had they been malicious, as we suppose the devil, the contrary tendency of the contrary sense would have excited their election of it. But is there nothing preferable or eligible antecedently to all affections too? No, certainly, unless there can be desire without affections, or superior desire, i.e., election, antecedently to all desire.

Some farther perplex this subject by asserting, 'that the same reasons determining approbation ought also to excite to election.' Here, (1) we often see justifying reasons where we can have no election, viz., when we observe the actions of others which were even prior to our existence. (2) The quality moving us to election very often cannot excite approbation, viz., private usefulness, not publicly pernicious. This both does and ought to move election and yet I believe few will say, 'They approve as virtuous the eating a bunch of grapes, taking a glass of wine, or sitting down when one is tired.' Approbation is not what we can voluntarily bring upon ourselves. When we are contemplating actions we do not choose to approve because approbation is pleasant; otherwise we would always approve, and never condemn, any action; because this is some way uneasy. Approbation is plainly a perception arising without previous volition, or choice of it, because of any concomitant pleasure. The occasion of it is the perception of benevolent affections in ourselves, or the discovering the like in others, even when we are incapable of any action or election. The reasons determining approbation are such as show that an action evidenced kind affections, and that in others as often as in ourselves. Whereas the reasons moving to election are such as show the tendency of an action to gratify some affection in the agent.

The prospect of the pleasure of self-approbation is indeed often a motive to choose one action rather than another; but this supposes the moral sense, or determination to approve, prior to the election. Were approbation voluntarily chosen from the prospect of its concomitant pleasure, then there could be no condemnation of our own actions, for that is unpleasant.

As to that confused word 'ought' it is needless to apply to it again all that was said about obligation.

Concerning that character of virtue and vice, the fitness or unfitness of actions

Section II

We come next to examine some other explications of morality which have been much insisted on of late.[a] We are told, 'that there are eternal and immutable differences of things, absolutely and antecedently; that there are also eternal and unalterable relations in the natures of the things themselves from which arise agreements and disagreements, congruities and incongruities, fitness and unfitness of the application of circumstances to the qualifications of persons; that actions agreeable to these relations are morally good, and that the contrary actions are morally evil.' These expressions are sometimes made of the same import with those more common ones, 'acting agreeably to the eternal reason and truth of things.' It is asserted that God who knows 'all these relations, etc., does guide his actions by them, since he has no wrong affection (the word 'wrong' should have been first explained) and that in like manner these relations, etc., ought (another unlucky word in morals) to determine the choice of all rationals, abstracting from any views of interest. If they do not, these creatures are insolently counteracting their Creator and, as far as they can, making things to be what they are not which is the greatest impiety.'

That things are now different is certain. That ideas, to which there is no object yet existing conformable, are also different, is certain. That upon comparing two ideas there arises a relative idea, generally when the two ideas compared have in them any modes of the same simple idea, is also obvious. Thus every extended being may be compared to any other of the same kinds of dimensions and relative ideas be formed of greater,

a. See Dr. Samuel Clarke's Boyle's Lectures and many late authors.

less, equal, double, triple, subduple, etc., with infinite variety. This may let us see that relations are not real qualities inherent in external natures but only ideas necessarily accompanying our perception of two objects at once and comparing them. Relative ideas continue when the external objects do not exist, provided we retain the two ideas. But what the eternal relations, in the natures of things, do mean is not so easy perhaps to be conceived.

To show particularly how far morality can be concerned in relations, we may consider them under these three classes. 1. The relations of inanimate objects as to their quantity, or active and passive powers, as explained by Mr. Locke. 2. The relations of inanimate objects to rational agents, as to their active or passive powers. 3. The relations of rational agents among themselves founded on their powers or actions past or continued. Now let us examine what fitnesses or unfitnesses arise from any of these sorts of relations in which the morality of actions may consist, and whether we can place morality in them without presupposing a moral sense. It is plain that ingenious author says nothing against the supposition of a moral sense. But many imagine that his account of moral ideas is independent upon a moral sense and therefore are less willing to allow that we have such an immediate perception, or sense of virtue and vice. What follows is not intended to oppose his scheme, but rather to suggest what seems a necessary explication of it by showing that it is no otherwise intelligible but upon supposition of a moral sense.

1. Relations of inanimate objects being known, puts it in the power of a rational agent often to diversify them, to change their forms, motions or qualities of any kind, at his pleasure. But nobody apprehends any virtue or vice in such actions where no relation is apprehended to a rational or sensitive being's happiness or misery; otherwise we should have got into the class of virtues all the practical mathematics and the operations of chemistry.

2. As to the relations of inanimate objects to rational agents, the knowledge of them equally puts it in one's power to destroy mankind as to perserve them. Without presupposing affections this knowledge will not excite to one action rather than another; nor without a moral sense will it make us approve any action more than its contrary. The relation of corn to human bodies being known to a person of kind affections was perhaps the exciting reason of teaching mankind husbandry. But the knowledge of the relations of arsenic would excite a malicious nature, just in the same manner, to the greatest mischief. A sword, an halter, a musket, bear the same relation to the body of an hero which they do to a robber. The killing of either is equally agreeable to these relations, but not equally good. The knowledge of these relations neither excites to actions nor justifies them without presupposing either affections or a moral sense. Kind affections with such knowledge makes heroes; malicious affections, villains.

3. The last sort of relations is that among rational agents, founded on their actions or affections, whence one is called Creator, another creature, one benefactor, the other beneficiary (if that word may be used in this general sense), the one parent, the other child, the one governor, the other subject, etc. Now let us see what fitnesses or unfitnesses arise from these relations.

There is certainly, independently of fancy or custom, a natural tendency in some actions to give pleasure, either to the agent or others, and a contrary tendency in other actions to give pain, either to the agent or others. This sort of relation of actions to the agents or objects is indisputable. If we call these relations fitnesses, then the most contrary actions have equal fitnesses for contrary ends; and each one is unfit for the end of the other. Thus compassion is fit to make others happy and unfit to make others miserable. Violation of property is fit to make men miserable, and unfit to make them happy. Each of these is both fit and unfit, with respect to different ends. The bare fitness then to an end is not the idea of moral goodness.

Perhaps the virtuous fitness is that of ends. The fitness of a subordinate end to the ultimate cannot constitute the action good unless the ultimate end be good. To keep a conspiracy secret is not a good end, though it be fit for obtaining a farther end, the success of the conspiracy. The moral fitness must be that of the ultimate end itself. The public good alone is a fit end, therefore the means fit for this end alone are good.

What means the fitness of an ultimate end? For what is it fit? Why, it is an ultimate end, not fit for anything farther, but absolutely fit. What means that word fit? If it notes a simple idea it must be the perception of some sense. Thus we must recur, upon this scheme too, to a moral sense.[b]

If fitness be not a simple idea, let it be defined. Some tell us that it is 'an agreement of an affection, desire, action, or end, to the relations of agents.' But what means agreement? Which of these four meanings has it? 1. We say one quantity agrees with another of equal dimensions every way. 2. A corollary agrees with a theorem when our knowing the latter to be truth leads us to know that the former is also a true proposition. 3. Meat agrees with that body which it tends to preserve. 4. Meat agrees with the taste of that being in whom it raises a pleasant perception. If any one of these are the meanings of agreement in the definition then one of these is the idea of fitness. (1) That an action or affection is of the same bulk and figure with the relation. Or, (2) when the relation is a true proposition, so is the action or affection or, (3) the action or affection tends to preserve the relation and contrary actions would destroy it so that, for instance, God would be no

b. A late author who pleads that wisdom is chiefly employed in choosing the ultimate ends themselves and that fitness is a proper attribute of ultimate ends, in answer to this short question, 'What are they fit for?' answers, 'They are fit to be approved by all rational agents.' Now his meaning of the word 'approved' is this, 'discerned to be fit.' His answer then is, 'they are fit to be perceived fit.' When words are used at this rate one must lose his labor in replies to such remarkers. See a paper called "Wisdom the Sole Spring of Action in the Deity." [Henry Grove (1684–1738), *Wisdom the First Spring of Action in the Deity*, London, 1734. This footnote not in ed. 1.]

longer related to us as Creator and Benefactor when we disobeyed him. Or, (4) the action raises pleasant perceptions in the relation. All these expressions seem absurd.[c]

These gentlemen probably have some other meanings to these words fitness or agreement. I hope what is said will show the need for explication of them, though they be so common. There is one meaning perhaps intended, however it be obscurely expressed, 'that certain affections or actions of an agent, standing in a certain relation to other agents, are approved by every observer, or raise in him a grateful perception, or move the observer to love the agent.' This meaning is the same with the notion of pleasing a moral sense.

Whoever explains virtue or vice by justice or injustice, right or wrong, uses only more ambiguous words, which will equally lead to acknowledge a moral sense.

c. Several gentlemen who have published remarks or answers to this scheme continue to use these words, agreement, conformity, congruity, without complying with this just request of explaining or fixing precisely the meaning of these words, which are manifestly ambiguous. [This footnote not in ed. 1.]

Mr. Wollaston's significancy of truth, as the idea of virtue, considered

Section III

Mr. Wollaston[a] has introduced a new explication of moral virtue, viz., significancy of truth in actions, supposing that in every action there is some significancy like that which moralists and civilians speak of in their tacit conventions and *quasi contractus*.

The word signification is very common but a little reflection will show it to be very ambiguous. In signification of words these things are included: (1) An association of an idea with a sound, so that when any idea is formed by the speaker the idea of a sound accompanies it. (2) The sound perceived by the hearer excites the idea to which it is connected. (3) In like manner a judgment in the speaker's mind is accompanied with the idea of a combination of sounds. (4) This combination of sounds heard raises the apprehension of that judgment in the mind of the hearer. Nothing farther than these circumstances seems to be denoted by signification.

Hearing a proposition does not of itself produce either assent or dissent, or opinion in the hearer, but only presents to his apprehension the judgment, or *thema complexum*. But the hearer himself often forms judgments or opinions upon this occasion, either immediately without reasoning, or by some short argument. These opinions are some one or more of the following propositions. (1) That a sound is perceived and a judgment apprehended. (2) Such a person caused the sound heard. (3) The speaker intended to excite in the hearer the idea of the sound and the apprehension of the judgment, or *thema complexum*. This judgment is not always formed by the hearer, nor is it always true, when men are heard speaking. (4) The speaker intended to

a. In his *Religion of Nature Delineated*. [London, Knapton, 1724. William Wollaston (1659–1724). 'Woolaston' in all editions.]

produce assent in the hearer. This judgment is not always true. (5) The speaker assents to the proposition spoken. This judgment in the hearer is often false, and is formed upon opinion of the speaker's veracity, or speaking what expresses his opinion usually. (6) The speaker does not assent to the proposition spoken. This judgment of the hearer is often false when what is spoken is every way true. (7) The speaker intended that the hearer should believe or judge 'that the proposition spoken was assented to by the speaker.' (8) The speaker had the contrary intention to that supposed in the last judgment. Both these latter judgments may be false when the proposition spoken is every way true. (9) The proposition spoken represents the object as it is, or is logically true. (10) The proposition spoken does not represent the object as it is, or it is logically false.

As to the first four circumstances which make up the proper significancy of speech, it is scarce possible that any one should place moral good or evil in them. Whether the proposition were logically true or false, the having a bare apprehension of it as a *thema complexum*, or raising this in another without intending to produce assent or dissent, can have no more moral good or evil in it than the reception of any other idea, or raising it in another. This significancy of falsehood is found in the very propositions given in schools as instances of falsehood, absurdity, contradiction to truth, or blasphemy. The pronouncing of which are actions signifying more properly than most of our other actions; and yet nobody condemns them as immoral.

As to the opinions formed by the hearer, they are all his own action as much as any other conclusion or judgment formed from appearances of any sort whatsoever. They are true or false according to the sagacity of the observer, or his caution. The hearer may form perfectly true opinions or judgments when the speaker is guilty of the basest fraud, and may form false judgments when the speaker is perfectly innocent and spoke nothing false in any sense.

The evils which may follow from false judgments of

the hearer are no otherwise chargeable on the speaker than as the evil consequences of another's action of any kind may be chargeable upon any person who cooperated or, by his action, or omission, the consequence of which he might have foreseen, did either actually intend this evil, or wanted that degree of kind affection which would have inclined him to have prevented it.

The intention of the speaker is what all moralists have hitherto imagined the virtue or vice of words did depend upon, and not the bare significancy of truth or falsehood. This intention is either, (1) to lead the hearer into a true or false opinion about the sentiments of the speaker, (2) to make the hearer assent to the proposition spoken or, (3) both to make the hearer assent to the proposition and judge that the speaker also assents to it or, (4) to accomplish some end by means of the hearer's assent to the proposition spoken. This end may be known by the speaker to be either publicly useful or publicly hurtful.

Some moralists[b] of late have placed all virtue in speech in the intention of the last kind, viz., accomplishing some publicly useful end by speaking either logical truth or falsehood; and that all vice in speaking consists in intending to effect something publicly hurtful by speech, whether logically true or false, and known to be such; or by using speech in a manner which we may foresee would be publicly hurtful, whether we actually intend this evil consequence or not. Some stricter moralists assert that the public evils which would ensue from destroying mutual confidence by allowing to speak propositions known to be false on any occasion are so great that no particular advantage to be expected from speaking known logical falsehoods can ever over-balance them; that all use of speech supposes a tacit convention of sincerity, the violation of which is

b. See Barbeyrac's notes on Pufendorf, lib. iv., c. 1, 7 [Samuel Pufendorf (1632–1694), *DeJure Naturae et Gentium*, Lund, 1672. Translated into French with extensive notes by Jean Barbeyrac (1674–1744), Amsterdam, 1706. Translated into English by Basil Kennett as *Of the Law of Nature and Nations*, Oxford, 1710.]

always evil. Both sides in this argument agree that the moral evil in speech consists either in some direct malicious intention or a tendency to the public detriment of society, which tendency the agent might have foreseen as connected with his action had he not wanted that degree of good affections which makes men attentive to the effects of their actions. Never was bare significancy of falsehood made the idea of moral evil. Speaking logical falsehood was still looked upon as innocent in many cases. Speaking contrary to sentiment, or moral falsehood, was always proved evil from some publicly hurtful tendency and not supposed as evil immediately, or the same idea with vice. The intention to deceive was the foundation of the guilt. This intention the speaker studies to conceal and does not signify it. It is an act of the will, neither signified by his words nor itself signifying any thing else.

This point deserved consideration because if any action be significant, it is certainly the act of speaking. And yet even in this the virtue is not the signifying of truth nor the vice the signifying falsehood.

The signification of some actions depends upon a like association of ideas with them, made either by nature, or arbitrarily, and by custom, as with sounds. Letters are by custom the signs of sounds. A shriek or groan is a natural sign of fear or pain. A motion of the hand or head may signify assent, dissent, or desire. The cutting down tall poppies was an answer. The sending spurs, advice to flight. Kindling many fires raises the opinion of an encampment. Raising a smoke will raise opinion of fire.

The most important distinction of signs is this, that[c] (1) some appearances are the occasion upon which an observer, by his own reasoning, forms a judgment without supposing, or having reason to believe, that the agent, who caused these appearances, did it with design to communicate his sentiments to others; or, when the actions are such as are usually done by the agents, without professing a design to raise opinions in observers.

c. See Grotius, *De Jure Belli.*, lib. 3, c. I.

(2) Some actions are never used but with professed design to convey the opinions of the agent to the observer or such as the observer infers nothing from but upon having reason to believe that the causer of the appearance intended to convey some sentiment to the observer. (3) Other signs are used when the signifier gives no reason to conclude any other intention, but only to raise an apprehension of the judgment, or the *thema complexum*, without professing any design to communicate his sentiments or to produce any assent in the observer.

To do actions from which the observer will form false opinions, while yet the agent is not understood to profess any intention of communicating to him his opinions or designs, is never of itself imagined evil, let the signs be natural or instituted, provided there be no malicious intention, or neglect of public good. It is never called a crime in a teacher to pronounce an absurd sentence for an instance; in a nobleman to travel without coronets; or a clergyman in lay-habit for private conveniency, or to avoid troublesome ceremony; to leave lights in a lodge to make people conclude there is a watch kept. This significancy may be in any action which is observed; but as true conclusions argue no virtue in the agent, so false ones argue no vice.

Raising false opinions designedly by the second sort of signs which reasonably lead the observer to conclude a profession of communicating sentiments, whether the signs be customary, instituted, or natural, is generally evil, when the agent knows the falsehood; since it tends to diminish mutual confidence. To send spurs to a friend, whom the sender imagines to be in no danger, to deceive by hieroglyphics or painting, is as criminal as a false letter. This significancy occurs in a very few human actions. Some of the most important virtues profess no design of communicating sentiments or raising opinions either true or false. Nor is there any more intention in some of the most vicious actions. Again, who can imagine virtue in all actions where there is this significancy of truth with intention? Is it virtue to say at

Christmas that the mornings are sharp? To beckon with the hand, in sign of assent to such an assertion? And in false propositions thus signified by actions or words there is no evil apprehended where the falsehood is only logical. When the falsehood is known by the agent the evil is not imagined in the significancy but in doing what one may foresee tends to breed distrust in society. And did all moral evil consist in moral falsehood there could be no sins of ignorance. If Mr. Wollaston alleges, 'that ignorance of some things signifies this falsehood, viz., we are not obliged to know the truth,' this falsehood is not signified with intention, nor is it moral falsehood, but only logical, since no man in an error knows that 'He is obliged to know the contrary truth.' Mr. Wollaston's use of the words 'ought' or 'obliged' without a distinct meaning is not peculiar to this place.

The third sort of significancy of falsehood is never apprehended as morally evil. If it were, then every dramatic writer drawing evil characters, every history-painter, every writer of allegories or epics, every philosopher teaching the nature of contradictory propositions, would be thought criminal.

But since only the first sort of significancy can be in all actions and that too supposing that every action whatsoever is observed by some being or other, let us see if this will account for morality. Perhaps either, first, 'Every action is good which leads the observer into true opinions concerning the sentiments of the agent, whether the agent's opinions be true or false.' Or, second, 'That action is good which leads the observer into true opinions concerning the object, the tendency of the action, and the relation between the agent and the object.'

Did virtue consist in this first sort of significancy of truth, it would depend not upon the agent but the sagacity of the observer. The acute penetration of one would constitute an action virtuous, and the rashness or stupidity of another would make it vicious. And the most barbarous actions would raise no false opinion of the sentiments of the agent in a judicious observer.

The second sort of significancy would also make virtue consist in the power of observers. An exact reasoner would receive no false opinion from the worst action concerning the object or relation of the agent to it. And a false opinion might be formed by a weak observer of a perfectly good action. An observer who knew an agent to have the basest temper would not from his worst action conclude any thing false concerning the object. And all such false opinions would arise only upon supposition that the agent was virtuous.

But may it not be said, 'that whether men reason well about actions or not, there are some conclusions really deducible from every action? It is a *datum* from which something may be inferred by just consequence, whether any one actually infers it or not. Then may not this quality in actions, whether we call it significancy or not, that only true propositions can be inferred from them by just reasoning, be moral goodness? And may it not be the very idea of moral evil in actions, that some false conclusions can by just consequence be deduced from them?' Or if we will not allow these to be the very ideas of moral good and evil, 'Are they not universal just characters to distinguish the one from the other?'

One may here observe in general that since the existence of the action is supposed to be a true premise or datum, no false conclusion can possibly be inferred from it by just reasoning. We could perhaps often justly infer that the agent had false opinions, but then this conclusion of the observer, viz., 'that the agent has false opinions' is really true.

But again, it will not make an universal character of good actions that a just reasoner would infer from them, 'that the opinions of the agent are true.' For it is thus men must reason from actions, viz., when the constitution of nature, the affections of agents, and the action, are given, to conclude concerning the opinions; or, more generally, given any three of these to conclude the fourth. Thus suppose the 'constitution of nature such that the private interest of each individual is connected with the public good.' Suppose an agent's affections selfish only, then from a publicly useful action we infer that the agent's opinions are true and from a publicly hurtful action conclude his opinions to be false.

The same constitution supposed with public affections as well as selfish, the observing a kind or publicly useful action, will not immediately infer that the agent's opinions are either true or false. With false opinions he might do publicly useful actions out of his public affections in those cases wherein they are not apparently opposite to his interest. A public action opposite to some present private interest would generally evidence true opinion or, if the opinions were false, that his public affections were in this case much stronger than his self-love. A cruel action would indeed evidence false opinions [1]or a very violent unkind passion.[1]

Suppose the same constitution in all other respects, with malicious affections in an agent. A cruel or ungrateful action would not always prove the opinions of the agent to be false but only that his malice in this instance was more violent than regard to his interest. A beneficent action would prove only one of these two, either that his opinions of the constitution were true or, that if he was mistaken about the constitution, he had also a false opinion of the natural tendency of the action. Thus false opinions may be evidenced by contrary actions.

Suppose a constitution wherein a private interest could be advanced in opposition to the public (this we may call an evil constitution). Suppose only self-love in the agent, then a publicly useful action, any way toilsome or expensive to the agent, would evidence false opinions, and the most cruel selfish actions would evidence true opinions.

In an evil constitution, suppose kind affections in the agent. A publicly useful action would not certainly argue either true or false opinions. If his opinions were true, but kind affections stronger than self-love, he

[1. Not in ed. 1.]

might act in the same manner as if his opinions were false and self-love the reigning affection.

In an evil constitution, suppose malicious affections in an agent. All publicly useful actions would argue false opinions and publicly hurtful actions would argue true ones. This may show us that men's actions are generally publicly useful, when they have true opinions, only on this account, that we neither have malicious affections naturally, nor is there any probability, in our present constitution, of promoting a private interest separately from, or in opposition to, the public. Were there contrary affections and a contrary constitution, the most cruel actions might flow from true opinions; and consequently publicly useful actions might flow from false ones.

In our present constitution, it is probable no person would ever do any thing publicly hurtful but upon some false opinion. The flowing from true opinions is indeed a tolerable character or property of virtue, and flowing from some false opinion a tolerable character of vice, though neither be strictly universal. But, (1) this is not proper signification. A judicious observer never imagines any intention to communicate opinions in some of the most important actions, either good or evil. (2) Did an action signify falsehood, it is generally only logical. (3) The false opinion in the agent is not the quality for which the evil action is condemned, nor is the true opinion that for which the good action is approved. True opinions in agents often aggravate crimes, as they show higher degrees of evil affection, or total absence of good. And false opinions generally extenuate crimes, unless when the very ignorance or error has flowed from evil affection, or total absence of good.

It is surprising, for instance, how any should place the evil of ingratitude in denying the person injured to have been a benefactor. The observer of such an action, if he supposed the agent had really that false opinion, would think the crime the less for it. But if he were convinced that the agent had a true opinion he would think his ingratitude the more odious. Where we most abhor actions we suppose often true opinions, and sometimes admire actions flowing even from false opinions when they have evidenced no want of good affection.

To write a censure upon a book so well designed as Mr. Wollaston's and so full of very good reasoning upon the most useful subjects would not evidence much good nature. But allowing him his just praise, to remark any ambiguities or inadvertencies which may lead men into confusion in their reasoning, I am confident would have been acceptable to a man of so much goodness when he was living.

One may see that he has had some other idea of moral good previous to this significancy of truth by his introducing, in the very explication of it, words presupposing the ideas of morality previously known, such as 'right,' 'obligation,' 'lie,' 'his' denoting 'property.'

Mr. Wollaston acknowledges that there may be very little evil in some actions signifying falsehood, such as throwing away that which is of but little use or value. It is objected to him that there is equal contrariety to truth in such actions as in the greatest villainy. He, in answer to it, really unawares gives up his whole cause. He must own that there may be the strictest truth and certainty about trifles, so there may be the most obvious falsehood signified by trifling actions. If, then, significancy of falsehood be the very same with moral evil, all crimes must be equal. He answers, that crimes increase according to the importance of the truth denied; and so the virtue increases as the importance of the truths affirmed.

Then,

Virtue and vice increase as the importance of propositions is affirmed or denied.
But signification of truth and falsehood does not so increase.
[2]Therefore, signification of truth or falsehood are not the same with virtue or vice.[2]

[2. Ed. 1 reads: 'Therefore virtue and vice are not the same with signification of truth or falsehood.']

But what is this importance of truth? Nothing else but the moment or quantity of good or evil, either private or public, which should be produced by actions concerning which these true judgments are made. But it is plain, the signification of truth or falsehood is not varied by this importance. Therefore virtue or vice denote something different from this signification.

But farther, the importance of actions toward public good or evil is not the idea of virtue or vice. Nor does the one prove virtue in an action, any farther than it evidences kind affections, or the other vice, farther than it evidences either malice or want of kind affections. Otherwise a casual invention, an action wholly from views of private interest, might be as virtuous as the most kind and generous offices. And chance medley, or kindly intended, but unsuccessful attempts, would be as vicious as murder or treason.

One of Mr. Wollaston's illustrations that significancy of falsehood is the idea of moral evil ends in this, 'It is acting a lie.' What then? Should he not first have shown what was moral evil, and that every lie was such?

Another illustration or proof is, 'that it is acting contrary to that reason which God has given us as the guide of our actions.' Does not this place the original idea of moral evil in counteracting the Deity, and not in signifying falsehood? But, he may say, 'Counteracting the Deity denies him to be our benefactor and signifies falsehood.' Then why is signifying falsehood evil? Why, it is counteracting the Deity, who gave us reason for our guide. Why is this evil again? It denies the truth, 'that he is our benefactor.'

Another illustration is this, 'that signifying falsehood is altering the nature of things and making them be what they are not, or desiring at least to make them be what they are not.' If by altering the natures be meant destroying beings, then moral evil consists in desiring the destruction of other natures, or in evil affections. If what is meant be altering the laws of nature, or desiring that they were stopped, this is seldom desired by any but madmen, nor is this desire evidenced by some of the worst actions, nor is such desire always criminal. Otherwise it were as great a crime as any to wish, when a dam was broken down, that the water would not overflow the country.

If making things be what they are not means, 'attempting or desiring that any subject should have two opposite qualities at once, or a quality and its privation,' it is certain, then, that according to the Stoics, all vicious men are thoroughly mad. But it is to be doubted that such madness never happened to even the worst of mankind. When a man murders he does not desire his fellow creature to be both dead and living. When he robs, he does not desire that both he and the proprietor should at the same time possess. If any says that he desires to have a right to that to which another has a right, it is probably false. Robbers neither think of rights at all, nor are solicitous about acquiring them. Or, if they retain some wild notions of rights, they think their indigence, conquest, or courage gives them a right, and makes the other's right to cease. If attempting to make old qualities or rights give place to new be the idea of moral evil then every artificer, purchaser, or magistrate invested with an office is criminal.

Many of Mr. Wollaston's propositions contradicted by actions are about rights, duties, obligation, justice, reasonableness. These are long words, principal names, or attributes in sentences. The little word 'his,' or the particles 'as,' 'according' are much better. They may escape observation and yet may include all the ambiguities of right, property, agreement, reasonableness. 'Treating things as they are, and not as they are not,' or, 'according to what they are, or are not,' are expressions he probably had learned from another truly great name, who has not explained them sufficiently.

It may perhaps not seem improper on this occasion to observe that in the *quasi contractus* the civilians do not imagine any act of the mind of the person obliged to be really signified, but by a sort of *fictio juris* supposing it, order him to act as if he had contracted, even when they know that he had contrary intentions.

In the tacit conventions it is not a judgment which is signified but an act of the will transferring right, in which there is no relation to truth or falsehood itself. The non-performance of convenants is made penal, not because of their signifying falsehoods, as if this were the crime in them. But it is necessary, in order to preserve commerce in any society, to make effectual all declarations of consent to transfer rights by any usual signs, otherwise there could be no certainty in men's transactions.

Showing the use of reason concerning virtue and vice, upon supposition that we receive these ideas by a moral sense

Had those who insist so much upon the antecedent reasonableness of virtue told us distinctly what is reasonable or provable concerning it, many of our debates had been prevented. Let us consider what truths concerning actions men could desire to know, or prove by reason. I fancy they may be reduced to these heads. (1) 'To know whether there are not some actions or affections which obtain the approbation of any spectator or observer and others move his dislike and condemnation?' This question, as every man can answer for himself, so universal experience and history show, that in all nations it is so; and consequently the moral sense is universal. (2) 'Whether there be any particular quality, which, wherever it is apprehended, gains approbation, and the contrary raises disapprobation?' We shall find this quality to be kind affection, or study of the good of others; and thus the moral senses of men are generally uniform. About these two questions there is little reasoning; we know how to answer them from reflecting on our own sentiments, or by consulting others. (3) 'What actions do really evidence kind affections or do really tend to the greatest public good?' About this question is all the special reasoning of those who treat of the particular laws of nature or even of civil laws. This is the largest field, and the most useful subject of reasoning, which remains upon every scheme of morals, [1]and here we may discover as certain, invariable, or eternal truths, as any in geometry.[1] (4) 'What are the motives which, even from self-love, would ex-

[1. Not in ed. 1.]

cite each individual to do those actions which are publicly useful?' It is probable, indeed, no man would approve as virtuous an action publicly useful, to which the agent was excited only by self-love, without any kind affection. It is also probable that no view of interest can raise that kind affection which we approve as virtuous, nor can any reasoning do it except that which shows some moral goodness, or kind affections, in the object for this never fails, where it is observed or supposed in any person, to raise the love of the observer.[2]

Yet since all men have naturally self-love as well as kind affections, the former may often counteract the latter, or the latter the former. In each case the agent is uneasy and in some degree unhappy. The first rash views of human affairs often represent private interest as opposite to the public. When this is apprehended, self-love may often engage men in publicly hurtful actions, which their moral sense will condemn; and this is the ordinary cause of vice. To represent these motives of self-interest, to engage men to publicly useful actions, is certainly the most necessary point in morals. This has been so well done by the ancient moralists, by Dr. Cumberland, Puffendorf, Grotius, Shaftesbury; it is made so certain from the divine government of the world, the state of mankind, who cannot subsist without society, from universal experience and consent, from inward consciousness of the pleasure of kind affections, and self-approbation, and of the torments of malice, or hatred, or envy, or anger, that no man who considers these things, can ever imagine he can have any possible interest in opposing the public good, or in checking or restraining his kind of affections. Nay, if he had no kind affections, his very self-love and regard to his private good might excite him to publicly useful actions and dissuade from the contrary.

What farther should be provable concerning virtue, whence it should be called reasonable antecedently to all affection, or interest, or sense, or what it should be fit for, one cannot easily imagine.

[2. Ed. 1 adds 'so that virtue is not properly taught.']

Perhaps what has brought the epithet reasonable, or flowing from reason, in opposition to what flows from instinct, affection, or passion, so much into use, is this, 'that it is often observed that the very best of our particular affections or desires, when they are grown violent and passionate through the confused sensations and propensities which attend them, make us incapable of considering calmly the whole tendency of our actions and lead us often into what is absolutely pernicious, under some appearance of relative or particular good.' This indeed may give some ground for distinguishing between passionate actions and those from calm desire or affection which employs our reason freely, but can never set rational actions in opposition to those from instinct, desire or affection. And it must be owned that the most perfect virtue consists in the calm, unpassionate benevolence, rather than in particular affections.

If one asks, 'How do we know that our affections are right when they are kind?' what does the word 'right' mean? Does it mean what we approve? This we know by consciousness of our sense. Again, how do we know that our sense is right, or that we approve our approbation? This can only be answered by another question, viz., 'How do we know we are pleased when we are pleased?' Or does it mean, 'How do we know that we shall always approve what we now approve?' To answer this, we must first know that the same constitution of our sense shall always remain and, again, that we have applied ourselves carefully to consider the natural tendency of our actions. Of the continuance of the same constitution of our sense we are as sure as of the continuance of gravitation or any other law of nature. The tendency of our own actions we cannot always know, but we may know certainly that we heartily and sincerely study to act according to what, by all the evidence now in our power to obtain, appears as most probably tending to public good. When we are conscious of this sincere endeavor, the evil consequences which we could not have foreseen never will make us condemn our conduct. But without this sincere endeavor we may often approve at present what we shall afterwards condemn.

If the question means, 'How are we sure that what we approve, all others shall also approve?' of this we can be sure upon no scheme. But it is highly probable that the senses of all men are pretty uniform, that the Deity also approves kind affections, otherwise he would not have implanted them in us nor determined us by a moral sense to approve them. Now since the probability that men shall judge truly, abstracting from any presupposed prejudice, is greater than that they shall judge falsely, it is more probable, when our actions are really kind and publicly useful, that all observers shall judge truly of our intentions, and of the tendency of our actions, and consequently approve what we approve ourselves, than that they shall judge falsely and condemn them.

If the meaning of the question be, 'Will the doing what our moral sense approves tend to our happiness and to the avoiding misery?' it is thus we call a taste wrong when it makes that food at present grateful which shall occasion future pains or death. This question concerning our self-interest must be answered by such reasoning as was mentioned above to be well managed by our moralists both ancient and modern.

Thus there seems no part of that reasoning which was ever used by moralists to be superseded by supposing a moral sense. And yet without a moral sense there is no explication can be given of our ideas of morality, nor of that reasonableness supposed antecedent to all instincts, affections, or sense.

'But may there not be a right or wrong state of our moral sense, as there is in our other senses, according as they represent their objects to be as they really are, or represent them otherwise?' So may not our moral sense approve that which is vicious, and disapprove virtue, as a sickly palate may dislike grateful food, or a vitiated sight misrepresent colors or dimensions? Must we not know therefore antecedently what is morally good or evil by our reason before we can know that our moral sense is right?

To answer this, we must remember that of the sensible ideas, some are allowed to be only perceptions in our minds, and not images of any like external quality, as colors, sounds, tastes, smells, pleasure, pain. Other ideas are images of something external, as duration, number, extension, motion, rest. These latter, for distinction, we may call concomitant ideas of sensation, and the former purely sensible. As to the purely sensible ideas, we know they are altered by any disorder in our organs and made different from what arise in us from the same objects at other times. We do not denominate objects from our perceptions during the disorder, but according to our ordinary perceptions, or those of others in good health. Yet nobody imagines that therefore colors, sounds, tastes, are not sensible ideas. In like manner many circumstances diversify the concomitant ideas, but we denominate objects from the appearances they make to us in an uniform medium, when our organs are in no disorder, and the object not very distant from them. But none therefore imagines that it is reason and not sense which discovers these concomitant ideas, or primary qualities.

Just so in our ideas of actions. These three things are to be distinguished, (1) the idea of the external motion, known first by sense, and its tendency to the happiness or misery of some sensitive nature, often inferred by argument or reason, [3] which on these subjects, suggests as invariable eternal or necessary truths as any whatsoever,[3] (2) apprehension or opinion of the affections in the agent, inferred [4] by our reason. So far the idea of an action represents something external to the observer, [5] really existing whether he had perceived it or not, and having a real tendency to certain ends.[5] (3) The perception of approbation or disapprobation arising in the observer, according as the affections of the agent are

[3. Not in ed. 1.]
[4. Ed. 1 has 'concluded']
[5. Not in ed. 1.]

apprehended kind in their just degree, or deficient, or malicious. This approbation cannot be supposed an image of any thing external, more than the pleasures of harmony, of taste, of smell. But let none imagine that calling the ideas of virtue and vice perceptions of a sense upon apprehending the actions and affections of another, does diminish their reality, more than the like assertions concerning all pleasure and pain, happiness or misery. Our reason often corrects the report of our senses about the natural tendency of the external action and corrects rash conclusions about the affections of the agent. But whether our moral sense be subject to such a disorder as to have different perceptions from the same apprehended affections in an agent, at different times, as the eye may have of the colors of an unaltered object, it is not easy to determine. Perhaps it will be hard to find any instances of such a change. What reason could correct if it fell into such a disorder I know not, except suggesting to its remembrance its former approbations and representing the general sense of mankind. But this does not prove ideas of virtue and vice to be previous to a sense, more than a like correction of the ideas of color in a person under the jaundice proves that colors are perceived by reason previously to sense.

If any say, 'This moral sense is not a rule' what means that word? It is not a straight rigid body. It is not a general proposition, showing what means are fit to obtain an end. It is not a proposition asserting that a superior will make those happy who act one way and miserable who acts the contrary way. If these be the meanings of rule, it is no rule; yet by reflecting upon it our understanding may find out a rule. But what rule of actions can be formed without relation to some end proposed? Or what end can be proposed without presupposing instincts, desires, affections, or a moral sense, it will not be easy to explain.

Showing that virtue may have whatever is meant by merit and be rewardable upon the supposition that it is perceived by a sense and elected from affection or instinct

Section V

Some will not allow any merit in actions flowing from kind instincts. 'Merit,' say they, 'attends actions to which we are excited by reason alone, or to which we freely determine ourselves. The operation of instincts or affections is necessary, and not voluntary; nor is there more merit in them than in the shining of the sun, the fruitfulness of a tree, or the overflowing of a stream, which are all publicly useful.'

But what does merit mean? or praiseworthiness? Do these words 'denote the quality in actions, which gains approbation from the observer, [1] according to the present constitution of the human mind?' [1] Or are these actions called meritorious, 'which, when any observer does approve, all other observers approve him for his approbation of it and would condemn any observer who did not approve these actions?' These are the only meanings of meritorious which I can conceive as distinct from rewardable, which is considered hereafter separately. [2] Let those who are not satisfied with either of these explications of merit endeavor to give a definition of it reducing it to its simple ideas and not, as a late author has done, quarreling these descriptions, tell us only that it is deserving or being worthy of approbation, which is defining by giving a synonymous term.[2]

Now we endeavored already to show, 'that no reason can excite to action previously to some end, and that no

[1. Not in ed. 1.]
[2. Not in ed. 1.]

end can be proposed without some instinct or affection.' What then can be meant by being excited by reason as distinct from all motion of instincts or affections? [3]Some perhaps take the word 'instinct' solely for such motions of will, or bodily powers, as determine us without knowledge or intention of any end. Such instincts cannot be the spring of virtue. But the soul may be as naturally determined to approbation of certain tempers and affections, and to the desire of certain events when it has an idea of them, as brutes are, by their lower instincts, to their actions. If any quarrel the application of the word instinct to any thing higher than what we find in brutes, let them use another word. Though there is no harm in the sound of this word, more than in a determination to pursue fitness, which they must allow in the Divine Will, if they ascribe any will to him at all.[3]

Then determining ourselves freely, does it mean acting without any motive or exciting reason? If it did not mean this, it cannot be opposed to acting from instinct or affections, since all motives or reasons presuppose them. If it means this, 'that merit is found only in actions done without motive or affection, by mere election, without prepollent desire of one action or end rather than its opposite, or without desire of that pleasure which[a] some suppose follows upon any election by a natural connection' then let any man consider whether he ever acts in this manner by mere election, without any previous desire. And again, let him consult

a. This is the notion of liberty given by the Archbishop of Dublin [William King (1650–1729)] in his most ingenious book, *De Origine Mali.* [London, 1702. English translation by Edmund Law, *Essay on the Origin of Evil,* 1731, with a preliminary essay by John Gay, "Dissertation Concerning the Fundamental Principle of Virtue or Morality."] This opinion does not represent freedom of election as opposite to all instinct or desire but rather as arising from the desire of that pleasure supposed to be connected with every election. Upon his scheme there is a motive and end proposed in every election and a natural instinct toward happiness presupposed, though it is such a motive and end as leaves us in perfect liberty since it is a pleasure or happiness not connected with one thing more than another, but following upon the determination itself.

[3. Not in ed. 1.]

his own breast whether such kind of action gains his approbation? Upon seeing a person not more disposed by affection, compassion, or love or desire, to make his country happy than miserable, yet choosing the one rather than the other, from no desire of public happiness, nor aversion to the torments of others, but by such an unaffectionate determination, as that by which one moves his first finger rather than the second, in giving an instance of a trifling action, let any one ask if this action should be meritorious, and yet that there should be no merit in a tender compassionate heart, which shrinks at every pain of its fellow-creatures, and triumphs in their happiness, with kind affections and strong desire laboring for the public good. If this be the nature of meritorious actions every honest heart would disclaim all merit in morals as violently as the old Protestants rejected it in justification.

But let us see which of the two senses of merit or praiseworthiness is founded on this (I will not call it unreasonable or casual, but) unaffectionate choice. If merit denotes the quality moving the spectator to approve then there may be unaffectionate election of the greatest villainy as well as of the most useful actions; but who will say that they are equally approved? But perhaps it is not the mere freedom of choice which is approved but the free choice of public good without any affection. Then actions are approved for public usefulness and not for freedom. Upon this supposition, the heat of the sun, the fruitfulness of a tree, would be meritorious or, if one says these are not actions, they are at least meritorious qualities, motions, attractions, etc. And a casual invention may be meritorious. Perhaps free election is a *conditio sine qua non,* and public usefulness the immediate cause of approbation; neither separately, but both jointly are meritorious. Free election alone is not merit, public usefulness alone is not merit, but both concurring. Then should any person by mere election, without any desire to serve the public, set about mines, or any useful manufacture, or should a person by mere election stab a man without knowing him to be a public robber, here both free election and public usefulness may concur. Yet will any one say there is merit or virtue in such actions? Where then shall we find merit, unless in kind affections, or desire and intention of the public good? This moves our approbation wherever we observe it. And the want of this is the true reason why a searcher for mines, a free killer of an unknown robber, the warming sun, or the fruitful tree, are not counted meritorious.

But it may be said that to make an action meritorious it is necessary not only that the action be publicly useful, but that it be known or imagined to be such, before the agent freely chooses it. But what does this add to the former scheme? Only a judgment or opinion in the understanding concerning the natural tendency of an action to the public good. Few, it may be presumed, will place virtue in assent or dissent, or perceptions. And yet this is all that is superadded to the former case. The agent must not desire the public good or have any kind affections. This would spoil the freedom of choice, according to their scheme, who insist on a freedom opposite to affections or instincts. But he must barely know the tendency to public good, and without any propensity to, or desire of the happiness of others, by an arbitrary election, acquire his merit. Let every man judge for himself whether these are the qualities which he approves.

What has probably engaged many into this way of speaking, 'that virtue is the effect of rational choice, and not of instincts or affections,' is this. They find, 'that some actions flowing from particular kind affections, are sometimes condemned as evil,' because of their bad influence upon the state of larger societies, and that the hurry and confused sensation of any of our passions, may divert the mind from considering the whole effect of its actions. They require therefore to virtue a calm and undisturbed temper.

There is indeed some ground to recommend this temper as very necessary in many cases, and yet some of the most passionate actions may be perfectly good.

But in the calmest temper there must remain affection or desire, some implanted instinct for which we can give no reason; otherwise there could be no action of any kind, as it was shown above in the first section.

If meritorious actions are these which whosoever does not approve is himself condemned by others, the quality by which they are constituted meritorious in this sense is the same which moves our approbation. We condemn any person who does not approve that which we ourselves approve. We presume the sense of others to be constituted like our own, and that any other person, would he attend to the actions which we approve, would also approve them, and love the agent. When we find that another does not approve what we approve we are apt to conclude that he has not had kind affections toward the agent, or that some evil affection makes him overlook his virtues, and on this account condemn him.

Perhaps by meritorious is meant the same thing with another word used in like manner, viz., rewardable. Then indeed the quality in which merit or rewardableness is founded is different from that which is denoted by merit in the former meanings.

Rewardable, or deserving reward, denotes either that quality which would incline a superior nature to make an agent happy or that quality of actions which would make a spectator approve a superior nature, when he conferred happiness on the agent, and disapprove that superior who inflicted misery on the agent or punished him. Let any one try to give a meaning to the word rewardable distinct from these, and not satisfy himself with the words worthy of, or deserving, which are of very complex and ambiguous signification.

Now the qualities of an action determining a powerful nature to reward it must be various according to the constitution and affections of that superior. If he has a moral sense, or something analogous of a more excellent sort, by which he is determined to love those who evidence kind affections and to desire their happiness, then kind affection is a quality moving to reward.

But farther, if this superior be benevolent, and observes that inferior natures can by their mutual actions promote their mutual happiness, then he must incline to excite them to publicly useful actions by prospects of private interest, if it be needful. Therefore he will engage them to such actions by prospects of rewards, whatever be the internal principle of their actions, or whatever their affections be. These two qualities in actions, viz., flowing from kind affections, and public usefulness concurring, undoubtedly incline the benevolent superior to confer happiness. The former alone, where, through want of power, the agent is disappointed of his kind intentions, will incline a benevolent superior to reward; and the want of power in the agent will never incline him to punish. But the want of kind affections, although there be publicly useful actions, may be so offensive to the moral sense of the superior nature as to prevent reward, or excite to punish; unless this conduct would occasion greater public evil, by withdrawing from many agents a necessary motive to public usefulness, viz., the hope of reward.

But if the superior were malicious with a moral sense contrary to ours, the contrary affections and tendency of actions would excite to reward, if any such thing could be expected from such a temper.

If actions be called rewardable, 'when a spectator would approve the superior mind for conferring rewards on such actions,' then various actions must be rewardable, according to the moral sense of the spectator. Men approve rewarding all kind affections. And if it will promote public good to promise rewards to publicly useful actions from whatsoever affections they proceed, it will evidence benevolence in the superior to do so. And this is the case with human governors, who cannot dive into the affections of men.

Some strongly assert (which is often the only proof) 'that to make an action rewardable, the agent should have had inclinations to evil as well as to good.' [4]What means this?[4] That a good governing Mind is only in-

[4. Ed. 1 has 'What does this mean?']

clined to make an agent happy, or to confer a reward on him when he has some evil affections, which yet are surmounted by the benevolent affections? But would not a benevolent Superior incline to make any benevolent agent happy, whether he had any weaker evil inclinations or not? Evil inclinations in an agent would certainly rather have some tendency to diminish the love of the superior mind. Cannot a good mind love an agent and desire his happiness unless he observes some qualities which, were they alone, would excite hatred or aversion? Must there be a mixture of hatred to make love strong and effectual, as there must be a mixture of shade to set off the lights in a picture? Is there any love where there is no inclination to make happy? Or is strong love made up of love and hatred?

It is true indeed, that men judge of the strength of kind affections generally by the contrary motives of self-love which they surmount. But must the Deity do so too? Is any nature the less lovely for its having no motive to make itself odious? If a being which has no motive to evil can be beloved by a superior, shall he not desire the happiness of that agent whom he loves? It is true, such a nature will do good actions without prospect of any self-interest; but would any benevolent superior study the less to make it happy on that account? But if they apply the word rewardable to those actions alone, which an agent would not do without prospect of reward, then indeed to make an action in this sense rewardable it is necessary that the agent should either have no kind affections, or that he should live in such circumstances wherein self-love should lead to actions contrary to the public good and overpower any kind affections, or that he should have evil affections, which even in a good constitution of the world his self-love could not over-balance without reward.

This poor idea of rewardableness is taken from the poverty and impotence of human governors. Their funds are soon exhausted; they cannot make happy all those whose happiness they desire. Their little stores must be frugally managed. None must be rewarded for what good they will do without reward, or for abstaining from evils to which they are not inclined. Rewards must be kept for the insolent minister who without reward would fly in the face of his prince; for the turbulent demagogue, who will raise factions if he is not bribed; for the covetous, mean-spirited, but artful, citizen who will serve his country no farther than it is for his private interest. But let any kind honest heart declare what sort of characters it loves, whose happiness it most desires, whom it would reward if it could, or what these dispositions are which, if it saw rewarded by a superior nature, it would be most pleased, and most approve the conduct of the superior. When these questions are answered we shall know what makes actions rewardable.

If we call all actions rewardable, the rewarding of which we approve, then indeed we shall approve the rewarding of all actions which we approve, whether the agent has had any inclinations or motives to evil or not. We shall also approve the promising of rewards to all publicly useful actions, whatever were the affections of the agents. If by this prospect of reward either malicious natures are restrained from mischief, or selfish natures induced to serve the public, or benevolent natures not able without reward to surmount real or apparent selfish motives; in all these cases the proposing rewards does really advance the happiness of the whole, or diminish its misery, and evidences benevolence in the superior mind, and is consequently approved by our moral sense.

In this last meaning of the word rewardable, these dispositions are rewardable. (1) Pure unmixed benevolence. (2) Prepollent good affections. (3) Such weak benevolence, as will not without reward overcome apparently contrary motives of self-love. (4) Unmixed self-love which by prospect of reward may serve the public. (5) Self-love which by assistance of rewards may over-balance some malicious affections. If in these cases proposing rewards will increase the happiness of the system, or diminish its misery, it evidences goodness in the governor, when he cannot so well otherwise accomplish so much good for the whole.

If we suppose a necessity of making all virtuous agents equally happy, then indeed a mixture of evil dispositions, though surmounted by the good, or of strong contrary motives over-balanced by motives to good, would be a circumstance of some importance in the distribution of rewards, since such a nature, during the struggle of contrary affections or motives, must have had less pleasure than that virtuous nature which met with no opposition. But as this very opposition gave this nature full evidence of the strength of its virtue, this consciousness may be a peculiar recompense to which the unmixed tempers are strangers. And there seems no such necessity of an equal happiness of all natures. It is no way inconsistent with perfect goodness to make different orders of beings and, provided all the virtuous be at last fully content, and as happy as they desire, there is nothing absurd in supposing different capacities and different degrees. And during the time of probation there is no necessity, not the least show of it, that all be equal.

Those who think 'no person punishable for any quality or action, if he had it not in his power to have had the opposite quality, or to have abstained from the action if he had willed it,' perhaps are not mistaken. But then let them not assert on the other hand that it is unjust to reward or make happy those who neither had any dispositions to evil nor could possibly desire any such dispositions. Now if men's affections are naturally good, and if there be in their fellows no quality which would necessarily raise malice in the observer but, on the contrary, all qualities requisite to excite at least benevolence or compassion, it may be justly said to be in the power of every one, by due attention, to prevent any malicious affections and to excite in himself kind affections toward all. So that the intricate debates about human liberty do not affect what is here alleged concerning our moral sense of affections and actions, any more than any other schemes.

Some allege that merit supposes, beside kind affection, that the agent has a moral sense, reflects upon his own virtue, delights in it, and chooses to adhere to it for the pleasure which attends it.[b] We need not debate the use of this word merit. It is plain, we approve a generous kind action, though the agent had not made this reflection. This reflection shows to him a motive of self-love, the joint view to which does not increase our approbation. But then it must again be owned that we cannot form a just conclusion of a character from one or two kind, generous, actions, especially where there has been no very strong motives to the contrary. Some apparent motives of interest may afterwards over-balance the kind affections and lead the agent into vicious actions. But the reflection on virtue, the being once charmed with the lovely form, will discover an interest on its side which, if well attended to, no other motive will over-balance. This reflection is a great security to the character, and must be supposed in such creatures as men are, before we can well depend upon a constancy in virtue. The same may be said of many other motives to virtue from interest which, though they do not immediately influence the kind affections of the agent, yet remove these obstacles to them, from false appearances of interest. Such are these from the sanctions of divine laws by future rewards and punishments and even the manifest advantages of virtue in this life, without reflection on which, a steady course of virtue is scarce to be expected amidst the present confusion of human affairs.

b. See Lord Shaftesbury's *Inquiry Concerning Virtue,* Part I. [Anthony Ashley Cooper, Third Earl of Shaftesbury, 1671–1713. The first edition of the *Inquiry* in 1699 was unauthorized. The official and best known version is in the three volume edition of 1711 entitled *Characteristics of Men, Manners, Opinions, Times.*]

How far a regard to the Deity is necessary to make an action virtuous

Section VI

I. Some imagine, 'that to make an action virtuous it is necessary that the agent should have previously known his action to be acceptable to the Deity and have undertaken it chiefly with design to please or obey him. We have not,' say they, 'reason to imagine a malicious intention in many of the worst actions. The very want of good affections in their just degree must constitute moral evil. If so, then the moral evil in the want of love or gratitude must increase in proportion to the causes of love or gratitude in the object. By the causes of love they mean those qualities in the object upon observation of which love or gratitude arise in every good temper. Now the causes of love toward the Deity are infinite, therefore the want of the highest possible degree of love to him must be infinitely evil. To be excited more by smaller motives or causes than by greater, to love those who are less lovely, while we neglect him in whom are infinite causes of love, must argue great perverseness of affections. But the causes of love in the Deity, his infinite goodness toward all, and even toward ourselves, from whence springs all the happiness of our lives, are infinitely above any causes of love to be found in creatures. Therefore to act from love to them without intention to please God must be infinitely evil.'

If this reasoning be just the best of men are infinitely evil. The distinction between habitual and actual intention will not remove the difficulty since these arguments require actual intention. An habitual intention is not a present act of love to the Deity influencing our actions more than actual love to creatures, which this argument requires, but a prior general resolution not at present repeated.

To find what is just on this subject we may premise

some propositions of which men must convince themselves by reflection.

II. There is in mankind such a disposition naturally that they desire the happiness of any known sensitive nature when it is not inconsistent with something more strongly desired; so that were there no oppositions of interest either private or public, and sufficient power, we would confer upon every being the highest happiness which it could receive.

But our understanding and power are limited, so that we cannot know many other natures, nor is our utmost power capable of promoting the happiness of many. Our actions are therefore influenced by some stronger affections than this general benevolence. There are certain qualities found in some beings more than in others which excite stronger degrees of good-will and determine our attention to their interests, while that of others is neglected. The ties of blood, benefits conferred upon us, and the observation of virtue in others, raise much more vigorous affections than that general benevolence which we may have toward all. These qualities or relations we may call the causes of love.

However these affections are very different from the general benevolence toward all, yet it is very probable that there is a regularity or proportion observed in the constitution of our nature; so that abstracting from some acquired habits, or associations of ideas, and from the more sudden emotions of some particular passions, that temper which has the most lively gratitude, or is the most susceptive of friendship with virtuous characters, would also have the strongest general benevolence toward indifferent persons. And, on the contrary, where there is the weakest general benevolence, there we could expect the least gratitude, and the least friendship, or love toward the virtuous. If this proportion be observed, then [1] we may denote the propensity of

[1. Ed. 1 reads: 'if we express all these desires of the good of others by the name of benevolence, we may denote the several degrees in which men possess these several kind dispositions by the *goodness of the temper*. And the degrees of desire toward the happiness of any person, we may call the *quantity of love* toward him. Then.']

mind, or the disposition to receive or to be moved with any tender or kind affections, by the goodness of temper. Then,

The degree of kind affection toward any person is in a compound proportion of the apprehended causes of love in him and of the goodness of temper in the observer.[1]

When the causes of love in two objects are apprehended equal the love toward either in different persons is as the goodness of temper.[2]

When the goodness of temper is the same or equal the love toward any objects will be [3]proportioned to the causes.[3]

The goodness of any temper is therefore as the quantity of love, divided by the apprehended causes.[4] And since we cannot apprehend any goodness in having the degree of love above the proportion of its causes, the most virtuous temper is that in which the love equals its causes, which may therefore be expressed by unity.[a]

Hence it follows, that if there were any nature incomparably more excellent than any of our fellow creatures from whom also we ourselves, and all others had received the greatest benefits, there would be less virtue in any small degree of desire of his happiness than in a like degree of love toward our fellow creature.

a. See Treat. II, Sect. 3, art. 11, last paragraph. [The London edition of 1738 reads: 'Since, then, benevolence or virtue in any agent is as M/A, or as $M+1/A$, and no being can act above his natural ability, that must be the perfection of virtue where $M=A$, or when the being acts to the utmost of his power for the public good; and hence the perfection of virtue in this case, or M/A, is as unity. And this may show us the only foundation for the boasting of the Stoics, "that a creature supposed innocent by pursuing virtue with his utmost power may in virtue equal the gods." For in their case if A, or the ability, be infinite, unless M, or the good to be produced in the whole, be so too, the virtue is not absolutely perfect and the quotient can never surmount unity.'

[In the Glasgow edition of 1772 this paragraph is modified to read: 'Since, then, in judging of the goodness of temper in any agent, the abilities must come into computation, as is above mentioned, and none can act beyond their natural abilities, that must be the perfection of virtue where the moment of good produced equals the ability, or when the being acts to the utmost of his power for the public good;

[2. Ed. 1 adds 'or, $L=C\times 1$']

[3. Ed. 1 reads: 'as the causes, or $L=G\times 1$.']

[4. Ed. 1 adds 'or $G=L/C$.']

But not loving such a being, or having a smaller degree of love, must evidence a much greater defect in virtue than a like want of love toward our fellow creatures. For the causes of love being very great, unless the love be also very great [5] there must be some depravation of the temper, some want of the natural proportion, or of that calm deliberation and calm affections, toward objects of the understanding.[5]

III. To apply this to the Deity is very obvious. Our affections toward him arise in the same manner as toward our fellows in proportion to our attention to the causes of love in him and the goodness of our temper. The reflection on his goodness raises approbation and complacence, his benefits raise gratitude, and both occasion good will or benevolence. [6]'His happiness is perhaps imagined [6] wholly detached from all events in this world, absolute and unvaried in himself.' And yet the same inclination of mind might remain in us, though we had this opinion. When the happiness of a friend is in suspense, we desire it; when he has obtained all that which we desired, the same inclination of mind seems to remain toward him, only without that uneasiness accompanying desire of an uncertain object. Thus gravity may be said to be the same when a body is resting on a fixed base as when it caused descent.

Upon this scheme of the divine happiness it is not easy to account how our love to him could excite us to promote the happiness of our fellows. Our frequent contemplation of such an amiable excellent nature might indeed tend to reform or improve our temper by presenting an example engaging our imitation.

and hence the perfection virtue in this case is as unity. And this may show us the only foundation for the boasting of the Stoics, "That a creature supposed innocent, by pursuing virtue with his utmost power may in virtue equal the gods." For in their case, if the ability be infinite, unless the good to be produced in the whole be so too the virtue is not absolutely perfect, and the quotient can never surmount unity.']

[5. Ed. 1 reads: 'the quotient which expresses the goodness of temper will be much below unity.']

[6. Ed. 1 reads: 'Some imagine that "his happiness is']

If we imagine that the Deity has such perceptions of approbation or dislike toward actions as we have ourselves, then indeed our love to him would directly excite us to do whatever he approves and shun what he condemns. We can scarce avoid imagining that the frequent recurring of events disapproved must be uneasy to any nature and that the observing approved actions must be delightful.

If we imagine that the divine happiness, or any part of it, is connected with the happiness of his creatures so that their happiness is constituted the occasion of his, then indeed our love to the Deity will directly excite us to all manner of beneficent actions. It is true, many good men deny these two last opinions yet it is probable, when their minds are diverted from speculations by opportunities of action, there recurs some imagination of offence, uneasiness, and resentment in the Deity, upon observing evil actions, of delight and joy in beholding good actions, of sorrow upon observing the misery of his creatures, and joy upon seeing them happy. So that by their love to the Deity they are influenced to beneficent actions notwithstanding their speculative opinions. In our conceptions of the Deity we are continually led to imagine a resemblance to what we feel in ourselves.

Whoever maintains these opinions of the Deity to be true must also 'suppose a particular determination of all events in the universe,' otherwise this part of the divine happiness is made precarious and uncertain, depending upon the undetermined will of creatures.

The diversity of opinions concerning the divine happiness may lead men into different ways of accounting for the influence which the love of God may have upon our actions toward our fellows. But the affections toward the Deity would be much the same upon both schemes. Where there were the same just apprehensions of the divine goodness in two persons, the love to the Deity in both would be proportioned to the goodness of temper. Though the highest possible degree of love to a perfectly good Deity would evidence no more virtue of temper than a proportioned love to creatures, yet the having only smaller degrees of love to the Deity would evidence a greater defect of goodness in the temper than any want of affection toward creatures.

Here it must be remembered that in arguing concerning the goodness of temper from the degree of love directly, and the causes of love inversely, actual attention to the causes of love is supposed in the person. For it is plain, that in the best temper no one affection or idea can always continue present, and there can be no affection present to the mind, toward any object, while the idea of it is not present. The bare absence therefore of affection, while the mind is employed upon a different object, can argue no evil in the temper farther than want of attention may argue want of affection. In like manner, in the best temper there can be no love toward an object unknown. The want therefore of love to an object unknown can argue no evil in the temper farther than ignorance may argue want of affection. It is certain indeed, that he who knows that there is a good Deity, and actually thinks of him, and of all his benefits, yet has not the strongest love and gratitude toward him, must have a temper void of all goodness; but it will not follow that the mind is void of goodness which is not always thinking of the Deity, or actually loving him, or even does not know him. How far the want of attention to the Deity, and ignorance of him, may argue an evil temper must be shown from different topics, to be considered hereafter.

IV. But previously to these inquiries we must consider 'what degrees or kinds of affections are necessary to obtain the simple approbation of innocence.' It is plain, the bare absence of all malice is not enough. We may have the general benevolence toward a mere sensitive nature which had no other desire but self-love; but we can apprehend no moral goodness in such a being. Nay, it is not every small degree of kind affections which we approve. There must be some proportion of kind affections to the other faculties in any nature, particularly to its understanding and active powers to obtain approbation. Some brutes evidence small degrees of good will, which make them be approved in their kind; but the same degrees would not be approved in a man. There is an higher degree expected in mankind to which, if they do not come up, we do not account them innocent. It is not easy to fix precisely that degree which we approve as innocent by our moral sense. Every kind affection, if it be considered only with relation to its own object, is indeed approved, such as natural affection, gratitude, pity, friendship. And yet when we take a more extensive view of the tendency of some actions proceeding even from these affections, we may often condemn these actions when they are apprehended as pernicious to larger systems of mankind. In the same manner, we often condemn actions done from love to a particular country when they appear to be pernicious to mankind in general. In like manner, self-preservation and pursuing private advantage abstractly considered, is innocent. But when it is apprehended as very pernicious in any case to the safety of others, it is condemned.

Mankind are capable of large extensive ideas of great societies. And it is expected of them, that their general benevolence should continually direct and limit, not only their selfish affections, but even their nearer attachments to others, that their desire of public good, and aversion to public misery, should overcome at least their desire of positive private advantages, either to themselves or their particular favorites; so as to make them abstain from any action which would be positively pernicious or hurtful to mankind, however beneficial it might be to themselves, or their favorites. To undergo positive evil for the sake of positive good to others seems some degree of virtue above innocence, which we do not universally expect, but to reject positive attainable good, either for ourselves or our particular favorites rather than occasion any considerable misery to others, is requisite to obtain the approbation of innocence. The want of this degree we condemn as positive evil, and an agent must rise above it by positive services to mankind, with some trouble and expense to himself, before we approve him as virtuous. We seem indeed universally to expect from all men those good offices which give the agent no trouble or expense. Whoever refuses them is below innocence. But we do not positively condemn those as evil who will not sacrifice their private interest to the advancement of the positive good of others unless the private interest be very small and the public good very great.[b]

But as the desire of positive private good is weaker than aversion to private evil, or pain, so our desire of the positive good of others is weaker than our aversion to their misery. It seems at least requisite to innocence that the stronger public affection, viz., our aversion to the misery of others, should surmount the weaker private affection, the desire of positive private good; so that no prospect of good to ourselves, should engage us to that which would occasion prepollent[7] misery to others. It is in like manner requisite to innocence that our aversion to the misery of greater or equal systems should surmount our desire of the positive good of these to which we are more particularly attached.

How far it may be necessary to the character of innocence to submit to smaller private pains to prevent the greater sufferings of others, or to promote some great positive advantages, or how far the happiness of private systems should be neglected for the happiness of the greater in order to obtain the approbation of innocence, it is perhaps impossible precisely to determine or to fix any general rules; nor indeed is it necessary. Our business is not to find out 'at how cheap a rate we can purchase innocence,' but to know what is most noble, generous and virtuous in life. This we know consists in sacrificing all positive interests and bearing all private evils for the public good and in submitting also the interests of all smaller systems to the interests

b. In many questions of this nature we must have recourse with Aristotle to a sense, which is the last judge in particular cases. [This footnote not in ed. 1.]

[7. Not in ed. 1.]

of the whole without any other exception or reserve than this, that every man may look upon himself as a part of this system and consequently not sacrifice an important private interest to a less important interest of others. We may find the same sort of difficulty about all our other senses in determining precisely what objects are indifferent, or where pleasure ends and disgust begins, though the higher[8] degrees of the grateful and ungrateful are easily distinguished.

It is also very difficult to fix any precise degree of affection toward the Deity which should be barely requisite to innocence. Only in general we must disapprove that temper which, upon apprehension of the perfect goodness of the Deity and of his innumerable benefits to mankind, has not stronger affections of love and gratitude toward him than those toward any other being. Such affections would necessarily raise frequent attention and consideration of our actions and would engage us, if we apprehended any of them to be offensive to him, or contrary to that scheme of events in which we apprehended the Deity to delight, to avoid them with a more firm resolution than what we had in any other affairs. Positive virtue toward the Deity must go farther than a resolute abstaining from offence, by engaging us with the greatest vigor to do whatever we apprehend as positively pleasing, or conducive to those ends in which we apprehend the Deity delights. It is scarce conceivable that any good temper can want such affections toward the Deity, when once he is known, as were above supposed necessary to innocence. Nor can we imagine positive degrees of goodness of temper above innocence, where affections toward the Deity do not arise proportionably.

What is here said relates only to the apprehensions of our moral sense, and not to those degrees of virtue which the Deity may require by revelation. And every one's heart may inform him whether or no he does not approve, at least as innocent, those who omit many good offices which they might possibly have done, pro-

[8. Ed. 1 has 'positive']

vided they do a great deal of good; those who carefully abstain from every apprehended offence toward the Deity, though they might possibly be more frequent in acts of devotion. It is true indeed, the omission of what we know to be required is positively evil, so that by a revelation we may be obliged to farther services than were requisite previously to it, which we could not innocently omit, after this revelation is known. But we are here only considering our moral sense.

V. Now let us inquire how far simple ignorance of a Deity, or unaffected atheism, evidences an evil disposition or defect of good affections below innocence.

1. Affections arising upon apparent causes or present opinions, though false, if they be such as would arise in the best temper, were these opinions true, cannot argue any present want of goodness in any temper, of themselves. The opinions indeed may often argue a want of goodness at the time they were formed, but to a benevolent temper there is no cause of malice, or [9]of the ultimate[9] desire of the misery or non-existence of any being for itself. There may be causes of dislike, and desire of misery or non-existence, as the means of greater good, or of lessening evil.

2. No object which is entirely unknown, or of which we have no idea, can raise affection in the best temper; consequently want of affection to an unknown object evidences no evil. This would be the case of those who never heard even the report of a Deity, if ever there were any such, or who never heard of any fellow-creatures, if one may make a supposition like to that made by Cicero.[c] And this is perhaps the case, as to the Deity, of any unfortunate children, who may have some little use of reason, before they are instructed in any religion.

If there really were an innate idea of a Deity so imprinted that no person could be without it, or if we are so disposed as necessarily to receive this idea as soon as we can be called moral agents, then no ignorance of a Deity can be innocent. All atheism must be affected,

c. De Nat. Deor., lib. 2, cap. 37. Ex. Aristotle.
[9. Not in ed. 1.]

or an opinion formed, either through evil affection or want of good affection below innocence. But if the idea of a Deity be neither imprinted, nor offer itself previously to any reflection, nor be universally excited by tradition, the bare want of it, where there has been no tradition or reflection, cannot be called criminal upon any scheme. Those who make virtue and vice relative to a law may say, 'Men are required to reflect, and thence to know a Deity.' But they must allow promulgation necessary before disobedience to a law can be criminal. Now previously to reflection it is supposed impossible for the agent to know the legislator or to know the law requiring him to reflect, therefore this law requiring him to reflect was not antecedently to his reflection published to him.

The case of human laws, the ignorance of which does not excuse, is not parallel to this. No person under any civil government can be supposed ignorant that there are laws made for the whole state. But in the present supposition, men antecedently to reflection may be ignorant of the Deity, or that there are laws of nature. If any subject could thus be unapprized, that he lived under civil government, he should not be accounted *compos mentis*. The supposition indeed in both cases is perhaps wholly imaginary; at least as to persons above childhood. One can scarce imagine that ever any person was wholly unapprized of a governing Mind, and of a right and wrong in morals. Whether this is to be ascribed to innate ideas, to universal tradition, or to some necessary determination in our nature, to imagine a designing Cause of the beautiful objects which occur to us, with a moral sense, let the curious inquire.

3. Suppose an idea formed in a benevolent mind of other sensitive natures, desire of their existence and happiness would arise.

4. A good temper would incline any one to wish that other natures were benevolent, or morally good, since this is the chief happiness.

5. A good temper would desire that the administration of nature were by a benevolent or good mind.

6. All desire of any event or circumstance inclines

any mind to search into the truth of that event or circumstance, by all the evidence within its power to obtain.

7. Where there is such desire, and sufficiently obvious evidence given in proportion to the sagacity of the desiring mind, it will come to the knowledge of the truth, if its desire be strong.

Now from these propositions we may deduce the following conclusions.[10]

1. Supposing the idea of a good Deity once apprehended, or excited either by report, or the slightest reflection; if there be objective evidence in nature proportioned to the capacity of the inquirer, for the existence of a good Deity, atheism directly argues want of good affection below innocence.

2. If there be only the simple tradition or presumption of a governing mind once raised, and if there be evidence as before for his goodness, to conclude the Deity evil or malicious must argue want of good affections as before.

3. Suppose the idea of an evil Deity once excited, and some presumptions for his malice from tradition, or slight reflection upon particular evils in nature; to rest in this opinion without inquiry, would argue want of good affection. To desire to reject this opinion, or confute it by contrary evidence, would argue good affection. Suppose such contrary evidences obvious enough in nature to one who inquired as diligently about it as about his own interest; to continue in his own interest; to continue in the false opinion cannot be innocent.

VI. In like manner concerning our fellow-creatures who are actually known to us.

4. To imagine fellow-creatures morally good, either according to evidence upon inquiry, or even by a rash opinion, evidences good affection.

5. Imagining them evil contrary to obvious evidence argues want of good affection below innocence.

6. Retaining and inculcating an opinion either of the causes of love in others, or of the causes of aversion,

[10. Ed. 1 has 'corollaries']

induces an habit and makes the temper prone to the affection often raised. Opinion of goodness in the Deity and our fellows increases good affection and improves the temper. Contrary opinion of either, by raising frequent aversions, weakens good affections and impairs the temper.

This may show how cautious men ought to be in passing sentence upon the impiety of their fellows, or representing them as wicked and profane, or hateful to the Deity, and justly given over to eternal misery. We may see also what a wise mark it is to know the true church by, 'that it pronounces damnation on all others.' Which is one of the characters of the Romish church by which it is often recommended as the safest for Christians to live in.

The same propositions may be applied to our opinions concerning the natural tendencies of actions. Where the evidence is obvious as before, good affection will produce true opinions, and false opinions often argue want of good affection below innocence. Thus, though in assent or dissent of themselves there can neither be virtue nor vice, yet they may be evidences of either in the agent, as well as his external motions. It is not possible indeed for men to determine precisely in many cases the quantity of evidence and its proportion to the sagacity of the observer which will argue guilt in him who, contrary to it, forms a false opinion. But men are no better judges of the degrees of virtue and vice in external actions. This therefore will not prove that all false opinions or errors are innocent, more than external actions. The searcher of hearts can judge exactly of both. Human punishments are only methods of self-defence in which the degrees of guilt are not the proper measure, but the necessity of restraining actions for the safety of the public.

VII. It is next to be considered how far want of attention to the Deity can argue want of good affections in any agent to whom he is known.

Every good temper will have strong affections to a good Deity and where there is strong affection there will be frequent reflection upon the object beloved, desire of pleasing, and caution of offense. In like manner every person of good temper, who has had the knowledge of a country, a system, a species, will consider how far these great societies may be affected by his actions, with such attention as he uses in his own affairs, and will abstain from what is injurious to them.

Attention to a Deity apprehended as good, and governing the universe, will increase the [11]disposition to[11] beneficence in any good agent various ways; [12]by prospects of reward, either present or future; by improving his temper through observation of so amiable a pattern; or by raising sentiments of gratitude toward the Deity, [13]to whom we may imagine the public happiness to be acceptable.[13] In like manner, the considering a species or system may increase our good offices, since their interests are advanced by good offices to individuals.

But then from a like reasoning to that in art. II, it is plain that in equal moments of good produced by two agents the goodness of the temper is rather[14] inversely as the several additional helps, or motives, to it. So that [15]where no more good is done, in equal abilities, by one agent who had presented to him the joint motives of piety toward God and humanity toward men, than is done by another from mere humanity, the latter gives a better evidence of a good temper. And where higher motives of gratitude to God are presented to one than to another, unless the good done from these stronger motives is greater, the temper must be so much the worse.[d] [15]

But an injurious action which appeared to the agent

d. See Luke x, 12, 13, 14.

[11. Ed. 1 has 'moment of']

[12. Ed. 1 adds 'such as']

[13. Ed. 1 reads: 'a part of whose happiness the agent may imagine depends upon the happiness of the universe.']

[14. Not in ed. 1.]

[15. Ed. 1 reads: 'more virtue is evidenced by any given moment of beneficence from good affections only toward our fellows, or particular persons, than by the same moment produced from the joint considerations of the Deity, or of a general system or species.']

not only pernicious to his fellows or to particular persons, but offensive to the Deity and pernicious to a system, is much more vicious than when the agent did not reflect upon the Deity or a community.

VIII. We must not hence imagine that in order to produce greater virtue in ourselves we should regard the Deity no farther than merely to abstain from offences. Were it our sole intention in beneficent actions, only to obtain the private pleasure of self-approbation for the degree of our virtue, this might seem the proper means of having great virtue with the least expense. But if the real intention which constitutes an action virtuous be the promoting public good, then voluntarily to reject the consideration of any motive which would increase the moment of public good or would make us more vigorous and steadfast in virtue, must argue want of good affection. [16] Good offices done from mere humanity, while the motives of piety were not present to the mind, provided they were not excluded by direct design or blameable inadvertence, may in this particular case be a better indication of good temper than offices only of equal importance done by another of equal abilities from the joint motives of piety and humanity; yet the retaining designedly and frequently recalling all these motives [16] with a view to increase the moment of public good in our actions, if they really do so, argues virtue equal to, or greater than that in the former case. And the affected neglect of these motives, that so we may acquit ourselves virtuously with the least expense to ourselves, or with the least moment of public good, must evidence want of good affections and base trick and artifice to impose upon observers or our own hearts.

Therefore, since gratitude to the Deity, and even consideration of private interest, tend to increase the moment of our beneficence and to strengthen good affections, the voluntary retaining them with this

[16. Ed. 1 reads: 'In any given moment of beneficence the unaffected want of regard to the Deity, or to private interest, does really argue greater virtue. But the retaining these motives']

view evidences virtue, and affecting to neglect them evidences vice.[e]

And yet if the moment produced by the conjunction of these motives be not greater than that produced, with unaffected neglect of these motives, from particular good affection, there is less virtue in the former than in the latter.

Men may use names as they please and may choose to call nothing virtue but 'what is intended chiefly to evidence affection of one kind or other toward the Deity.' Writers on this scheme are not well agreed about what this virtuous intention is, whether only to evidence submission, or submission and love, or to [17] express gratitude by compliance with the divine will, or to express a disinterested esteem, or to obtain our own happiness by means of the divine favor. This last intention may influence a very corrupt mind in some things. And the former more generous intentions must really increase the goodness of every action, and are the highest virtues of themselves.[17] But let them not assert, against universal experience, that we approve no actions which are not thus intended toward the Deity. It is plain, a generous compassionate heart which, at first view of the distress of another, flies impatiently to his relief, or spares no expense to accomplish it, meets with strong approbation from every

e. This may sufficiently justify the writers of morality in their proving 'that virtue is the surest means of happiness to the agent.' It is also plain from universal experience that a regard to the Deity, frequent reflection on his goodness, and consequent acts of love, are the strongest and most universally prevailing means of obtaining a good temper. Whatever institution therefore does most effectually tend to raise men's attention, to recall their minds from the hurry of their common affairs, to instruct them in the ways of promoting public good farther than the busy part of the world without assistance would probably apprehend, must be so wise and good that every honest mind should rejoice in it, even though it had no other authority than human to recommend it. Everyone will understand that by this is meant a public worship on set days, in which a stop is put to commerce and the busy part of mankind instructed in the duties of piety and humanity.

[17. Ed. 1 reads: 'obtain the divine benevolence and private happiness to the agent, or to give pleasure to the Deity.']

observer who has not perverted his sense of life by school-divinity or philosophy. [18] Joining frequently and habitually the acts of piety with those of humanity is, no doubt, the perfection of goodness and virtue. But we must not deny the reality of virtue in these actions which are not of the most perfect sort.[18]

To be led by a weaker motive where a stronger is alike present to the mind, to love a creature more than God, or to have stronger desire of doing what is grateful to creatures than to God, when we equally attend to both, would certainly argue great [19] perversion of our affections; or to study the particular good of one more than that of a system, when we reflected on both. But as no finite mind can retain at once a multiplicity of objects, so it cannot always retain any one object. When a person, therefore, not thinking at present of the Deity, or of a community, or system, does a beneficent action from particular love, he evidences goodness of temper. The bare absence of the idea of a Deity, or of affections to him, can evidence no evil; otherwise it would be a crime to fall asleep, or to think of any thing else. If the bare absence of this idea be no evil, the presence of kind affections to fellow-creatures cannot be evil. If indeed our love to the Deity excited to any action and at the same time love to a creature excited to the omission of it, or to a contrary action, we must be very criminal if the former do not prevail; yet this will not argue all actions to be evil in which pleasing the Deity is not directly and chiefly intended. Nay, that temper must really be very deficient in goodness which ever needs to recall the thoughts of a [20] divine command and its sanctions, or even the thoughts of the interests of greater societies or systems, before it can be engaged into any particular acts of kindness. Accordingly, we find in nature that the particular kind passions gen-

[18. Ed. 1 reads: ''Tis to be suspected that some vanity must be at the bottom of these notions which place virtue in some nicety which active tempers have not the leisure to apprehend and only the recluse student can attain to.']

[19. Ed. 1 has 'some']

[20. Ed. 1 reads: 'Deity, or a community, or a system.']

erally move the mind first. And upon reflection, more extensive motives begin to occur, and regards to the great head of the rational system.[20] The frequent recalling these thoughts, indeed, does strengthen all good affections and increases the moment of beneficence to be expected from any temper; and with this view frequently to recall such thoughts, must be one of the best helps to virtue, and evidence high degrees of it. Nay, one cannot call that temper entire and complete which has not the strongest affection toward the greatest benefactor and the most worthy object.

Beings of such degrees of knowledge, and such extent of thought as mankind are not only capable of but generally obtain when nothing interrupts their inquiries, must naturally arise to the knowledge of the Deity, if their temper be good. They must form general conceptions of the whole and see the order, wisdom, and goodness in the administration of nature in some degree. The knowledge and love of the Deity, the universal mind, is as natural a perfection to such a being as man as any accomplishment to which we arrive by cultivating our natural dispositions; nor is that mind come to the proper state and vigor of its kind where religion is not the main exercise and delight.

IX. There is one very subtle argument on this subject. Some allege, 'that since the Deity is really the cause of all the good in the universe, even of all the virtue or good affection in creatures, which are the seeming causes of love toward them, it must argue strange perversion of temper to love those in whom there is no cause of love, or who are (as they affect to speak) nothing, or emptiness of all goodness. The Deity alone is amiable, in whom there is infinite fullness of every amiable quality. The Deity, say they, not without some reason, is the cause of every pleasant sensation, which he immediately excites according to a general law, upon the occasion of motions arising in our bodies; that likewise he gave us that general inclination, which we modify into all our different affections; God therefore, say they, is alone lovely. Other things are not to be beloved, but only the goodness of God appearing in them. Nay, some make the loving of them, without considering God as displaying his goodness in them, to be infinitely evil.'

In answer to this it must be owned, 'that God's being the cause of all the good in the universe will no doubt raise the highest love to him in a good temper when it reflects upon it.'

1. But, first, had all men this apprehension that 'there was no good in any creature,' they really would not love them at all. But men generally imagine, with very good ground, that there are good beings distinct from God, though produced by him. And whether this opinion be true or false, it evidences no evil.

2. As upon this scheme God is the cause of all pleasant sensation, so is he the cause of all pain. He is, according to them, the cause of that inclination which we modify into evil affection as well as into good. If then we are to love God only, for what we call good affection in creatures, and not the creatures themselves, we must also only love God upon observing evil affections in creatures, and have no aversion to the basest temper, since God gave the general inclination alike in both cases.

3. If we may suppose real beings distinct from God, that their affections are not God's affections, if God is not the only lover and hater, if our moral sense is determined to approve kind affections, and our love or benevolence must arise toward what we approve; or if we find an instinct to desire the happiness of every sensitive nature, we cannot avoid loving creatures, and we must approve any kind affections observed in others toward their fellows. It is true, we must approve the highest affections toward the Deity and condemn, as a deficiency of just affections toward God, any degree which is not superior to our other affections. But still, affections towards creatures, if they be distinct natures, must be approved.

4. If to make a mind virtuous, or even innocent, it be necessary that it should have such sublime specula-

tions of God, as the τὸ πᾶν in the intellectual active system (if we call one agent in many passive organs an active system), then God has placed the bulk of mankind in an absolute incapacity of virtue, and inclined them perpetually to infinite evil by their very instincts and natural affections. Does the parental affection direct a man to love the Deity, or his children? Is it the divinity to which our pity or compassion is directed? Is God the object of humanity? Is it a design to support the divinity which we call generosity or liberality? Upon receipt of a benefit does our nature suggest only gratitude toward God? Affections toward the Deity may indeed often accompany affections toward creatures and do so in a virtuous temper. But these are distinct affections. This notion of making all virtuous affections to be only directed toward God is not suggested to men by any thing in their nature, but arises from the long subtle reasonings of men at leisure, and unemployed in the natural affairs of life.

5. If there be no virtue or cause of love in creatures, it is vain for them to debate wherein their virtue consists, whether in regard toward the Deity, or in any thing else, since they are supposed to have none at all.

To conclude this subject. It seems probable that however we must look upon that temper as exceedingly imperfect, inconstant, and partial, in which gratitude toward the universal benefactor, admiration and love of the supreme original beauty, perfection and goodness, are not the strongest and most prevalent affections; yet particular actions may be innocent, nay, virtuous, where there is no actual intention of pleasing the Deity influencing the agent.

Appendix

The Correspondence between Gilbert Burnet and Francis Hutcheson

LETTERS

Between the Late

Mr. GILBERT BURNET,

AND

Mr. HUTCHINSON,

CONCERNING

The true Foundation of VIRTUE or MORAL GOODNESS.

Formerly published in the LONDON JOURNAL.

To which is added,

A PREFACE and a POSTSCRIPT,

Wrote by

Mr. BURNET some time before his Death.

Ita fiet, ut Animi Virtus *Corporis* Virtuti *anteponatur ; Animique* Virtutes *non voluntarias vincant* Virtutes *voluntariæ ; quæ quidem proprie* Virtutes *appellantur, multumque excellunt, propterea quod ex* Ratione *gignuntur, qua nihil est in Homine divinius.*
In Homine autem summa omnis Animi est ; &, in Animo Rationis ; *ex qua* Virtus *est, quæ* Rationis Absolutio *definitur ; quam etiam atque etiam explicandam putant.*

Cicero de Fin. Bon. & Mal.

LONDON:

Printed by W. WILKINS in *Lombard-Street*, 1735.

(Price One Shilling.)

Preface

The occasion of this small controversy was owing to a very ingenious book, entitled, *An Inquiry into the Original of our Ideas of Beauty and Virtue.*[1]

In the *Inquiry into Virtue,* I apprehended that the beautiful structure the author had raised, wanted a sufficient foundation and, though the conclusions were generally true and right in themselves and were capable of demonstrative proof, yet he seemed to me to have left them unsupported.

As I was unwilling that so many excellent truths and such a worthy conduct of life as the ingenious author recommends to us should remain under the accusation of being but slightly grounded, I took the liberty to represent the defect of his reasoning and the needfulness of a further and deeper search into the very bottom of virtue in order to discover the true and solid foundation of it.

Such a firm foundation has been laid down by several very great men who have writ on this subject, in particular, by the learned Bishop Cumberland, in his *Disquisitio Philosophica de Legibus Naturae;*[2] after him by the Rev. Dr. Clarke, in the beginning of his second Boyle's Lectures;[3] and lately, by the excellent author of *The Religion of Nature Delineated.*[4]

[1. By Francis Hutcheson, London, 1725.]

[2. Richard Cumberland (1632–1718) was successively chaplain to the Lord Keeper of London, rector at Brampton in Northamptonshire, rector at Allhallows at Stamford, and bishop of Peterborough. *De Legibus Naturae, Disquisitio Philosophica* was first published in London in 1672; English translation by John Maxwell, London, 1727.]

[3. Samuel Clarke (1675–1729) was successively chaplain to the bishop of Norwich, rector of Drayton, Boyle Lecturer, rector of St. Bennett's, chaplain to Queen Anne, and rector of St. James, Westminster. The first series of Boyle Lectures was given in 1704 and published in London in 1705 as *Demonstration of the Being and Attributes of God.* The second series was given in 1705 and published in 1706 as *A Discourse Concerning the Unchangeable Obligations of Natural Religion.* Both series were delivered as sermons in St. Paul's.]

[4. William Wollaston (1659–1724) was assistant master of the Birmingham grammar school. He returned to London at 29 with an in-

These are the principles maintained in the following papers, subscribed Philaretus. And they all amount to this one proposition, "that virtue, or moral goodness, is founded on truth."

As this debate is now closed I make bold to offer it again in one view to the world hoping that, with all its defects, it may not be wholly useless nor unacceptable to those persons who desire always to know for what reason they ought to perform any action or office of life.

I thought it the fairest way to publish my own and my correspondent's letters together in the order in which they were writ, that the reader might have the opportunity of examining more easily whether I have mistaken or misrepresented him or not.

It is with no small comfort that I look back and observe that in this controversy the rule of candor and good manners have not been transgressed through an impatient zeal for our respective sentiments, a conduct which certainly nothing can excuse, either in writing or conversing on any subject, but much less where the most important truths are concerned. For it is not the way to promote any truth, and in the present case would have been inconsistent with the truths we were both defending, though in different methods. And, sure, anyone, who is capable of feeling the least ardor for the discovery of truth must be much above the low pleasure of triumphing at the expense of it.

I should not have said this if I had not thought it an acknowledgment due to my correspondent and were not conscious to my self of endeavoring to keep close to the example he showed me.

I have added a postscript concerning the several meanings of the word *good* which I hope will not be thought superfluous, since it is pretty evident that most of the mistakes in moral science are in a good measure owing to the unwary use of words, by which well-meaning men are often led insensibly, and undesign-

---

heritance and was the father of eleven children. *The Religion of Nature Delineated* was first privately printed in 1722; it was published in 1724 in London and reached an eighth edition in 1759.]

edly, to drop into their conclusions a sense which never subsisted in their premises.

I am apt to think that the ingenious author of the *Inquiry*, if he had thoroughly searched into the different acceptations of the words *good* and *evil*, and in what manner they were all derived from the primary and proper sense, would not have rested satisfied with the bare description of moral good and evil, by the effects the apprehension of them work in us to excite internal pleasure and pain or, which amounts to the same, love or aversion; nor have doubted whether we had really such ideas and whether there was any general foundation in nature for the difference of actions as morally good or evil as he does, pp. 111, 112.

His description will only hold as to relative good and evil. It is very true that what affords us pleasure is good relatively to us, and what brings us pain is evil to us. But still what is good to us may be, notwithstanding its being relatively good to us, very evil in itself, as well as relatively evil to others; as, if one creature were to be made happy by means of the undeserved misery of all other creatures. Happiness, in that case, would be good relatively to that one creature but would be relatively evil to all other creatures; and, because undeserved, would be evil in itself. And the author of such a supposed constitution of things as should render one creature happy at the expense of universal misery could never be denominated good in the proper sense though still he would be relatively good to that single creature.

In the divine mind the ideas of moral good and evil must be immutably fixed. If those words only mean what he approves and loves, or is averse to and dislikes, they are useless and supernumerary words, and should not needlessly be introduced into philosophical discourse. If, when you affirm that God is good, you only mean that he approves and likes something you know not why, you seem to say some great thing of him but in reality say nothing that implies any moral perfection. For aught we know, upon the supposition that we know not why he approves anything, he may approve tomorrow just the contrary of what he approves today. Will then moral good and evil, in that case, change places and what is morally good today be morally evil tomorrow? To be sure it must if moral good means only what he approves and moral evil what he disapproves. But, if this be too absurd to be maintained, it remains that moral good and evil have an immutable foundation in the nature of things; as immutable as the truths of geometry have, which even the divine mind cannot be conceived to alter. It follows, that things are not morally good because God approves them, nor morally evil because he disapproves them. But he is immutably good himself, in the moral sense of the word, because he always, and unchangeably, approves what is in itself good, and disapproves what is in itself evil, and always acts conformably.

And if the intelligence of men is capacious enough to attain the knowledge of the existence, the ground of the existence, the modes of it, and the attributes of the supreme being, how can it be conceived that they should come short of the capacity of knowing the differences of things that come within their reach, and their relations to one another and to their common author, and the immutable results of such differences and relations, once supposed to exist, which seem to lie much more within the sphere of their intelligence than those higher truths; especially if we take into the consideration how far men are advanced in the knowledge of the more abstruse and remote truths of geometry and arithmetic and natural philosophy?

But I shall not pursue this subject farther at present. I am only here giving a sketch of those principles of morality which very able men before me have maintained and which I should scarce have presumed to trace after them in public if the present occasion had not called for it. How I have acquitted myself of my undertaking I must leave to the judgment of my reader if any one shall think it worth his while to peruse these papers.

To Britannicus

10 April 1725

Sir:

It was with great pleasure that I read the letter you lately published from Philopatris relating to the *Inquiry into the Original of our Ideas of Beauty and Virtue,* both because in it he recommends to the world a very ingenious treatise and because he professes his design and hopes were to excite the curiosity of men of leisure and inquisitiveness to enter into such subjects, to study the philosophy of virtue and the nature of true religion. And I am the more pleased with his design because I am much afraid that without some study and cultivation the bare moral sense of virtue, which the author of the *Inquiry* very justly observes to be implanted in men, would continue lurking in their breasts without ever exerting itself in any constant and regular course of useful and agreeable products. Without this, it may indeed ferment and annoy them within, but it will never spring up sufficiently to have any lasting and uniform influence on their actions without. It may make them sensible when they are in the wrong, but it will scarce have force enough to prevail upon them to keep themselves always in the right, unless they will afford some time and some pains to consider coolly of it and suffer themselves to feel the weight of the arguments and reasons for it.

And, as nothing seems to me more likely to stir up the attention of mankind to this study than the hearing the different opinions of men on such subjects when they are delivered in a truly philosophical manner and appear to proceed from a real desire of truth without any mixture of contention and cavil, I have taken the liberty to send you my thoughts on this subject, leaving it wholly to your judgment whether they deserve to be conveyed into the world or not.

I could not but be sensibly touched with the noble design of the author of the *Inquiry* to deduce the excellency and obligation of moral actions from one plain and simple principle in nature which he calls a moral sense. And, allowing his principle, his conclusions are most justly and accurately drawn. But when I considered his principle itself more closely, I could not find in it that certainty which principles require. I saw, indeed, there was some such thing in human nature. But I was at a loss to know how it came there and whence it arose. I could not be sure it was not a deceitful and wrong sense. The pleasure arising from the perceptions it afforded did not seem sufficient to convince me that it was right. For I knew that pleasure was very apt in many things to mislead us and was always ready to tinge the objects it was concerned in with false and glaring colors. And I could not see any good reason to trust it more in one case than in another. It appeared to me too uncertain a bottom to venture out upon in the stormy and tempestuous sea of passions and interests and affections.

I wanted, therefore, some further test, some more certain rule, whereby I could judge whether my sense (my moral sense, as the author calls it), my taste of things, was right and agreeable to the truth of things or not. And till I obtained this satisfaction, I could not rest contented with the bare pleasure and delight it gave me. Nay indeed, without this I could not indulge myself in this pleasure without a secret uneasiness arising from my suspicions of its not being right and from a kind of constant jealousy I entertain of every pleasure till I am once satisfied it is a reasonable one.

The perception of pleasure, therefore, which is the description this author has given of his moral sense (p. 106), seems to me not to be a certain enough rule to follow. There must be, I should think, something antecedent to justify it and to render it a real good. It must be a reasonable pleasure before it be a right one or fit to be encouraged or listened to.

If it be so, then it is the reason of the thing and not the pleasure that accompanies it which ought to conduct us. And the first question must always be, "Is the action reasonable; is it fit that I should allow myself to accept of the pleasure it promises me?"

The constitution of all the rational agents that we know of is such indeed that pleasure is inseparably annexed to the pursuit of what is reasonable. And pleasure ought never to be considered as something independent on reason, no more than reason ought to be reckoned unproductive of pleasure. But still, the ideas of reason and right are quite different from those of pleasure and must always in reasoning be considered distinctly; reason as the ground of inward pleasure and that pleasure as the encouragement to follow reason.

Reason and pleasure may both of them be properly enough styled internal sense and, with relation to moral actions, moral senses. But still they must be conceived as different senses; reason as the sense of the agreement or disagreement of our simple ideas or of the combinations of them resulting from their comparison; pleasure as the sense of joy which any ideas afford us.

Now this internal or moral sense, which we call reason, is the rule by which we judge and the only rule we can judge by of truth and falsehood and, in moral actions, of moral good or evil, of what is right or wrong, fit or unfit. And the other internal or moral sense of pleasure or pain, whereby we conceive joy in discerning truth or pain in feeling ourselves embarrassed with falsehood—or, in moral actions, by reflecting upon in ourselves or observing in others moral good or moral evil—is not itself the rule by which we judge or can judge of truth or falsehood, of moral good or evil, but only the consequence of finding that we judge right and according to reason. And this latter sense indeed constitutes our idea of beauty, by which word, I think, we mean no more than what pleases us.

But things do not seem to us to be true or right because they are beautiful or please us, but seem beautiful or please us because they seem to us to be true or right. And always, in our apprehensions of things (I mean those apprehensions of things about which we are now concerned), the reason of the thing or the sense of its being true or right is antecedent to our sense of beauty in it or of the pleasure it affords us.

Thus, in a theorem or problem in geometry we perceive beauty. But we first discern truth or we should never find out any beauty in it. And so in moral science we first conclude that a certain action is right and then it appears to us likewise beautiful. But while we are in any suspense about it and doubt whether it is in itself right or wrong, or if we know it to be wrong, we can never feel any beauty in it. I do not say there is always a distance of time between these two sentiments, viz., of truth or right and beauty. If there is, the perceptions of our mind are often in this case too nimble for us to measure it. But I speak only of the order in which we should consider them and the dependence they have on one another. And in this sense, I say, beauty in the nature of things follows or depends upon our previous apprehension of truth or of right.

It may be said indeed, by way of objection to what I have advanced, that the sense of beauty or pleasure moves faster than the sense of truth or right; that, in particular, the former is immediate upon many moral actions proposed to us, but the latter does not operate but after a long deduction of reasoning which many are incapable of who yet discern beauty and feel pleasure in such actions. But the answer is pretty easy. It is true we often find beauty and pleasure in propositions and actions where there is no truth or right. But then it must be where we imagine we find truth or right in them. In this we may deceive ourselves, but still that deception is the ground of our sense of beauty or pleasure in such a case though it may be a false ground. And if we know or imagine that there is an absence of truth or right, we shall never feel any such sense of beauty or pleasure there. Sometimes we perceive truth or right by a kind of natural penetration and sagacity of the mind before we have stayed to weigh distinctly every one of the steps which lead to it. And then, taking the conclusion for granted, we esteem it beautiful or pleasant.

This may happen to some in the abstruser sciences who have heads perfectly well turned for them. Whenever a proposition is named to them, if it be not of too complex a nature, they shall immediately discern whether it is true or false even before they go through every step of the demonstration. And upon this confidence in their own penetration and sagacity they shall perceive beauty or pleasure in the proposition. And when they enquire further, if they find they judged right, it confirms them in that beauty or pleasure which they conceived from a more partial and slight view and increases it. If they find they judged wrong, the beauty immediately vanishes away and a sentiment of the contrary succeeds. Few, indeed, are capable of such quick perceptions in those kinds of sciences where the conclusions are forced to pass through many steps. But almost all mankind are capable of them in moral science where the conclusion and the premises lie within a narrower compass.

To instance in benevolence. Every man of any degree of understanding who has observed himself and others, immediately with one glance of thought perceives it reasonable and fit that the advantage of the whole should be regarded more than a private advantage or the advantage of a part only of that whole. And taking this quick conclusion for granted even before he has examined every step that conduces to it, he sees beauty in every moral action by which the advantage of the whole is designed—not because it is advantageous or useful to himself or even to the whole, but because he sees or thinks he sees it to be fit and reasonable that the advantage of the whole should take place. And the beauty he apprehends in the action seems to consist in this, that it agrees or seems to agree with what is in itself fit and reasonable. And the more he considers the proposition, viz., that it is fit and reasonable that the advantage of the whole should be preferred, and by proving it feels the truth of it more strongly in his mind, the more he will be confirmed in esteeming benevolence to be beautiful as a disposition conducing to that which is fit and reasonable in itself; and the same as to actions proceeding from that disposition. But if it were possible a mind could be so framed as to feel the contrary to be truth and right, no doubt all the beauty of benevolence or benevolent actions would immediately vanish out of that mind. And I am afraid that men may, by long endeavoring to deceive themselves into this false opinion, bring themselves at last to believe it or at least to imagine they do and by that means destroy in themselves all sense of beauty in benevolence as well as work out by degrees the disposition itself which nature has fixed so deeply in their breasts. But I hope there are few such monsters in human nature or at least that ever arrive at the highest pitch of this depravity.

I do not mean by what I have advanced to diminish the force of the strong motives to virtue arising from the beauty or pleasure which our natural affections make us perceive and feel in morally good actions. I know they are the most successful solicitors to everything that is right and reasonable if duly attended to and not mistaken or misused. And we should be comfortless and forlorn creatures if we had no affections and inward warmth of sentiments to spur us on to what dry reason approves of. But I would not have men depend upon their affections as rules sufficient to conduct them, though they are the proper means to animate them to and support them in such a conduct as reason directs. I would have them search still higher for the foundation and ground of those very motives. And I am persuaded they will find that reason is as necessary to account for them and to justify their effect as it is needful to guide and direct them afterwards.

And I have no small pleasure in observing that all the accurate deductions and reasonings of the author of the *Inquiry* may easily be adapted to the principle here laid down, viz., reason—or our internal sense of truth and falsehood, moral good and evil, right and wrong—accompanied and fortified by another succeeding internal sense of beauty and pleasure, feeling those things which are reasonable and true to be at the same time delightful and, on the reverse, of deformity and pain terrifying us from following after falsehood or giving ourselves up to anything that is unreasonable.

But I find too many thoughts on this subject crowding into my mind to dispose them within the compass of a letter. And therefore, if it be acceptable, I shall take some further opportunity of addressing myself to you. And, in the meanwhile, am

Sir, yours, etc.
Philaretus [Burnet]

Sir:

I send you the following thoughts upon the subject of Philaretus's letter of April 10 and shall study to imitate his gentlemanly and truly philosophical manner of writing on so useful a subject.

There are certain words frequently used in our discourses of morality which, I fancy, when well examined, will lead us into the same sentiments with those of the author of the late *Inquiry into Beauty and Virtue*. The words I mean are these, when we say that actions are reasonable, fit, right, just, conformable to truth. Reason denotes either our power of finding out truth or a collection of propositions already known to be true. Truths are either speculative—as when we discover, by comparing our ideas, the relations of quantities or of any other objects among themselves—or practical—as when we discover what objects are naturally apt to give any person the highest gratifications, or what means are most effectual to obtain such objects. Speculative truth or reason is not properly a rule of conduct; however, rules may be founded upon it. Let us inquire then into practical reason both with relation to the end which we propose and the means.

To a being which acts only for its own happiness, that end is reasonable which contains a greater happiness than any other which it could pursue; and when such a being satisfies itself with a smaller good for itself while a greater is in its power, it pursues an unreasonable end. A being of this temper as to the means would call those reasonable which were effectual to obtain their end with the smallest pain or toil to the agent. With such a being the cruelty of the means, or their bad influence on a community, would never make them pass for unreasonable provided they had no bad influence on his own happiness.

But if there are any beings which by the very frame of their nature desire the good of a community or which are determined by kind affections to study the good of others and have withal a moral sense which causes them necessarily to approve such conduct in themselves or others and count it amiable and to dislike the contrary conduct as hateful, to such beings that end is reasonable which contains the greatest aggregate of public happiness which an agent can procure; and the pursuing of the good of a small party or faction with neglect of more universal good to such natures would seem unreasonable. If these beings have also self-love as well as natural benevolence and a moral sense and at the same time find that their own highest happiness does necessarily arise from kind affections and benevolent actions, that end which would appear reasonable would be universal happiness, the very pursuit of which is supposed to be the greatest happiness to the several agents themselves, for thus both desires are at once gratified as far as they are capable of doing it by their own actions. By such beings as these the means of public good will be counted unreasonable when they occasion evil to the agent greater than the good obtained by them to the public or when other means equally in our power might have obtained the same or an equal public good with less detriment either to the agent himself or to other persons. And in like manner the means of private good will be reputed unreasonable by such beings when they contain a prepollent public evil or a greater evil towards others than is contained in means equally effectual for obtaining the same or equal private good. Under this class of beings the author of the *Inquiry* seems to rank our own species, mankind.

If any one should ask concerning public and private good, 'Which of the two is most reasonable?' the answers would be various, according to the dispositions of the persons who are passing judgment upon these ends. A being entirely selfish and without a moral sense will judge that its own pursuit of its greatest private pleasure is most reasonable. And as to the actions of others, it can see whether the actions be naturally apt to attain the ends proposed by the agents or whether their ends interfere with its own ends or not; but it would never judge of them under any other species than that of advantage or disadvantage and only be affected with them as we are now with a fruitful shower or a destructive tempest. Such a being might have the abstract idea of public good but would never perceive anything amiable in the pursuit of it. The only debate which such a mind could entertain concerning ends would be only this, whether this object or another would conduce most to its own greatest advantage or pleasure.

But if the same question be proposed to beings who have a moral sense of excellence in public affections and a desire of public good implanted in their nature, such beings will answer that it is reasonable that smaller private good should yield to greater public good, and they will disapprove of a contrary conduct. But without this sense and affections I cannot guess at any reason which should make a being approve of public spirit in another farther than it might be the means of private good to itself.

If one should still farther inquire, 'Is there not something absolutely reasonable to any possible mind in benevolence or a study of public goood? Is it not absolutely reasonable that a being who does no evil to others should not be put to pain by others?' It is very probable every man would say that these things are reasonable. But then all mankind have this moral sense and public affections. But if there were any natures disjoined from us who knew all the truths which can be known but had no moral sense nor anything of a superior kind equivalent to it, such natures might know the constitution of our affairs and what public and private good did mean, they would grant that equal intenseness of pleasure enjoyed by twenty was a greater sum of happiness than if it were enjoyed only by one, but to them it would be indifferent whether one or more enjoyed happiness if they had no benevolent affections. Such natures might see from the constitution of our affairs that a social conduct would be the most probable way for each single person of mankind to secure his own happiness in the neighborhood of a set of beings like themselves with social affections and a sense of honor and virtue; but these disjoined natures without a moral sense would see nothing reasonable in the good affections of one man towards another abstractly from considerations of the advantage of the virtue to the virtuous agent. And if this disjoined nature observed such a conjecture wherein a man who had stupified his moral sense so as to be above remorse could with privacy, force, or cunning management furnish himself with the highest pleasures he then could relish at the expense of misery to multitudes, if this disjoined nature had no notion of a good Deity and of a state of future rewards or punishments, it would see perhaps that the conduct of this man was not apt to promote the public good, not the reasonable means for that end; but it would also acknowledge that this was reasonable conduct in the agent in order to obtain private happiness to itself. If there be any other meaning of this word reasonable when applied to actions, I should be glad to hear it well explained and to know for what reason besides a moral sense and public affections any man approves the study of public good in others or pursues it himself antecedently to motives of his own private interest.

What has been said of reasonable and unreasonable may be also applied to that fitness and unfitness of things which some speak of in their moral writings. It is certain that abstracting from the observation or relish and approbation of any other mind some objects are apt or fit to give greater pleasures to the person who enjoys them than others. It is certain also that some means are more effectual to obtain an end than others. In this sense there is a natural fitness and unfitness both in ends and means. Thus one tenor of conduct is naturally more fit among men to promote public good than another; and to men who have a moral sense and public affections a benevolent conduct is more fit to promote the happiness of the agent than the contrary, more fit to engage the favor of a good deity than a malicious conduct. And any mind whatsoever who knew our state and believed a good Deity might perceive this fitness in benevolence to promote both public happiness and that of the agent both in this life and the next. But a mind without a moral sense, although it saw this natural fitness of benevolence to obtain these ends, would never approve of benevolence unless this observing mind had kind affections toward mankind so that the happiness of men were an end agreeable to this mind, or a moral sense did determine it to admire and approve a public spirit wherever it observed it. Without a moral sense, a mind would approve nothing but what was fit for its own ends, although it might also observe what was fit to promote the ends of others. That absolute antecedent fitness in the nature of the things themselves, of which some talk, must either mean this sensation of excellence which we necessarily receive by our moral sense or it is to me perfectly unintelligible, since it is supposed antecedent to any views of private interest or any sanctions of laws; and for public interests, it must be a moral sense or a benevolent instinct which can make any man regard them.

As to the words just, right, and their opposites, unjust and wrong, antecedently to any opinion of laws or views of interest the same may be said of them which was said of the former words, reasonable, fit, and unfit; they seem to have no other meaning but agreeable or disagreeable to a moral sense.

As to another character of actions, viz., agreeable to truth, we know that by custom words or sounds are made signs of ideas and combinations of words signs of judgments. We know that men generally by words express their sentiments and profess to speak, as far as they know, according to what is matter of fact, so that their profession is to speak truth. In like manner we judge of actions; we know what is the usual conduct of men upon certain occasions from the dispositions which we generally imagine to be in mankind, if they have the same opinions of objects which we have and which men generally profess to have. And hence we conclude from a man's acting otherwise that he has either other opinions of objects or other affections than those which we have ourselves and expect to find in other men.

Thus a man who kills another who had done him no harm, by his action declares or gives us occasion to conclude either that he does not take that object which he treats in this manner to be a man or, if he knows what object he acts upon (as we generally imagine he does on such occasions), he declares or gives us ground to conclude that he has not those affections or that moral sense of actions which we generally expect in mankind. So that this disagreeableness to truth in such an action at last must end in a moral sense, unless the person be mad and really have false appearances of objects.

As to these phrases—treating things as they are or according to what they are or are not—they arise from our moral sense. This sense suggests to us what treatment of objects is amiable and what is odious. Virtue or a regard to public good in conformity to this sense is so universally professed by mankind and acknowledged to be the only conduct which they can approve that we say, 'Men do not act suitably to the nature of things who do not pursue public good.' But it is our moral sense of excellence in a public spirit which suggests to us this idea of suitableness of conduct to natures, which suitableness we involve in the particles 'as,' 'according,' and such like. Had we ourselves been wholly selfish and lived in a system of beings wholly selfish without a moral sense in which system we should have had no ground to have expected any regard to the good of each other in our fellows, their doing evil to each other or procuring private pleasure by the pains of multitudes when they had force to do it successfully would have been treating things as they would have been upon this supposition, nor should we have perceived any opposition to truth in such actions.

It were to be wished that writers would guard against, as far as they can, involving very complex ideas under some short words and particles which almost escape observation in sentences, such as 'ought,' 'should,' 'as,' 'according'—nay, sometimes in our English gerunds, 'is to be done,' 'is to be preferred,' and such like. Some writers treat the pronoun 'his' as if it were the sign of a simple idea and yet involve under it the complex ideas of property and of a right to natural liberty, as the Schoolmen made space and time to vanish into nothings by hiding them in the adverbs when and where or by including them in the compound words coexistent, corresponding, etc.

As to Philaretus's letter, he has not happened to observe the author of the *Inquiry's* definition of the moral sense (p. 124) and seems by this means to have misapprehended him in some things.

As to his questions, 'Whence this sense arose?' the author of the *Inquiry* takes it to be implanted by the author of nature. Philaretus wants to be sure that this sense is not deceitful or wrong. If by a wrong or deceitful sense he means a sense which shall make that pleasant for the present which shall have pernicious consequences, the author of the *Inquiry* had attempted to prove that the pleasures of the moral sense are the most lasting and solid in human life. And as he does not profess to give a complete treatise of morality he recommends to us Cumberland and Puffendorf, who show that benevolence and a social conduct are the most probable ways to secure to each individual happiness in this life and the favor of the Deity in any future state to be expected, that so all obstacles to our moral sense and our kind affections, from false views of interest, may be removed. (See p. 251 of the *Inquiry*.)

Philaretus wants to know if this moral sense of something amiable in benevolence be right and reasonable or fit and justifiable. If by these words he means whether the actions which this sense at any time makes him approve shall be always approved as morally good by him, the author tells him that this moral sense and our benevolent affections do make us pursue public good as the end, find our greatest pleasure in such pursuits, and approve of all benevolent actions in others; but then the author also in many places recommends the most serious application of our reason to inquire into the natural tendencies of our actions as the means to attain this end that we may not be led by every slight appearance of particular good to do actions which may have prepollent evil consequences. And this inadvertence he makes one great source of immoral actions which both we ourselves and all others will condemn when we observe the prepollent evil consequences which the agent might have foreseen. (See Art. 8, 9, 10 of the third section, and p. 250, and the whole fourth section.) If he means, 'Will this sense lead me to my own greatest happiness to a constant self-approbation and engage the favor of the Deity if my actions be conformable to this sense according to the best knowledge of the natural tendencies of my actions?' the author partly proves this and partly refers to other writers for what was not to his present design (p. 251). Our moral sense and affections determine our end, but reason must find out the means.

Philaretus thinks that this sense is not a proper rule. The author recommends to moralists to examine also into the state of human affairs to know what course of action will be most effectual to promote public good, the end which our kind affections and moral sense incline us to pursue (p. 253). And if a further rule be necessary, it must come from revelation.

Philaretus fears that 'this bottom is too uncertain to set out upon amidst the storms of our passions and self-interests.' The author suggests that we have benevolent passions as well as selfish and recommends it to moralists to explain, as he partly does himself, how all our selfish affections would conspire, if we understood our own true interest, to persuade us to the same actions which benevolence excites us to and our moral sense determines us to approve. And the author of the *Inquiry* frequently suggests that in the present state of human nature many other additional motives to the study of public good are very necessary besides our moral sense and kind affections. These motives or reasons for pursuing public good and preferring it to private, which he hints at, are such as some way or other may prove that the pursuit of public good does most effectually promote the truest interest of the agent, either as the pursuit of public good is acceptable to the Deity and will be rewarded by him, or as this pursuit gives the agent pleasant reflections upon his own conduct, or as it engages the love, esteem, and mutual good offices of mankind and is withal generally consistent with the highest and truest enjoyment of other pleasures, nay, is the very spirit and life of the most of our pleasures, whereas a contrary temper has all the contrary pernicious effects. We have a perception of moral good and evil, of something amiable or hateful in actions, antecedently to any of these reasons, and yet the author of the *Inquiry* knows no other reasons for virtuous actions; and hence he concludes that our first ideas arise from a sense. All action is designed for some end; if the end be reasonable and the action with all its consequences naturally apt to attain it, the action is reasonable. The end must be either the good of the agent or of the public, or both consistently with each other. Philaretus owns that actions are reasonable, fit, right, etc., without regard to the interest of the agent; they are reasonable, then, with regard to public interests. Now for what reason should the public interest be regarded? What means that 'should'? Is it that this regard to the public is the interest of the agent or that it will be rewarded by the Deity? No, it is fit antecedently. Fit! For what end? For public good or private good? Public good, to be sure, because that the advantage of the whole should take place is fit. Again, fit for what end? Not for private but public good. Why should I in my actions regard public good? For what reason? Why, it is fit for public good that I should do so. In this circle we must run until we acknowledge the first original of our moral ideas to be from a sense or, which is to the same purpose, till we acknowledge that they arise from a determination by the author of nature, which necessitates our minds to approve of public affections and of consulting the good of others. And then we have room enough for our reason to direct us in that tenor of action which shall produce the greatest and most extensive good in our power and to confirm our public spirit by motives of self-interest and to prove it to be reasonable in that sense. I mistake Philaretus very much from his letter if his zeal for the reasonableness of virtue does not flow from a lively moral sense and very noble affection,

And am his and your most obedient, obliged servant,
Philanthropus [Hutcheson]

31 July 1725

Sir,

When I read Philanthropus's letter in the journals of the 12th and the 19th of June, I was mighty glad to meet with a person of his ingenuity and candor so willing and so able to examine my sentiments of things. And as I conceive no small hopes, by his means, to be either convinced that I am in the right by hearing all that he has to say against my opinion, I shall beg the favor of you—if you judge it proper—to convey these speculations to him by publishing them to the world.

I entirely agree with him as to the method he proposes in arguing on these subjects, viz., to examine into the meaning of the words used in our discourses of morality. And therefore, I will immediately define what I mean by the words which Philanthropus mentions, viz., reasonable, fit, right, just, conformable to truth, that we may see whether they stand for the same ideas with him that they do with me, and that if they do not, we may agree what ideas they shall stand for.

By 'reason' I understand, strictly speaking, that method of thinking whereby the mind discovers such truths as are not self-evident by the intervention of self-evident truths and such truths as are less evident by such as are already supposed to be more so. The perception of evident truths is knowledge which is, therefore, acquired and improved by reasoning, i.e., by connecting remote or less evident truths with self-evident or more evident ones. All propositions which we perceive as true, whether immediately or by the means of other intermediate perceptions, we call truths. They are all, strictly speaking, speculative, i.c., they are seen and perceived by the mind. But when such truths are relative to the actions of rational agents they are in common usage styled practical truths. And they are always the conclusions made from those which, by way of distinction, are called speculative truths. Speculative truths are not themselves rules of action, but only the practical truths or conclusions drawn from them. The instance which Philanthropus gives of practical truth, according to these definitions, seems rather to belong to speculative truth. For the discovering what objects are naturally apt to give any person the highest gratifications, or what means are most effectual to obtain such objects, is discovering the same species of truth with the relations of quantities or of any other objects among themselves, both speculative truths or theorems. But the inferring from thence in what manner persons are obliged to act toward such objects, or what means they are obliged to employ in order to obtain them, would be the discovering practical truths properly so called. 'Reasonable' signifies the result of employing reason. But this is in a less proper and strict sense. When, again, the word reason is used to denote a collection of propositions already known to be true, it is likewise improperly and figuratively used and means no more than reasonable or the result of reasoning.

Now I think it will plainly follow from this definition of the word reasonable, if it be a right one, that the reasonableness of the ends of moral agents does not depend on their conformity to the natural affections of the agent nor to a moral sense representing such ends as amiable to him, but singly on their conformity to reason. Reason would always represent the end in the same manner to the rational agent, whatever his affections or inward sense of amiableness were. And supposing a being framed so as to have only selfish affections and yet to be endued with a faculty of reasoning, such a being, if he employs that faculty, must see it to be highly unreasonable that his private interest or pleasure should take place to the destruction of the interest or pleasure of all other beings like himself, though for want of kind affections he would be void of any collateral disposition to act in that manner which to his understanding must necessarily appear reasonable. Nay, such a being would perceive his natural affections to be very unreasonable affections. I do not believe, indeed, he could possibly have a sense of amiableness in a conduct agreeable to such affections, because it seems absurd that anything should appear amiable to a rational creature which so evidently contradicted reason. But if he could be supposed to have such a sense, it would be a sense as unreasonable as his affections were. And neither of them, nor both together, could possibly render a conduct pursuant to them reasonable.

That which perhaps may be apt to mislead us in this point is that we find in fact, it is always reasonable to act according to natural affection and the moral sense. And thence we may too hastily conclude that such a conduct is reasonable for this reason, because our natural affections and moral sense move us to it. But, if we examine more closely, I believe we shall find the reverse to be the truth, viz., that we deem our affections and our moral sense to be reasonable affections, and a reasonable sense, from their prompting us to the same conduct which reason approves and directs. And thus, reason is the measure of the goodness or badness of our affection and moral sense and, consequently, of the actions flowing from them, and not vice versa.

Philanthropus acknowledges that every man would say that benevolence, or a study of the public good, is absolutely reasonable to any possible mind. But he thinks they would say so only because all mankind have a moral sense and public affections. And he thinks they would not say so if they had not, but would be indifferent.

I agree with him that they would be indifferent as to any affection they would feel toward others, disposing them to do or to wish them any good. But they would not, they could not, be indifferent as to perceiving it reasonable that the public good should be preferred to private good and, consequently, that it was in itself reasonable that every rational agent should study the public good. They would not only see the speculative truth that an equal intenseness of pleasure enjoyed by twenty was a greater sum of happiness than if it were enjoyed only by one. But they would likewise see this practical truth to be the consequence of it, 'that it was therefore reasonable that the happiness of the twenty should be considered preferably by all rational agents to the happiness of the one, where all things else were supposed equal and there were no peculiar circumstances to justify a distinction.'

And it is from this perception of the reasonableness of regarding the happiness of many more than the happiness of a few that we discern and admire the wisdom of our maker in implanting social and public affections in his creatures to be subservient to this wise and reasonable end. Whereas if we had not this previous apprehension of reasonableness antecedent to and independent on any affections or sense of them, we could not judge it to be more wise or reasonable to have bestowed such social affections on men than to have given them only selfish affections prompting them to take care of themselves alone without any respect to the cruelty of the means or the bad influence on a community. In short, without such a previous apprehension of what is reasonable in itself, all conceivable constitutions of creatures would have been equally wise, which is evidently absurd.

'Reasonable,' therefore, when said of actions or of the ends of rational agents, denotes the agreeableness of those actions and those ends, not to the natural affections of such agents, not to a moral sense rendering the compliance with those affections amiable, but to reason only. And those affections, as well as that moral sense, are themselves denominated reasonable when they move us to such actions or ends as reason prescribes to us and directs us to; and they must be styled unreasonable if they diverted us from them or disposed us to the contrary.

The next word, fit, is a relative word expressing the relation of means to an end. And, therefore, an absolute antecedent fitness in the nature of things, meaning thereby antecedent to any end, either existing or in supposition, is absolute nonsense. But when moralists speak of antecedent fitness, they mean only antecedent to the actual constitution of things and fit upon supposition of certain circumstances existing which, perhaps, may never really exist. As, for instance, if never any creatures had been produced it would nevertheless have been always antecedently true that, if they should ever be so and so constituted, it would be fit that they should act toward one another in such and such a manner. For upon supposition that the perfectly wise and good author of nature should produce any rational agents, it was always antecedently fit that they should use the best means to happiness, since their happiness must be the chief end for which the wise and good author would bring them into being. And further, supposing they should be framed with natural affections leading to this end, it was likewise antecedently fit that they should exercise those affections and follow their motions, not barely because they are supposed to have such affections (for that consideration alone discovers no end, and consequently no fitness), but because they are supposed to have such affections leading to such an end. It is not fit that they should perform such offices barely because they have such affections. But because it was antecedently fit that they should perform such offices, it was likewise fit that they should be endued with such affections. And for the same reason it was fit that they should exert those affections when they have them.

This explanation of the word fit may easily clear up that seeming circle which Philanthropus observes in arguing upon this proposition, 'It is fit that the advantage of the whole should take place.' Fit, says he, for what end? Not for private, but public good. Now, indeed, to argue that it is fit for public good, that public good should take place is arguing in a circle and proving nothing. But, if we consider that when we say, 'It is fit that public good should be regarded,' the end to which the fitness there relates is not public good considered barely in itself, but the wise and good end of the creator to render all his creatures as happy as their constitution will admit of, then it will be no circle to argue that the regard of public good is a fit means for obtaining this wise and good end of the creator. If the question be, 'Why should I in my actions regard public good?' the proper and first answer is, 'Because it is the fit means of obtaining the public good that every constituent member of the public should regard it.' But if it be further demanded, 'Why ought the public good to be sought after?' then the right answer is, 'Because it is fit for the accomplishing the wise end of our creator to make all his creatures happy that it should be so.' And if it be further urged, 'Why is that end to be regarded?' the answer is, 'Because it is a wise and reasonable end.'

Indeed, the fitness of means to an end lays no obligation but as the end is reasonable. And therefore, when moralists say that any thing is antecedently fit, they always suppose the end to be reasonable. Means may be very apt to promote a very unreasonable end. But in a moral sense of the word, such means would never be said to be fit and far less to constitute such an antecedent fitness as moralists speak of in their writings. I will trouble you with what remains next week, and am,

Yours, etc.
Philaretus.

7 August 1725

Sir:

The next to be considered is the word right, which denotes nothing more in effect than reasonable, only taking it for granted that reason represents to us the nature of things truly as it is.

The word just denotes only right applied specially to what we owe to other persons. And therefore what has been said of the word reasonable may be applied to these words right and just.

The expression 'agreeable to truth,' when used with respect to actions, is to the same effect with 'agreeable to reason.' For though truth, meaning thereby such propositions as express the nature of things as it is, is the real foundation of all moral good or evil, yet as this truth must be apprehended by the agent before it can be a rule for his actions, so truth considered as a rule to act by, i.e., moral truth, is the same with reason or what reason dictates. And acting agreeably to truth can mean no more than acting agreeably to our knowledge of it, i.e., to reason, for reason leads us to that knowledge. Reason informs us how things are, as far as it goes. And if we treat things not as our reason tells us they are but as our reason tells us they are not, we act contrary to our apprehension of truth or to moral truth and, acting therein perversely, become morally evil agents, whereas if we act the reverse, we are denominated morally good agents. Acting contrary to our natural affections does not immediately render us morally evil agents nor acting agreeably to them morally good agents, because our affections do not of themselves immediately inform us how things are or are not. But immediately the acting agreeably or disagreeably to them may denominate us morally good or morally evil as those affections are indications of the will and design of our creator and as the acting in opposition to his will is acting as if he had not been our benefactor and as if we owed him no return of gratitude and obedience. And further, the thwarting our natural affections may constitute us morally evil agents as being in effect the denying that we have such affections by acting as if we had them not. And in this case, the moral evil will consist in acting contrary to this truth, that we have such affections. But still all this supposes these affections to be good, right, reasonable affections. For if they are not so, then the thwarting them will not render us evil but good agents.

For in that case, reason would be a much surer indication of the will and design of our creator than the affections can be, and the acting as if we had not natural evil affections would render us morally good agents.

But, as such a supposition of natural evil affections can only be put for argument's sake and can never really exist, it being impossible that a wise and good Being should give his creatures a natural bias to evil, the conclusions from reason and from natural affection duly examined will always be the same. For the natural affections, and the moral sense attending them, are so ordered by the author of nature, that they coincide with the dictates of reason. And therefore whatever follows from the consideration of their movements will likewise follow from a due attention to the discoveries of truth which our reason will open to us. The only difference is that the one is a sufficient principle to argue from, the other is not. For when in the regress of the analysis, as I may call it, we arrive at natural affections or a moral sense accompanying them and take them for our ultimate principle, we do not feel sufficient satisfaction to make any demonstrative conclusion from them. Whereas, when we go back to reason in our investigation, i.e., when we resolve the propositions into self-evident or evident truths, then we find no further doubt in our minds but meet with a principle which we cannot but acquiesce in. In one case we still leave our principle to be proved. In the other, we reach a principle which is self-evident or certainly demonstrable. When we have observed certain natural affections in ourselves, the question still remains whether these natural affections are good or evil, right or wrong, i.e., agreeable to reason or disagreeable to it, which requires further proof to determine it. But when we rest our foot upon such truths as are evident or demonstrated, we leave nothing unproved but arrive at as much certainty as we are capable of and can go no farther.

Thus I have examined all the terms which Philanthropus proposes. And, as I understand them, they would lead me to look upon reason as that which alone discovers and delivers to us the proper rule and measure of action as that which lays the proper and indeed, strictly speaking, the only obligation upon us to act in a certain manner, since we are always self-condemned whenever we contradict its conclusions and directions. And as for all those natural affections, whether social or selfish, which the author of our nature has interwoven in our frame, all the consequent relishes and tastes which he has enduced us with, they are indeed additional motives to right acting, as they render our duty pleasant and comfortable to us and the contrary displeasing and comfortless; they render us the more inexcusable in departing from the rules of reason since they were given us to promote the observance of them. But they can never fix upon us any proper and strict obligation farther than as they are made objects of reason and furnish us with topics to reason from and are found to agree with reason.

And I believe, if we consider the matter closely, we shall find that we cannot so much as form an idea of obligation without introducing reason as its foundation. Supposing we have natural affections disposing us to certain action, how are we obliged to comply with such dispositions? Why, because it is reasonable to do so. Have we a moral sense or relish for such actions and dispositions? How are we at all obliged to consult our own interest or pleasure? Are we not at liberty to give up that interest or pleasure? No, it is unreasonable to do it. We are self-condemned if we do it in such and such cases. And therefore we are obliged in such cases not to do it. In short, all sort of obligation to anything implies some reason to give it force, without which it is a mere phantom of the imagination.

Philanthropus thinks I have not happened to observe the author of the *Inquiry's* definition of the moral sense (p. 124) and that I have by this means misapprehended him in something. If I have, I shall be extremely glad to be set right. But I think I have all along understood him to mean by his moral sense, as he defines it, a determination of our minds to receive amiable or disagreeable ideas of actions when they occur to our observation antecedently to any opinions of advantage or loss to redound to ourselves from them. That there is such a sense implanted in us by the author of our nature, I make no question. I believe every one may feel it in himself. And when I asked, 'Whence this sense arose?' I did not mean to express any doubt about its existence, but only to signify the necessity of inquiring into the original of it in order to determine whether it was a right sense or not; by which I meant whether it prompted us to right actions or to judge rightly of actions or not, and whether the actions or agents in which it delighted or to which it was averse were really morally good or morally evil in themselves; the test of which inquiry I took to be reason and that this sense was good or bad, right or wrong, as it agreed or disagreed with reason and not reason as it agreed or disagreed with this sense. As to Philanthropus's admonition against squeezing too much meaning into some short words and particles by which means the crowded sense often passes almost unobserved in the sentence, I think it very just and have endeavored to avoid that fault in writing this as much as I could.

I am persuaded that Philanthropus is no more an enemy to the reasonableness of virtue than I am to the amiableness of it. But the question at present is, 'From what principle moral obligation is to be deduced and what it is that immediately denominates actions and agents morally good or morally evil?' In which inquiry I shall always be glad of, as I shall be ever ready to receive, further information from so ingenious a writer as Philanthropus.

I am, sir, his and your
obliged humble servant,
Philaretus.

9 October 1725

Sir:

After hearty thanks to Philaretus for engaging me in a further inquiry into the foundation of virtue, please to communicate to him these thoughts on his letters of 31 July and August 7.

Our debate is drawn into narrower bounds by his reducing ultimately all other moral attributes of actions to reasonableness or conformity to truth. I allow his definitions, nor do I apprehend he would have disallowed my instance of practical truth had he defined the word obligation.

The reasonableness of an action or its conformity to truth or the power of finding out truth, I fancy, needs further explication. True propositions may be made concerning all objects, good or evil; there must be a conformity between every true proposition and its object; if then all conformity between an object and a truth be goodness, all objects must be good. If there be any particular kind of conformity which constitutes moral goodness, I wish it were explained and distinguished from that conformity between every object of our knowledge and the truths which we know.

In every truth some attribute is affirmed or denied of its subject. In truths about actions some attribute is affirmed or denied of actions. Whatever attribute is affirmed of any action, the contrary attribute may be as truly affirmed of the contrary action or omission. Both these propositions shall be true and their objects, viz., the actions, shall be conformable to them. If then this conformity be moral goodness, the most contrary actions shall both be good, being both conformable to their several truths. This conformity then cannot denominate the one good more than the other. It must be some other attribute which can be ascribed to one and not to the other which must make the distinction and not the agreeing with a truth; for any one may make as many truths about villainy as about heroism by ascribing to it the contrary attributes.

But not to pass over this debate with a logical or metaphysical argument. When we ask the reason of an action, we sometimes mean the truth which excites the agent to it by showing that it is apt to gratify some inclination of his mind. Thus, why does a sensual man pursue wealth? The reason in this meaning of the word is this truth, viz., wealth is useful to purchase pleasures. At other times by the reason of actions we mean the truth which shows a quality in the action of any person engaging the approbation either of the agent or the spectator or which shows it to be morally good. Thus, why do I observe the contracts I have made? The reason is this, mutual observation of contracts is necessary to preserve society. The former reasons, after Grotius, I call exciting reasons; the latter, justifying reasons.

Now Philaretus seems to me to maintain that there is some exciting reason to virtue, antecedent to all kind affections or instinct toward the good of others, and that in like manner there are some justifying reasons or truths antecedent to any moral sense causing approbation. The author of the *Inquiry*, I apprehend, must maintain that desires, affections, instincts must be previous to all exciting reasons and a moral sense antecedent to all justifying reasons.

The exciting reasons are such as show an action to be fit to attain its end. But nothing can be an end previous to all desires, affections, or instincts determining us to pursue it. They must then be previous to all exciting reasons or truths, unless we say that there may be exciting reasons to actions where no end is intended or that ends are intended previously to all desire or affection.

But are there not exciting reasons even antecedent to any end moving us to propose one end rather than another? To this Aristotle long ago answered that there are ultimate ends not desired with a view to anything further and subordinate ends desired with a view to something further. There are exciting reasons, or truths about subordinate ends showing their tendency toward the ultimate end; but as to the ultimate ends, there is no truth or reason exciting us to pursue them. Were there exciting reasons for all ends, there could be no ultimate end, but we should desire one thing for the sake of another in an infinite series.

Thus ask a being who has selfish affections why he pursues wealth. He will assign this truth as his exciting reason, that wealth furnishes pleasures or happiness. Ask again why he desires his own happiness or pleasure. I cannot divine what proposition he would assign as the reason moving him to it. This is indeed a true proposition, there is a quality in his nature moving him to pursue happiness; but it is this quality or instinct in his nature which moves him and not this proposition. Just so this is a truth, that a certain medicine cures an ague; but it is not a proposition which cures the ague, nor is it any reflection or knowledge of our own nature which excites us to pursue happiness.

If this being have also public affections, what are the exciting reasons for observing faith or hazarding his life in war? He will assign this truth as a reason, such conduct tends to the good of mankind. Go a step further, why does he pursue the good of mankind? If his affections be really disinterested, without any selfish view, he has no exciting reason; the public good is an ultimate end to this series of desires.

When Philaretus to evade a circle brings in the end of the Deity as a reason of pursuing public good, if he means an exciting reason, let him express the truth exciting men to pursue the end proposed by the Deity. Is it this, no creature can be happy who counteracts it? This is a reason of self-love exciting all who consider it. But again, what reason excites men to pursue their own happiness? Here we must end in an instinct. Is this the truth, the Deity is my benefactor? I ask again the reason exciting to love or obey benefactors. Here again we must land in an instinct. Is this the truth, the end of the Deity is a reasonable end? I ask again, what is the truth, a conformity to which makes the desire of public good reasonable in the Deity? What truth either excites or justifies the Deity in this desire? As soon as I hear a pertinent proposition of this kind, I shall recant all I have said. If the exciting reason of men's complying with the Deity be this truth, men are obliged to comply or it is their duty, then we are excited because we are obliged or bound in duty and not because it is reasonable so to do or because it is conformable to a truth. For this also is a truth, disobedience is contrary to obligation; yet no body imagines that conformity to this truth either makes disobedience morally good or excites to pursue it. But whoever will define the words oblige, owe, duty will find himself at as great a loss for ultimate exciting reasons, previous to affections, as ever.

In like manner, where he says that to a being void of public affections, the pursuing the happiness of twenty rather than his own is reasonable, I want to know the truth exciting such a nature to pursue it. Sure it is not this, that the sum of twenty felicities is a greater quantity than any one of them. For unless by a public affection the happiness of others be made desirable to him, the prospect of a great sum in the possession of others will never excite him more than the knowledge of this truth, that one hundred equal stones are a greater bulk than one, will excite a man who had no desire of heaps to cast them together.

If Philaretus intended in these two last cases justifying reasons, then it leads to the next part of our debate about justifying reasons. The true way of deciding it is not a frequent assertion that we approve actions antecedently to a sense but producing the very truths for conformity to which we approve actions ultimately. Here the former argument might be repeated, that we may form true propositions concerning all sorts of actions, good or evil; each sort of action is conformable to the truths formed concerning it; this conformity, then, cannot distinguish good actions from evil. But to pass this argument.

Philaretus owns that truths which only show an action to be fit to attain its end do not justify it. The justifying truths must be about the ends themselves. Now what are the justifying truths about ultimate ends? What is the truth for conformity to which we approve the desire of public good as an end or call it a reasonable end? Is it this, public good is a reasonable end? This amounts to a very trifling argument, viz., it is reasonable because it is reasonable. Is it this one, this desire excites to actions which really do promote public happiness? Then for conformity to what truth do men approve the promoting of public happiness? Is it this truth, public happiness includes that of the agent? This is only an exciting reason to self-love. Is this the justifying truth, public happiness is the end of the Deity? The question returns, what truth justified concurrence with the Divine ends? Is it this, the Deity is our benefactor? Then what truth justified concurrence with benefactors? Here we must end in a sense. Or shall we assign this reason, concurrence with the Divine ends is morally good because those ends are reasonable ends? Then what is the reason or truth for conformity to which we call the Divine ends reasonable? They are not good or conformable to reason because he wills them to be so. Here I own I must ultimately resolve all approbation into a moral sense as I was forced to resolve all exciting reasons into instincts.

Philaretus often insinuates two objections, first, there must be some antecedent standard by which we judge the affections or moral senses themselves to be right or wrong. As to affections, we judge of them ultimately by the moral sense according as they are kind or malicious. But as to the moral sense itself, it can no more be called morally good or evil than we call the sense of tasting sweet or bitter. Each person judges the sense of others by his own. But no man can immediately judge of his own moral sense or sense of tasting whether they be right or wrong. Reason may show men that their moral sense, as it is now constituted, tends to make the species happy and that a contrary sense would have been pernicious, and therefore we may by a metonymy call it happy as we call our taste healthy when it leads us to delight in objects tending to our health.

The other objection is this, that if there is no moral standard antecedent to a sense, then all constitutions of senses had been alike good and reasonable in the Deity. To this it may be answered that we can conceive no exciting reasons of the divine actions antecedent to something in the divine nature of a nobler kind corresponding to our kindest and sweetest affections by which the Deity desires universal happiness as an end. The divine wisdom did, no doubt, suggest the implanting of such a sense in men to be the fittest means of obtaining this end. The justifying reasons of the divine actions, when we judge of them, must end in our moral sense which makes us approve such a kind, beneficent constitution of our nature. Had we wanted a moral sense, yet the Deity might have judged of his own actions as he does now, but we should have had no moral ideas either concerning the Deity or ourselves. Our reason might have suggested indeed that if the Deity did study our happiness as an end, the omitting to give us such a sense if we could have had an idea of it was omitting the proper means for obtaining his end. But moral good or evil would have been to us unknown.

I am his and your
very humble servant,
Philanthropus

27 November 1725

Sir:

If you are not already tired with this debate yourself I would by your means presume once more on Philanthropus's patience and beg you to convey these thoughts to him in answer to his last letter of Oct. 9.

He observes rightly that the argument is drawn into narrower bounds and seems willing to put the issue of the whole upon this single question, whether or no there are reasons previous to all desires, affections, instincts, or any moral sense arising from them.

The question then is whether truth, apprehended by our reason, is the principle from which we must argue to prove anything to be morally good or evil, or whether our desires, affections, instincts, and a moral sense attending them distinct from the faculty of reason compose that principle.

Philanthropus thinks truth cannot be the principle, because we may form true propositions concerning all sorts of actions, good and evil, and each sort of action is conformable to the truths formed concerning it, and therefore this conformity cannot distinguish good actions from evil. But upon this principle, all objects must be good, and the most contrary actions shall be both good. This is the substance of his logical or metaphysical argument.

But he, by a great mistake here, puts the conformity or agreeing with a truth, i.e., any one single truth, for the conformity with truth as truth signifies the true state and connection and relation of things taken all together. For, when it is said that moral goodness consists in the acting in conformity to truth, the meaning is not that it consists in a conformity to any one single and detached true proposition but to the whole chain and compages of truth in acting agreeably to the state and connection and mutual relation of things.

For instance, though it is a true proposition that such an action gives me pleasure, yet it may not be a morally good action because it may contradict and interfere with other truths, as that, though it pleases me, it hurts another; and that the nature of that other requires pleasure as well as mine; or that, though it gratifies me for the present, it may probably be followed by pain afterwards; and the like; and because it may be contradictory to the nature and constitution of things, which is the chain and series of truth.

But not to dwell longer on this logical or metaphysical objection, which is entirely founded upon his mistaking the sole idea which is annexed to the word truth in this question. I shall proceed to examine his moral objections.

Philanthropus divides reasons for actions, after Grotius, into two sorts, exciting reasons and justifying reasons. And I am willing to follow him in this partition, though in truth the exciting reason to an action and the justifying reason for it ought always to be the same in substance and should only differ in the form of putting them. The exciting reason should amount to this in order to be a valid reason, this action is right, therefore I will do it; and the justifying reason, it was right, therefore I did right in doing it.

But the dispute is what method we are to take to prove that this action is, or was, right.

Now this I would prove from its conformity to the nature and constitution of things, about which I form in my mind certain true propositions and thence call it truth. And in this disquisition I would take into consideration my own nature, the nature of things without me, and my relation to them and theirs to me. And under this head all natural desires, affections, passions, appetites, instincts, relishes, and senses both in myself and others come to be examined as indications of the condition and end of nature. And when from all these considerations I find certain true propositions resulting concerning the nature of things, then moral goodness, I say, consists in acting agreeably to those true propositions and moral badness in acting disagreeably to them.

But Philanthropus thinks this point may be proved singly from the ends which our desires and affections propose to us and from a moral sense or taste approving of what is agreeable to them, wherein I think he wants ground to rest upon. He esteems that to be the whole proof which seems to me but a branch of the reasoning and the quarry whence we are to fetch some of the materials which help us in examining those propositions which are the foundations of our rules for acting.

He proceeds to sustain his own and overturn the contrary opinion by this principle, that there can be no exciting reason to an ultimate end. In which I agree with him and Aristotle. But the very point in question is, what is, or ought to be, the ultimate end of action. And the greatest part of moral goodness consists in choosing a right ultimate end. He who proposes his pleasure as his ultimate end can scarce be a very good man, whereas he who makes truth his ultimate end can scarce be a bad man. He acts like a rational creature and does not desire or wish that truth may lie on this side or that side of the question but studiously and sincerely pursues it whithersoever it leads him.

The question is not what is seen in experience to lead men to act. I confess their passions and affections generally do lead them. And it is their happiness and the wisdom of their creator that they have such affections and passions as naturally tend, till they corrupt them, to produce in many instances the same effects which reason both dictates before and approves afterwards. But still it is reason alone which informs us beforehand that such actions would be right as well as afterwards that such actions were right. And of this indeed I think there can be no doubt to anyone who has ever felt reason working in his breast.

Philanthropus observes that to avoid a circle I bring in the end of the Deity. But I must remind him that this was only under the definition of the word fit which, being a relative word respecting some end or other, must have a correlative answering it, whereas the words true, reasonable, right are absolute and not relative terms and therefore need no correlate. Now I said if we form this proposition, 'It is fit the public good should be regarded,' it must be fit for the attaining some end. And this fitness is a moral fitness and right in itself, if the end be a wise and reasonable end. I mentioned that Deity not as meaning that this end was wise because it was the end of Deity, but because all ends must subsist in some intelligent agent and the Deity is an intelligent agent who is perfectly wise and always proposes wise ends to himself.

Philanthropus proceeds to ask, 'What is the truth exciting men to pursue the end proposed by the Deity?' And he offers me my choice of several truths which, though they are all very weighty truths, yet are not those I should choose to build upon in this argument. The single truth I would pitch upon is, 'Because the end is a reasonable end.' And the truth which makes this end, viz., public good or happiness, a reasonable end is that it is best that all should be happy. This is the truth a conformity to which makes the desire of public good reasonable in the Deity and, I add, in all rational creatures who would imitate the wisdom and goodness of the Deity.

If anyone asks why it is best, I would answer him as I would do if he asked me why four is more than two. It is self-evident. I should be sorry indeed to argue, as Philanthropus afterwards puts it, that public good is a reasonable end because it is a reasonable end. I should think it sufficient to prove it to be best and should not be afraid of affirming it to be reasonable to pursue what is best. The only point is to prove what is best. And this can only be done by considering and examining by reason, not feeling by instinct or sense, how the matter of fact stands and what is actually best in itself. Just as when I am examining whether I ought to assent to a proposition, I would not say, 'It is true because it is true,' but would consider the evidence of it and, if I perceived it to be true, would assent to it.

The self-evident truth then, that it is in itself best that all should be happy, is immediately perceivable by all rational natures. But the question of fact, wherein that best consists, makes the difference of more or less moral goodness in intelligent agents, according to the greater or narrower extent of their knowledge considered together with their disposition to act and, in fact, acting agreeably to their knowledge and also using the means to acquire and improve that knowledge. In this the all-knowing author of nature, being infallible and unchangeable, he is most perfectly good in a moral sense. Inferior beings are more or less capable of being so proportionably to their capacity of knowledge and are, in fact, morally good or evil as they act according to, or contrary to, that knowledge which they are possessed of or may acquire.

But that which I fancy misleads Philanthropus in this point is that by exciting he means exciting as the passions and affections do by giving us uneasiness when we do not follow their movements, which is indeed a guard to our virtue but not the ground of it, whereas by reason's exciting I mean only its proposing an action to us as most eligible and right, which, though it may be attended with pleasure or uneasiness from an additional moral sense, yet is distinct from it and not dependent upon it. And on the same ground he often confounds a thing's being desirable to us with its being esteemed reasonable by us, whereas men often desire what they think and are conscious is very unreasonable and know that to be very reasonable which they by no means desire. For which I appeal to the common experience of mankind.

What I have said about exciting reasons may be easily applied to all that Philanthropus demands concerning justifying reasons, and therefore I need not consume the time in doing it nor mistrust the judgment of my readers so far. But I may possibly say more on this head if ever I come to examine Philanthropus's answers to the two objections, which he says I often insinuate.

I shall conclude at present with giving my meaning of the word obligation, since Philanthropus desires it more than once, though I thought I had in effect done it in my last.

Obligation is a word of a Latin original signifying the action of binding which, therefore, in a moral sense (for the question here is not about corporal force), must import the binding an intelligent agent by some law, which can be no other than that of reason. For all other ties are reducible to this, and this is primary and reducible to no other principle. I find I can thwart my desires and affections and yet approve what I do in contradiction to them. I can approve of actions by a moral sense and yet, upon examination by reason, rectify that sense as I can my external senses and condemn what it approved. But my reason I can never contradict but it flies in my face; I stand self-condemned and bring myself in guilty though all the earth should acquit me. And I never heartily comply with its dictates but I acquit myself, though all the world should condemn me. And I do not find that desire or affection or passion or any kind of sensation has any influence in the case except it be to increase or diminish pleasure and self-complacency as we comply with or reject the dictates of reason and are thereby a kind of natural rewards and punishments or, perhaps, to extenuate our guilt and excuse us in some degree on the strength and violence of the temptation.

I am, sir, yours, etc.
Philaretus

25 December 1725

Sir:

I would fain, methinks, clear the account I have in several former letters given of the basis and groundwork of true virtue from all seeming and plausible difficulties. And therefore I now beg leave to conclude by examining the answers which Philanthropus gives to the two objections he says I often insinuate.

The first objection is that there must be a standard to judge of the affections and moral sense themselves whether they are right or wrong.

To this Philanthropus returns for answer that, 'We judge of the affections by the moral sense. But as to the moral sense itself, it can no more be called morally good or evil than we call the sense of tasting sweet or bitter. No man can immediately judge of his own moral sense or sense of tasting whether they be right or wrong.'

Now the question is not whether the moral sense can be called morally good or evil, which I admit it cannot, properly and strictly speaking, because moral good and evil belong to agents and their actions, not to affections or inclinations. For the person chooses and his action arises from his own choice, and therefore he is accountable. But his affection or inclination or sense is implanted in him and not in his own power, and therefore he is not accountable either for having it or for wanting it; and consequently it has nothing moral in it, since morality implies the being accountable and answerable and cannot take place where force is used or power is wanting. A man is no more a morally good man for being made affectionate than for being made hungry when his stomach is craving. But as hunger prompts us to eat when the machine requires repair where perhaps reason might forget or neglect it were it left to itself, so natural affection and the sentiments belonging to it urge us to render good offices to others which our reason, though it approves them and even proposes them to our thoughts as the best things we can do, yet might be too slack and remiss in stirring us to perform them without such indefatigable solicitors continually prompting us. But still the doing such good offices is a morally good action not because affection or sentiment inclines us so (for then cruelty, in case a cruel affection or sentiment was natural to us, would be morally good, too), but because our mind perceives it to be best to do so, perceiving immediately and intuitively this truth, that it is best that the species should be happy; and deducing this further truth by reason, that benevolence is the properest and fittest means to procure the happiness of the species.

But the true question is whether the moral sense may be called right or wrong or not. For we grant it cannot be properly called morally good or evil. And this it certainly may, as well as any other sense. It is not parallel to the calling the sense of tasting sweet or bitter, as Philanthropus has wrongly put it and in doing so directly begs the question. For sweet and bitter are on all hands allowed to be denominations of sensations but of particular distinct sensations, whereas we deny that moral good and evil are at all denominations of dispositions and actions of agents. But it is exactly parallel to the calling the sense of tasting right or wrong.

Now this we certainly may do, and in fact very frequently do, in this and all other senses, internal as well as external. We judge any sense to be wrong, or vitiated, when it represents things otherwise than we know it would do if we were in a right state of body. And even in our best state, our senses often deceive us and are, or may be, rectified by our reason, a truth so well known to all natural philosophers that I need not spend time in proving it. In the same manner the moral sense must be esteemed wrong, or vitiated, where it contradicts our reason in which the health and vigor of the mind consists. If all men were naturally selfish and ill-natured to others and by any internal sense found delight in reflecting on actions conformable to such a malign affection, still all men endued with reason and employing their reason in examining such things must perceive it to be a wrong sense that relished such actions, a sense which represented things very differently from what they really were. And it would be as ill reasoning to conclude from such a vitiated internal sense the moral goodness or badness of an action as it would be to conclude the true taste or color of a body, that is, what sensation of tasting or seeing it would give us in a right habit of body, from the taste or color which a fever or a jaundice makes it put upon us. But, as in the external senses our reason must be the test to inform us whether they are perfect in their kind or defective and vitiated, so it is likewise in the internal senses. And without this standard of reason to recur to, all senses would be equally right merely because they were senses, which we know is contrary to fact.

But I think Philanthropus here gives the point up in effect

himself. For he admits that reason may show men that their moral sense, as it is now constituted, tends to make the species happy and that a contrary sense would have been pernicious. Why, if this be allowed, we have the greatest truth we wanted and the most complex and difficult to be demonstrated. And one truth more, and that a self-evident one, will afford us a solid bottom on which the whole structure of morality may safely rest. And that is that it is better that the species should be happy than that it should not. This is such an unmoveable truth that it will bear all the weight we can lay upon it. And consequently whatever actions or dispositions of the mind are the proper means to this end, viz., to obtain the happiness of the species, are in themselves evidently morally good, being agreeable to this self-evident truth that it is best that the species should be happy. And if we find in ourselves affections or sentiments leading to this end, we judge them to be right affections, though I would not choose to style them morally good. And so, vice versa.

But if it be farther asked why it is best that the species should be happy, I own no reason can be assigned for it, no more than a reason can be assigned why the whole is equal to all its parts, or a part is less than the whole, or things equal to the same third are equal to one another. No reason can be ever given for a self-evident axiom, for all reasoning is only an appeal to some self-evident principle or other. And if I could find a man of so different a make of understanding from mine that what was self-evident to me was not so to him, I should have no medium by which I could argue with him any longer on that head, but we must part and own that we cannot understand each other. Only in that case we should not be angry at one another for what neither of us could help.

Again, if it be farther demanded for whom is it best that the species should be happy, I answer, for themselves and for everyone who has anything to do with them and who is capable of perceiving that happiness is better than misery and of seeing this consequence, that therefore he does for the better who promotes happiness anywhere than he who promotes misery. And this I should think every intelligent being must perceive if he applies his mind to it at all.

The other objection Philanthropus takes notice that I insinuate is that if there is no moral standard antecedent to a sense, then all constitution of senses had been alike good and reasonable in the Deity. I meant for the Deity to appoint and cause.

To this he answers that we can conceive no exciting reasons of the Divine actions antecedent to something in the Divine nature of a nobler kind, corresponding to our kindest and sweetest affections, by which the Deity desires universal happiness as an end. The justifying reasons of the Divine actions must end in our moral sense, which makes us approve such a kind beneficent constitution of our nature.

But I would here ask Philanthropus by what kind of reasoning it is that we attribute benignity to the Deity. Is it only because we find benign affections in ourselves? If so, then on the same ground we may attribute pain and uneasiness to Him because we sometimes feel them, or any other imperfect sentiment which is familiar to us. But the truth is, we conclude that the Deity cannot but be benign because, by some previous standard in our own minds, we judge benignity to be a perfection, something in itself right and excellent, and therefore cannot be wanting where there is infinite perfection. And this brings us back to the inquiry, how, and by what standard, we are to judge of our affections and senses; which was fully considered under the former objection and needs not be repeated here. So that we go much higher in our inquiry than the bare consideration of affection or a moral sense in ourselves. I own, indeed, we cannot but conceive something in the Deity in some measure analogous to our kindest affections as that He takes infinite pleasure in communicating good to His creatures. But this consideration by itself would only lead us to conclude Him infinitely happy and not good in a moral sense. We esteem Him essentially good because He knows all truth and always acts according to it. He infallibly knows what is best and will always do what is best upon the whole, all things considered. For instance, His infinite knowledge represents to Him happiness as something that is better than misery. And thence we firmly conclude that He will always propose the happiness and not the misery of His creatures as His end in creating them. And if He creates them with a capacity for happiness, He will not make it impossible for them to be happy, though perhaps it may be in the nature of things impossible to make them capable of the happiness of intelligent and free agents without leaving it in their own power to make themselves miserable if they will, which will therefore still be best to put in their own election, though the consequence may be evil to them through their own perverse choice.

And I think here Philanthropus again gives up the cause

when he admits that our reason might have suggested that, if the Deity did study our happiness as an end, the omitting to give us such a sense, if we could have had an idea of it, was omitting the proper means for obtaining His end.

Then surely there can be no doubt that the Deity intended us to be happy when He created us, nor can we suppose that He intends us to be happy and yet withholds from us the necessary means of happiness. For the not doing the one would be acting contrary to what He knows to be best, and the other would be acting contrary to His own design, neither of which can find place in an intelligent, free, and perfect being.

So that upon the whole, I think, these objections have not been answered by Philanthropus. And indeed they seem to me such as cannot be removed and must entirely overturn his notions of moral good and evil.

But I cannot part with Philanthropus till I assure him once more that I think the *Treatise of the Original of Virtue*, which gave occasion to this debate as well as the other, *Concerning Beauty and Order*, exceedingly ingenious and well argued from the principles laid down. And if the author had laid his principles deeper, he would have made his discourse as useful and solid as it is delightful and entertaining. And I should not esteem my labor lost if by what I have said I could provoke him to undertake the proof of the rectitude and excellence, as well as of the existence, of his moral sense. I am fully persuaded he would be much more capable of deducing that series of truths which is necessary to the compassing such a design than

Yours, etc.
Philaretus

Postscript

Concerning the Meaning and Different Acceptions of the Words GOOD and EVIL

There having been frequent occasion in the foregoing papers to mention the words moral good and moral evil, it may not be thought improper to subjoin something here, by way of further inquiry into the original and strict meaning of the words good and evil and how the derived senses of those words are formed from the original ones, that so we may the more readily attend to the true importance of them when they are applied to moral subjects.

If this inquiry is pursued with regard to any one of these words it will be sufficient because, signifying direct opposite ideas, whatever is affirmed of the one is to be denied of the other.

I shall therefore confine myself to the word good as the most eligible to describe. And what shall be said of good will be easily applicable, by reversing it, to evil, provided the reader proceed cautiously in applying it.

By good, when taken in the primary and proper sense of the word, we denote the idea of some perfection or excellence of nature, which commonly goes by the name of physical goodness. When the nature of the thing which we say is good is absolutely or infinitely perfect in every sense, then it constitutes absolute or infinite goodness, or goodness in the highest sense and utmost extent of the word. When the nature is limited and consequently not absolutely perfect every way then, if the thing we speak of be at all good, it constitutes respective goodness or goodness according to the measure and limits of that nature supposed always to have some degree of goodness in it. And a thing is said to be more or less good, or its respective goodness to be greater or less, as it is thought to approach nearer to, or to keep a greater distance from absolute goodness, still supposing it to have some positive goodness; or, by comparing it with some other respectively good thing and finding the difference of its respective goodness, i.e., the excess or deficiency of it. These operations are both performed by the mind when it considers one thing as better or worse than, or as good as, another. Whatever, likewise, is the result, or proper consequence of good, is good in this primary sense. And if good is ever the occasion of evil, it is by accident and from some other extrinsic cause; which will not interfere with the foregoing self-evident proposition.

From this primary and strict sense of good we deduce a secondary and relative sense. Thus when the constitution and nature of any thing suits it for a particular end we say it is good, meaning relatively to that end. And it is called better or worse, in this relative sense, as it answers that end more or less perfectly. In this sense an eye or ear is said to be good to see or hear with, a house is good to dwell in, etc.

But then, unless the end to be served be a good end in the primary sense of good, the thing which serves that end is not good in that primary sense, though it be called good relatively; which word in that case means no more than useful or apt for that purpose. Thus meat is not good in the strict sense, though it please the taste, if the consequence of eating it be sickness or pain, though, in the common speech what pleases the taste is said to be good, i.e., good relatively to the taste.

Another relative sense of good is when any thing is said to answer one particular relation. And here that may be relatively good which is not good in the primary sense, as an ill man may be a good scholar or workman. And what is relatively good may, at the same time, be relatively bad, as a good father may be a bad friend, or subject, etc., whereas that which is good in the primary sense can never be bad in the primary sense. Therefore, before relative goodness can coincide with primary goodness, it must be goodness with respect to all the relations in which the thing stands, or universal relative goodness.

A third relative sense of goodness is when it denotes the aptness of any thing to give us pleasure. We call such a thing good, i.e., relatively good for us, in this relative sense; and yet it may be far from being good in itself. As, if the causing undeserved misery to others or the committing any crime should be a source of pleasure to us or to any other person.

Therefore what causes pleasure, though it be always relatively good, is yet never good in the primary sense unless that pleasure be the result of a good nature or of acting agreeably to that nature.

When pleasure is the result of perception, intelligence, power, rectitude of nature, inclining us to use our power according to our intelligence joined with a consciousness of willing and acting so, then pleasure is the result of a good nature and a good manner of acting and, consequently, that which procures it is good in the primary as well as in the relative sense of the word.

But where pleasure is the result of perception and power with a wrong apprehension of things, or with a right apprehension and a wrong and perverse nature inclining to will and act contrary to that apprehension, or with a right apprehension and a rightly disposed nature and yet at the same time a consciousness of willing and acting in a manner contrary to that intelligence and rectitude of nature; in all these cases, I say, it is evidently the result of an evil nature or evil manner of acting and, consequently, cannot be good in the primary sense of good, though it is still good relatively, i.e., it is good to us.

Hence, by-the-by, we may collect that God, who is the author of nothing but what is good in the primary sense, will never annex pleasure upon the whole to an evil nature nor to the acting contrary to a good nature; and therefore, that moral goodness must upon the whole be attended with happiness and moral badness cannot. I speak not of particular incidental pleasures and pains, which limited and imperfect creatures may enjoy or suffer contrary to this rule for wise reasons, and perhaps for their greater good upon the whole, but of happiness, which is the excess of their whole pleasures above their whole pains.

When the word good means goodly or beautiful it is taken in this last relative sense. For by beauty we understand no more than what occasions pleasure by the contemplation of it. There is no need at present of inquiring into the other metaphorical senses of the word. What has been said will be sufficient to explain the importance of this term good when applied to moral subjects.

Having thus far inquired into the different acceptations of the word good, it is easy to deduce from thence the analogy they all bear to the original and primary sense.

The relative goodness or aptness for an end is properly enough styled goodness because it is a degree of perfection and excellence of nature to answer the end which the nature of the thing suits it for, though to render it strictly, and upon the whole, good, the end must be likewise a good end.

Again, the relative goodness of answering any one relation is, so far as that relation reaches, good in the proper sense, though it is but partial goodness unless all the relations are at the same time answered.

Lastly, the relative goodness of what affords pleasure is

properly termed good in one view as being the result of something which, in itself, and considered alone, is good, viz., perception and power; though this pleasure is evil in another view, as it arises from a mixture of evil ingredients, viz., a perverse understanding, a wrong nature, or an incongruous manner of acting; and as perception and power in conjunction with those evil properties are themselves corrupted and rendered evil. Or, rather, the being who perceives and has power without right intelligence and right nature is an evil being.

From all that has been said it will appear what is understood by moral goodness.

It is plain, moral goodness means the goodness of a moral person, i.e., of an intelligent agent.

Now, as agency implies freedom, i.e., a power to act, it is evident an agent is a good agent when he employs this power well; and employing power well is the employing it agreeably to a good nature. And the associating the ideas of intelligence and of a propensity to act according to intelligence gives us the complex idea of a good nature. It follows that to employ power or exert freedom agreeably to intelligence and to the propensity of nature to act according to it, is employing power well and consequently being a good agent. And because intelligence is always supposed to be right intelligence, or the intelligence of truth and, further, because it cannot be conceived that an intelligent being should in his nature be propense to act contrary to his intelligence, therefore it is said that moral goodness consists in acting agreeably to truth.

Moral goodness depends on the power of the agent, since by withdrawing or not exerting that power he ceases to be a good agent, were his intelligence and natural disposition never so good. And, on the other hand, moral goodness supposes a good nature, i.e., intelligence and rectitude of natural disposition because without these the agent cannot act well. No one can do what he knows not how to do nor can be expected to do what he is no ways disposed to do.

If there was no such thing as liberty or agency the distinction of moral and physical good would be a mere distinction of words without any differences in the things. If there was no physical good then moral good would be an impossible idea, having no ground to rest upon. For it would be frivolous to say an agent is good if we had no idea of good.

When we say an agent employs his power well, if we mean only that he employs it so as to produce a good effect, this imports no goodness of agency but only the physical goodness of the cause and effect; which is the same whether the cause be supposed to act in the strict sense of the word or only to be acted upon, i.e., to be an instrumental cause which, in strict speech, is no proper cause at all but only an effect serving as an instrument to work another effect.

But if, when we say an agent employs his power well, we preserve the idea of agency and speak accurately, we then mean that the agent intends and desires to produce a good effect and acts agreeably to that intention and inclination. But he cannot intend it without intelligence, i.e., without knowing what is a good effect, and will not desire it unless his nature disposes him to act agreeably to his intelligence. And intelligence and an inclination to act intelligently are evidently physically good qualities or perfections of nature. Consequently, an intelligent nature disposed to act intelligently is a good nature in the physical and primary sense. It follows that an agent who employs his power well is an agent who employs his power agreeably to such a good nature. And the idea of such an agent is the idea of a morally good person.

Goodness, when applied to agents, bears the same primary and relative senses which it bears when applied to any other subject. The primary sense of moral goodness implies the absolute or respective perfection of agency. The relative senses of moral goodness imply the perfection of agency with regard to the relations in which the agent stands.

And moral goodness in the relative sense must be relative with respect to all the relations in which the agent stands before it can coincide with moral goodness in the primary and strict sense of the word.

There is a particular relative sense of good which, though it falls under the foregoing definitions, yet deserves to be considered apart, as being the most common acceptation of the word. It is when the word is applied with regard to the communication of good from one agent to another.

Goodness in this respect bears sometimes a physical and sometimes a moral sense.

When it carries a physical sense it is termed benignity, which is physical goodness, as it is a high perfection of nature. And it appears to be a perfection of nature because it is the result of intelligence, which perceives good as good, and evil as evil, and of a propensity or disposition of nature to act agreeably to that intelligence; which properties are in themselves perfections of nature. And whatever is the result of a perfection of nature is a perfection of nature itself. Only it must be observed that this relative goodness, in order to fall in with primary goodness, must be relative to all, not partial, not goodness to some and evil to others. It must be goodness to the whole. And the general term of goodness is appropriated to benignity, as benignity is one of the noblest and most exalted perfections that can denominate any nature good in the primary sense of the word.

When the word goodness, in this respect of communicating good to others, carries a moral sense, it means the acting agreeably to this natural benignity. And is then styled benevolence which, when it takes effect, is called beneficence. This benevolence goes by the name of goodness of an agent as such, acting agreeably to a good, which is in this case a benign, nature. And this branch of moral goodness has the general title of goodness, as it bears a moral sense, conferred upon it, because it is justly placed in the foremost rank of moral excellency and is seldom found to stand alone.

I shall only further examine in what sense the word good is applied to the affections of the mind.

The affections are proper to those agents to whom a certain system of matter is annexed which they direct within certain limits and which again influences them to a certain degree, not so indeed as to take away their agency but so as to affect their inclination or desire to act. These influences are sometimes distinguished into appetites, passions, affections and sometimes go under the general denomination of affections. They are considered as something different from the propensity which must be conceived in every intelligent agent to act agreeably to his intelligence, and arise from our particular constitution and frame of soul and body. We find by experience that the consciousness of some actions, over and above the immediate uneasiness it gives the mind, creates such a disturbance and disorder in the material system to which we are joined as reflects back a further pain and uneasiness to the mind, i.e., to the intelligent agent. And, on the other hand, the consciousness of other actions gives such a kindly motion to the parts of the material system as returns to the mind a pleasing and grateful sensation.

Now when these affections are said to be good it is always in the physical, never in the moral, sense because they are not in our power and do not depend on our choice or will. They are relatively good in this physical sense as far as they afford us pleasure. But still, if that pleasure be the result of evil the affections will not be good in the primary and proper sense, though they will be still good to us as far as they serve to increase our happiness.

Again, these affections are relatively good with respect to the end they are adapted to. This end is to deter us from some actions and to prompt us to others by increasing the pleasure or pain of being conscious of such actions.

And the affections are apt and proper instruments to serve this end. But still we cannot determine that these affections are good in the primary sense till we have examined the end they are subservient to and have found it to be a good end in the primary sense of good; that is, till we have by some other test tried whether the actions they prompt us to are in themselves good actions and those they deter us from are evil ones. This test is to us the true nature of things as far as it may be perceived and understood by our intelligence. It follows that only our intelligence can inform us when these affections are good in the strict and proper sense. And we can never infer it from the sensations which the affections themselves give us nor, consequently, from any internal or moral sense which is only the result of those sensations.

I said these affections are peculiar to intelligent agents united to a system of matter as their organ and sensorium. For the supreme being who is of an absolutely perfect nature, who sees every instant whatever is every where true and is by the necessity of his nature always disposed to use his power agreeably to his intelligence, i.e., to act wisely, and who is infinitely happy from the result of those perfections of his nature and of his consciousness of always acting in conformity to them, stands in need of no such assistance from affections to redouble his happiness and, thereby, to augment his disposition to do right, as he has made us to want and has therefore afforded us. And as he does not stand in need of such assistance, so neither could he possibly receive it, being of a perfectly independent nature whom therefore nothing from without can influence or act upon.

FINIS.

Index